Account-Based Marketing

for
dummies®
A Wiley Brand

Account-Based Marketing

for **dummies®**

A Wiley Brand

by Sangram Vajre

for **dummies®**
A Wiley Brand

Account-Based Marketing For Dummies®

Published by: **John Wiley & Sons, Inc.,** 111 River Street, Hoboken, NJ 07030-5774, www.wiley.com

Copyright © 2016 by John Wiley & Sons, Inc., Hoboken, New Jersey

Media and software compilation copyright © 2016 by John Wiley & Sons, Inc. All rights reserved.

Published simultaneously in Canada

No part of this publication may be reproduced, stored in a retrieval system or transmitted in any form or by any means, electronic, mechanical, photocopying, recording, scanning or otherwise, except as permitted under Sections 107 or 108 of the 1976 United States Copyright Act, without the prior written permission of the Publisher. Requests to the Publisher for permission should be addressed to the Permissions Department, John Wiley & Sons, Inc., 111 River Street, Hoboken, NJ 07030, (201) 748-6011, fax (201) 748-6008, or online at www.wiley.com/go/permissions.

Trademarks: Wiley, For Dummies, the Dummies Man logo, Dummies.com, Making Everything Easier, and related trade dress are trademarks or registered trademarks of John Wiley & Sons, Inc. and may not be used without written permission. All trademarks are the property of their respective owners. John Wiley & Sons, Inc. is not associated with any product or vendor mentioned in this book.

LIMIT OF LIABILITY/DISCLAIMER OF WARRANTY: THE PUBLISHER AND THE AUTHOR MAKE NO REPRESENTATIONS OR WARRANTIES WITH RESPECT TO THE ACCURACY OR COMPLETENESS OF THE CONTENTS OF THIS WORK AND SPECIFICALLY DISCLAIM ALL WARRANTIES, INCLUDING WITHOUT LIMITATION WARRANTIES OF FITNESS FOR A PARTICULAR PURPOSE. NO WARRANTY MAY BE CREATED OR EXTENDED BY SALES OR PROMOTIONAL MATERIALS. THE ADVICE AND STRATEGIES CONTAINED HEREIN MAY NOT BE SUITABLE FOR EVERY SITUATION. THIS WORK IS SOLD WITH THE UNDERSTANDING THAT THE PUBLISHER IS NOT ENGAGED IN RENDERING LEGAL, ACCOUNTING, OR OTHER PROFESSIONAL SERVICES. IF PROFESSIONAL ASSISTANCE IS REQUIRED, THE SERVICES OF A COMPETENT PROFESSIONAL PERSON SHOULD BE SOUGHT. NEITHER THE PUBLISHER NOR THE AUTHOR SHALL BE LIABLE FOR DAMAGES ARISING HEREFROM. THE FACT THAT AN ORGANIZATION OR WEBSITE IS REFERRED TO IN THIS WORK AS A CITATION AND/OR A POTENTIAL SOURCE OF FURTHER INFORMATION DOES NOT MEAN THAT THE AUTHOR OR THE PUBLISHER ENDORSES THE INFORMATION THE ORGANIZATION OR WEBSITE MAY PROVIDE OR RECOMMENDATIONS IT MAY MAKE. FURTHER, READERS SHOULD BE AWARE THAT INTERNET WEBSITES LISTED IN THIS WORK MAY HAVE CHANGED OR DISAPPEARED BETWEEN WHEN THIS WORK WAS WRITTEN AND WHEN IT IS READ.

For general information on our other products and services, please contact our Customer Care Department within the U.S. at 877-762-2974, outside the U.S. at 317-572-3993, or fax 317-572-4002. For technical support, please visit www.wiley.com/techsupport.

Wiley publishes in a variety of print and electronic formats and by print-on-demand. Some material included with standard print versions of this book may not be included in e-books or in print-on-demand. If this book refers to media such as a CD or DVD that is not included in the version you purchased, you may download this material at http://booksupport.wiley.com. For more information about Wiley products, visit www.wiley.com.

Library of Congress Control Number: 2016935142

ISBN 978-1-119-22485-3 (pbk); 978-1-119-22486-0 (epub); 978-1-119-22488-4 (epdf)

Manufactured in the United States of America

10 9 8 7 6 5 4 3 2 1

Contents at a Glance

Table of Contents

Foreword

Nothing makes me happier than seeing the market embrace a good idea that works. For account-based marketing (ABM), that time is now. Why is ABM the new big thing in business-to-business (B2B), especially when it's not really a "new" idea at all? There are a number of reasons why you may be opening this book and starting on the road to ABM. Here are my thoughts on why reading it and deploying ABM will be a smart investment for you.

The first reason that ABM is getting so much attention these days is that marketing and sales leaders have determined that the natural next step in their relationship requires account focus. Marketing has made great strides over the last few years toward building credibility with sales. Unfortunately, the last mile to ideal alignment with sales has eluded marketing, because they've maintained a focus on delivering volumes of leads. What's the problem with that model? If you ask a sales person where growth will come from, he or she will name a list of accounts. Marketing, on the other hand, typically starts talking about personas and segments. Now, with ABM, marketing is speaking the language of sales. Efficient revenue growth requires focus on the specific accounts, and the people in them, who are most likely to deliver that growth. To sales, and now for those who embrace account-based marketing, anything else is a waste of time.

The second reason is the reality of how buyers buy. Marketing and sales finally agree it's no longer a battle for who plays the most critical role in the buying cycle. Instead, common sense and ample research evidence show that marketing and sales together are needed to support buyers on their journey. This requires a balanced strategy, where sales and marketing understand their respective roles and how those need to be coordinated in every stage of buying. ABM is the way to operationalize that strategy as a partnership that's focused on delivering growth.

The third reason for ABM's rise, which Sangram points out in this book, is that *both* sales and marketing have been ignoring the most critical driver of B2B buying: the post-sale customer experience. Fully 71 percent of the reason that B2B buyers choose to buy from a specific company is based on either their own direct experience with a company, or what they hear about the experience others have with the company. This means that the funnel as we know it makes very little sense. The real battle for customer hearts, minds, and investments happens after customers buy. It's essential to balance pre- and post-sale requirements when building an account-based plan, because those non-selling investments in customer success deliver both retention and growth. Marketing's toolkit is essential to both customer acquisition and customer engagement.

The fourth reason is around technology. You may wonder why now there's so much fuss about a marketing concept that has been around for more than a decade. That's a fair question. In the past, ABM had to be executed as a one-to-one, customized approach, with a focus on just a small number of very significant accounts. This custom approach was, and remains, labor-intensive and not the right model for every business. What's changed to support the current wave of ABM adoption is the availability of technology and analytics to make one-to-few (or more than a few) much more realistic, even for small teams with limited budgets. The current wave of ABM is fueled by a data-driven approach to marketing that begins with the identification of ideal companies and contacts to target, and then uses technology to engage with them at scale in useful ways, both pre- and post-sale. The traditional one-to-one model still makes sense, and is successfully used by many companies who commit the resources to do it, but technology has democratized ABM.

If you're reading this book and just getting started with ABM, let me be the first to welcome you to the future of what B2B marketing can be: insight led, technology enabled and, above all, customer focused. Happy reading!

Megan Heuer (@megheuer)

Vice President & Group Director, SiriusDecisions

Introduction

Our world is becoming increasingly connected. Today, the modern marketer is an innovator, creating new ways to connect with potential customers that defy the status quo. Technology has given a platform for business-to-business (B2B) marketers to reach customers, but it's a blessing and a curse, because buyers are inundated with thousands of messages every day. This is why it's essential for marketers to identify their best-fit customers before ever creating that first message. By targeting your ideal customers and determining how to engage them on digital channels such as mobile, social media, display advertising, and video, you can connect with your buyers on their own terms. This is called *account-based marketing* (ABM).

B2B marketing and sales teams have been doing ABM as a side project for years, but now it's time to take ABM mainstream by making it a core part of your company's go-to-market strategy. ABM is a program of various marketing activities, not using a particular software product. There are many elements to engaging individual accounts on their terms that go beyond just online or offline conversations. The question to ask is "Are you a B2B company that knows which accounts you want to target?" Focusing your marketing efforts on the best-fit accounts will allow your team to become more efficient and grow sales revenue faster.

In this book, I tell you all about account-based marketing: how it has evolved from traditional lead generation and why you should strongly consider using ABM in your B2B marketing and sales efforts. I show you how to use marketing technology (MarTech) and software to target your best-fit prospects, create contacts that expand into accounts, and engage them through content and marketing activities generating sales velocity to drive new revenue for your company. I discuss how to retain your accounts through customer advocacy, continuously engaging your clients throughout the customer lifecycle (and reducing churn). I will walk through a game plan with real-life examples based on my experience in seeing how more than 100 companies implemented ABM in their go-to-market strategies.

About This Book

This book exists to help you understand this new trend called account-based marketing. Whether you are new to the world of B2B marketing, work as a salesperson for a B2B organization, or you're an experienced CMO, having a strong understanding of account-based marketing is a must. The reason account-based marketing has become such a buzzword in the B2B marketing world is because it solves an issue of how to target and engage your best-fit prospects and customers *at scale*.

I will give you an overview and blueprint of how to do account-based marketing unlike any other publication available on the market. I've laid out this book to give you a foundation of B2B marketing, how account-based marketing takes your efforts to the next level utilizing readily available MarTech solutions, and increase new and existing revenue for your company.

Here are some terms used in this book that you should know:

>> ABM is the abbreviation of account-based marketing. I interchange with this across the start of each chapter.

>> When possible, I've included the Twitter handles of key people, companies, or technology solutions when possible so you can follow them on social media. Using social media is an essential part of ABM.

>> Web addresses and programming code appear in monofont. If you're reading a digital version of this book on a device connected to the internet, you can click the web address to visit that website.

Foolish Assumptions

The most foolish assumption you can make about this book is that you already know all the intricacies about B2B marketing and therefore can do account-based marketing. The basic concepts for account-based marketing are different than the traditional lead-based marketing techniques used in B2B marketing, especially for the sales funnel. With account-based marketing, I literally flip the funnel on its head so B2B marketing teams are no longer concerned with generating tons of leads to pour into the top of the funnel. I show you how to think correctly about account-based marketing so you identify your best-fit contacts, expand those contacts into accounts, and engage them on their terms through digital channels to accelerate pipeline velocity and close deals faster.

If you're a beginner in the field of B2B marketing, I want to encourage you to start reading from the beginning of this book to understand the basics of our industry. The world of B2B marketing is different from business-to-consumer (B2C) marketing, or the world of mass consumer advertising. B2B marketing is about selling your company's products and services to companies who can and want to use what you're selling successfully. B2B and B2C marketing require different activities and tactics, and account-based marketing adds another layer of complexity. However, if you're new to the world of B2B marketing, starting your experience with account-based marketing early will help put you ahead of the curve. Because you aren't used to the old ways of lead-based marketing, you can start your career in B2B marketing as an innovator who already understands the principles of ABM.

If you've already established a career and are experienced in the world of B2B marketing, you can skip around the different chapters of this book. Make use of the information you want to learn to help improve your existing marketing and sales techniques. If you're doing traditional lead-based marketing, which most B2B marketers are, then approach this book as a new way of taking the good data you already have about your customers and prospects and make it work even better using targeted account-based marketing strategies.

Lastly, if you work for a B2B organization that's using a customer relationship management (CRM) software (such as Salesforce), plus a marketing automation tool (such as Marketo, HubSpot, Eloqua, or Pardot), and you have a website and social media, then you *must* read this book. You already have all the tools to do account-based marketing. I will show you how to use these technologies to impact your marketing efforts for increased sales revenue.

If you approach account-based marketing without having an appreciation and understanding of marketing technology solutions such as a CRM, marketing automation system, and digital presence on the web then you will not accomplish your goal as a B2B marketer, which is to help drive business for sales. In the end, you will end up having to hire a consultant who can set up your CRM and create a process for your marketing and sales teams to do account-based marketing, which could potentially cost tens of thousands of dollars. Reading this book will save you time and resources as it will give you the steps to implement account-based marketing strategies: the basic elements of identifying accounts, targeting them using technology, and how to improve your marketing campaigns over time.

The B2B marketing industry has new buzzwords every day. Account-based marketing is more than just a buzzword because it's a proven strategy to make more money for your business. ABM is laser-focused B2B marketing.

Icons Used in This Book

TIP

The Tip icon marks tips and tricks which you can use to make account-based marketing even more successful.

REMEMBER

The Remember icon notes the pieces of information which are especially important to keep in mind. You'll need this information while you read this book, and as you go beyond this book to implement your own account-based marketing campaigns.

WARNING

The Warning icon tells you what not to do (like wasting time in a Dummies book explaining a Warning icon). Seriously though, you should keep an eye out for the Warning icons because I give you useful information which can help you from making mistakes as you do account-based marketing.

TECHNICAL STUFF

The Technical Stuff icon notes where I call out certain technology providers which you will need for ABM. It is also an icon to note where I tell you how to set up data in your CRM, create workflows, and segment lists.

Beyond the Book

I have written extra articles you won't find in the book itself. Go online to find the following

>> **Online articles covering additional topics**: www.dummies.com/extras/account-based-marketing

Here you'll find resources such as the ten ways to get started with account-based marketing, building a game plan for your company to switch from lead-based marketing to ABM, and much more.

>> **The Cheat Sheet for this book at**

www.dummies.com/cheatsheet/account-based-marketing

Here you'll find additional articles about the stages of account-based marketing, including how to identify, engage, and accelerate your accounts across all stages of the buyer's journey, creating customer advocates.

Where to Go from Here

I wrote this book with the goal of having you read modularly. You can jump between different parts of this book to find the information you need to be successful with account-based marketing. Use it as a guide to start doing B2B marketing campaigns from scratch, or to take the contacts you already have in your CRM to create accounts and segment into lists to tailor your messaging based on the particular needs of your best-fit customers or personas. Keep it on your desk at the office or where your marketing and sales teams sit so they can have it handy.

If you follow me on Twitter (@sangramvajre) and Tweet a photo of yourself (even a "selfie") reading this book, then I'll send you an autographed copy to help share the good news about account-based marketing and how it will revolutionize the B2B marketing world.

1

Getting Started with Account-Based Marketing

Chapter 1

Introducing the Basics of Account-Based Marketing

A ccount-based marketing (ABM) is a hot topic. #ABM and #FlipMyFunnel are trending on Twitter. At business-to-business (B2B) marketing events, featured speakers illustrate the value of account-based marketing. If you're unfamiliar with ABM, this chapter shows exactly what account-based marketing is, and how it can change the status quo of how your company measures its success metrics.

This chapter defines account-based marketing, and shows why ABM is such a powerful movement in the B2B marketing industry. I list the major reasons why companies need to implement account-based marketing, and how you flip the traditional B2B sales and marketing funnel. Instead of collecting tons of leads at the top of the funnel, I describe how to quickly identify your best-fit customers, then convert these prospects into your accounts for targeted marketing.

Defining Account-Based Marketing

The essential definition of account-based marketing is *focused* B2B marketing. The term *account-based marketing* isn't new. Identifying and targeting key accounts has always been a best practice for B2B marketing and sales teams. What's different today about account-based marketing is that improved technology gives marketing teams the tools for account-based marketing *at scale*.

REMEMBER

Scale means the ability to reach the right contacts instead of either blasting emails to the thousands of people in your database or manually reaching out to each individual prospect.

Account-based marketing is about identifying your best-fit prospects, then focusing all your efforts on engaging these prospects on their own terms. For B2B marketing, this is essential, as it's the most efficient way to use your time, energy, and resources. You target businesses that are most likely to buy from your company. This is very different from old-fashioned B2B marketing.

Pouring leads into the funnel

The forecasting model that is used by B2B marketing and sales professionals to monitor potential new revenue is the *sales pipeline.* The pipeline is commonly referred to as the *funnel.*

The traditional B2B marketing and sales funnel tracks the various stages of a revenue opportunity as it moves through the sales process. The pipeline itself is named from the funnel. A lead became an opportunity as it progressed through the funnel, or pipeline, where it eventually became a closed deal. Marketing and sales teams are familiar with the CEO or President examining all of the opportunities in the sales pipeline. This is why marketing has been focused on pouring leads into the top of the funnel. New leads were acquired through purchasing lists, advertising, sending emails with content, and a variety of marketing efforts. When more leads came in, more potential deals entered the pipeline. Figure 1-1 illustrates the traditional B2B sales funnel.

From beginning to end, your prospect moves through a few predictable stages in this funnel. These are the stages of the traditional B2B buyer's journey:

1. **Awareness:** A potential new customer hears about your company's product or service.

   This potential client is called a *prospect,* or *lead.* Leads are the most common metric that B2B marketers use to measure the success of their marketing activities and programs. In the Awareness stage, marketers pour leads into the top of the funnel to identify any and all prospects who want to learn about your product or service.

2. **Interest:** A lead becomes a marketing qualified lead (MQL).

The marketing team examines the lead's title, company information, and other attributes to determine whether this prospect should be forwarded to sales. If the lead becomes an MQL, then it's time to start engaging the prospect at a deeper level. The lead is passed on to sales, becoming a sales accepted lead (SAL). Now, the salesperson engages in a series of calls and emails to engage the SAL in an in-depth conversation or discovery call. In the discovery call, the salesperson learns more about the issues or pain points the SAL is experiencing. During the call, if your salesperson and SAL agree that there is a potential opportunity to do business, the SAL becomes a sales qualified lead (SQL).

3. **Consideration:** The time when your SQL becomes an opportunity.

Often, this stage is the breaking point for a lead. Your SQL is getting more people from his or her company involved. In B2B purchases, the decision rarely is left to a single decision maker. Your original lead, or champion, probably must persuade his or her internal stakeholders that they should purchase your product or service. This is when you negotiate with your potential new customer. At the Consideration stage, the marketing and sales teams must work in alignment to provide content that can overcome objections. The more handholding your team does during this stage of the traditional funnel, the more likely that a deal closes. Advancing a deal through Consideration always is an uphill battle for B2B sales.

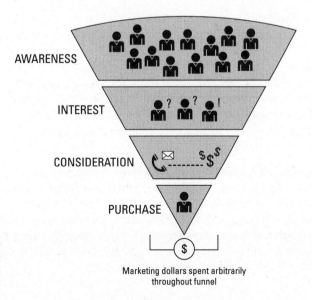

FIGURE 1-1:
The stages of the traditional B2B funnel.

Marketing dollars spent arbitrarily throughout funnel

4. **Purchase:** The final stage of the traditional B2B marketing and sales funnel ends with a decision.

   Your prospect has progressed from an MQL, SAL, or SQL to opportunity. Now, the opportunity either chooses your company, chooses another competitor's products or services, or abandons the purchase. Your business either has won the deal, or wasted a lot of time and energy on the sales process.

Moving away from lead-based marketing

Working in B2B marketing is tough. According to Forrester Research, only 0.75 percent of leads become closed revenue. If you can induce a lead to purchase, you deserve praise for making it to the bottom of the funnel. Your team hustles all quarter to pour leads into the funnel. However, sometimes it doesn't generate revenue, because not all of the leads marketing generates become sales opportunities.

Not all leads are created equal.

REMEMBER

The biggest problem with the traditional funnel is that leads fall out as they move through these stages. Only a small percentage of the leads collected at the top of the funnel in Awareness will make it all the way to Purchase at the bottom, which is why the traditional sales funnel looks like an upside-down triangle. With the traditional funnel, four major problems can cause lead-based marketing efforts to fail:

>> **The funnel isn't optimized for B2B marketing**. Because the traditional funnel comes from a sales process, it isn't optimized for marketing. Also, the traditional funnel is designed for a single customer, and isn't optimized for multiple decision makers. This model is better attuned for a B2C process, where the stages are well known, there are quick cycles, and the progression is very linear. If fewer than 1 percent of your leads ever become closed deals, the other 99 percent of leads are a huge waste of your time and resources. B2B marketers have to think differently about what's generating revenue, and focus on those efforts.

>> **Marketing is focused on acquiring leads instead of accounts.** The VP of Sales or the CEO says, "Our company needs to double revenue!" In the past, that's when the marketing executive tells the team to crank up demand generation so they can double the amount of leads, adding more to the top of the funnel *and* closing more revenue. Sadly, at the end of the quarter, the marketing team will have decreased cost per lead (CPL) and increased leads, but they won't have increased revenue produced.

>> **Lead volume is more important than precise targeting.** With lead-based marketing, it's easy to look at your conversion rate and decide that you need to add more leads to the funnel to close more revenue. That isn't exactly the answer.

>> **A linear path is assumed for all customers' journeys.** When you're looking at the traditional funnel, it looks like logical steps in a progression, which isn't always the case for a customer journey, No prospect wakes up and says "I've got to solve this problem today." For the Awareness stage, your marketing team created content that answers that problem and blasted it everywhere, hoping to find people who need this problem solved. That's another reason why lead-based marketing fails: You're putting your message in front of people who aren't trying to solve this problem.

FLIP THE FUNNEL, ACCORDING TO JOSEPH JAFFE

Joseph Jaffe is the author of *Flip The Funnel,* and several other books. He enlightens the B2B industry on the fact that marketers spend their marketing dollars and resources on the wrong area of the business. "If 80 percent of your revenue comes from repeat business, then why are you spending less than 20 percent on the 80 percent revenue contribution? What we see in the marketing world is this constant obsession with acquisition."

Jaffe challenges marketers to view retention as the new acquisition by focusing on customer advocacy programs to acquire new customers through existing customers. "At the end of the day when you think about it, the real magic is the magic between a company and its customer base. It's not your grandfather's customer service. It's about customer service 2.0, where we are super-consumers, promoters, and influencers."

According to Jaffe, marketers should be thinking about the migration from the voice of the customer to the brain of the customer. He said the customer's voice is linked to innovation and the research and development of a company. By hearing the ideas and suggestions of your customers, this helps evolve the company's offering to suit the needs of your customers.

Jaffe estimates that the cost of acquiring a new customer through an existing one is about one-third of the cost of other acquisition methods. Therefore, marketers *shouldn't* spend their time, energy, or money by blasting out their message to acquire as many leads as possible. The moral of his story? *Don't buy attention, pay attention.* Focus on your customers and give them an incredible experience. Their good references and word-of-mouth referrals will drive new clients to your company.

But what if your company flipped this funnel, so that your customers are at the top and the channels you're targeting are second? Instead of asking which technologies and channels you should use to target your buyers, you should ask "Which customers?"

Flipping the Funnel

In 2006, renowned author Seth Godin wrote about flipping the funnel to give your fans a "megaphone." Through the rise of the Internet, your customers can voice their opinions more loudly than ever before, and they will get louder. Your marketing and sales team also can flip the funnel with account-based marketing. Figure 1-2 shows how we flip the funnel.

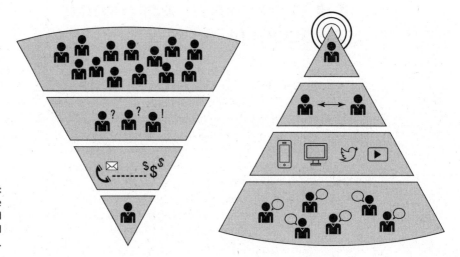

FIGURE 1-2:
Comparing the lead-based and account-based funnels.

The traditional lead-based sales and marketing funnel has been turned into a cone by using account-based marketing. The tip of the cone is your initial lead. This lead becomes your first *contact* and is then developed into an *account*. That's how account-based marketing got its name. You're identifying the accounts you want to engage, then strategically marketing to each contact in the account. Throughout this book, I discuss all levels of account-based marketing, and I show you how to use technology for marketing to these contacts.

There are four stages of account-based marketing: *Identify, Expand, Engage* and *Advocate.* The four stages of account-based marketing apply different processes and components of technology. By using technology, you can implement account-based marketing. Figure 1-3 shows the stages of account-based marketing.

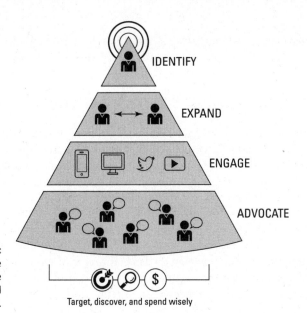

IDENTIFY

EXPAND

ENGAGE

ADVOCATE

Target, discover, and spend wisely

FIGURE 1-3:
Examining the stages of the account-based marketing funnel.

I cover each of the four stages in detail in each of the parts of this book. Part 2 shows how to identify your contacts. Part 3 shows how to expand contacts into accounts. Part 4 shows how to engage accounts. Part 5 shows how to turn accounts into your customer advocates. Part 6 provides the metrics to determine whether your account-based marketing activities are successful. Part 7 has additional resources and tools for account-based marketing.

In the rest of this chapter, I provide a high-level overview of each of the four stages.

Identifying your best-fit contacts

The first step of account-based marketing is to *identify*. With traditional lead-based marketing, your marketing team focused on feeding as many leads as possible in the top of the funnel. With the account-based marketing funnel, you start the sales process by focusing on a single point of contact. You target your best-fit lead and create a contact. This contact potentially is a good fit for your business. You determine whether they're a good fit by using a set of criteria. This set of criteria aligns with your *ideal customer profile*. After you have determined that this contact meets your ideal customer profile, you begin the process of turning the contact into a full account.

TIP

Would you rather go fishing with a net or a fish-finder? Knowing where trout congregate in a stream is a first step toward catching the exact type of fish that you want, but how much easier is your job with a fish finder? Not only can you see where the fish are located, you also get more insight into the size of the fish.

Think of account-based marketing as your fish finder, so you can reel in the biggest fish.

Expanding contacts into accounts

The second stage of account-based marketing is to *expand.* This involves expanding your contact into an account. After the account is created, you further expand the account by adding more contacts. Your ideal customer profile is the type of company (the *account*) you want to work with. Within those accounts, there are *contacts* (the people who will use your product or service).

WARNING

Often, expanding is the toughest stage for marketers who are used to traditional lead-based marketing. With lead-based marketing, you're starting big at the top of the funnel, then slimming down the leads through different stages of qualification. Switching from lead-based marketing to account-based marketing requires a fundamental shift in the mindset of an organization.

Engaging accounts on their terms

The third stage of account-based marketing is to *engage.* Engagement is where your content and channels come to life. This stage is by far the broadest, because there are so many ways to engage with your prospects. Engagement often is where marketers become scientists. They test different types of content to find which types resonate with specific types of contacts and accounts.

Using personalized marketing, your marketing and sales teams engage all of the contacts within an account. You target your marketing messages to your best-fit customers on the channels where your ads are most likely to be seen, whether that's social media, display advertising, video, or mobile. This creates more energy to close deals sooner.

Engagement is the broadest stage of account-based marketing, because there are so many ways to engage with your prospects. Think about email, webinars, ebooks, targeted ads, videos, events, and any programmatic or automated ways you use to get in front of your target audience (target audience is the key phrase).

While this is the first step in the traditional funnel, the flipped funnel waits until you've identified key accounts before developing the targeted content needed for engagement. This gives sales and marketing the opportunity to dive deeper and understand the motivations, pain points, and demographics of each account.

Here's an example: A healthcare company is actively targeting enterprise employers in the San Francisco area. With a list of employers in hand, the healthcare company can both target specific leads with which they may have already engaged, and automatically present personalized ads to other decision makers in those accounts on the same channels that they're already using. This increases the reach within those accounts and makes it more likely that those contacts will already have been exposed to marketing messaging by the time the sales team is actively reaching out. The key here is to present marketing messages on the buyer's schedule, not on yours. This is a huge differentiator between traditional and account-based marketing. This outreach is called *engagement*.

TIP

Your sales reps are on the front lines, so they're a valuable source of information about your prospects. Ask your sales team what's going on with each of your target accounts. What are the pain points of these specific accounts? Which decision makers are you trying to reach? Which features of your product are most important to buyers?

Creating customer advocates

The final stage of account-based marketing is *advocate*. This is when your accounts are customers. Your new goal is to turn your customers into raving fans of your business. This is the creation of customer advocates. Customer word-of-mouth marketing through referrals, reviews, and talking to their peers is the most organic and impactful type of marketing.

Traditional B2B marketing lacks alignment between the marketing, sales, and customer success teams. In this book, I show you how to work with your entire company to continue your account-based marketing efforts beyond the buyer journey and throughout the customer lifecycle.

Chapter 2

Making the Case for Account-Based Marketing

Account-based marketing provides a strategy for B2B companies that want to grow revenue by focusing on the best-fit prospects and customers. The key metric is revenue. For too long, the B2B marketing industry has considered lead generation the primary metric. B2B marketing teams worked hard to pour leads into the top of the funnel for sales. Now that you want to start with account-based marketing, you have to sell the executives at your company on the idea that you aren't focusing on leads. Enticing the stakeholders in your company to agree to focus on accounts, not leads, can be a very daunting task.

The C-level executives have always used leads to determine whether the B2B marketing team is successful. The job of the marketing team is to create opportunities for sales; this was accomplished by generating leads. But the most important metric for your company is *revenue*. By focusing on accounts, not leads, your company can both grow revenue from new sales and generate additional revenue from existing customers.

This chapter covers how account-based marketing can transform your B2B marketing and sales organization. I show where your company can gain the most value from account-based marketing by investing your resources in strategic accounts. I show how you can convince your marketing team, executive leadership, and other stakeholders that account-based marketing helps you generate more qualified opportunities, close more new business, and retain your existing customers.

Understanding Why B2B Companies Need Account-Based Marketing

Proving how account-based marketing is transformational to your organization can be done using data. Good data enhances your credibility for making the case for account-based marketing; numbers support your words. Bad data can be detrimental to your marketing efforts.

REMEMBER

The right data to support your company's revenue goals is essential for account-based marketing.

TIP

You can use data from your current lead generation efforts. Show the amount of money your team spent on marketing and a potential return on investment (ROI). Data demonstrating why your team needs account-based marketing should include the following items:

>> **Leads generated year-to-date (YTD):** The number of leads that marketing generated over the past year; it can be presented as the number of leads generated monthly or quarterly.

>> **Revenue from leads generated by marketing:** If your company had $1 million in new revenue this year, how much of it came from new leads that marketing brought in? If you have a marketing automation system, a report can show the lead source tied to revenue. I show how to use your marketing automation system for attributing activities at the account level in Chapter 9.

>> **Revenue from existing customers:** While reviewing your revenue, you can determine how much came from either your current client base or new leads generated by marketing. You'll compare year-to-date new revenue against your current annual recurring revenue (ARR).

REMEMBER

The goal is to demonstrate that lead-based marketing is extremely inefficient. The data should show that marketing isn't focused on the right business metric: growing revenue for your company. If your marketing team is focused on creating new leads for sales, and those leads don't turn into revenue, then it's a waste of resources that could have been allocated to other activities.

In a recent survey I conducted with my marketing team, we received responses from more than 200 B2B marketing professionals about their goals for account-based marketing. Almost 50 percent of respondents cited pipeline acceleration and revenue generation as their main goal for implementing ABM. Even more interesting is that this includes marketers from organizations that range from SMB to enterprise. That's an awesome business case for marketers to acquire the right tools and create the right programs to build revenue generating programs.

STATISTICS IN FAVOR OF ACCOUNT-BASED MARKETING

When you compare how much it costs for a lead to become closed revenue for your organization, you can make a compelling case for why your company should switch from traditional lead generation to account-based marketing:

- Only 0.75 percent of leads generated become closed revenue (Forrester).

- Generating high-quality leads is the number-one challenge for B2B marketers (IDG Enterprises).

- More than 90 percent of B2B marketers acknowledge account-based marketing as either important or very important (SiriusDecisions).

- B2B companies have begun utilizing targeted account strategies, as 86 percent of marketing and sales professionals stated (LeanData).

- More than 60 percent of B2B marketers surveyed said they plan to implement an ABM program within the next year (Terminus).

- ABM had higher ROI than other marketing activities, according to 97 percent of marketers in a survey (Alterra Group).

- Almost 85 percent of marketers who measure ROI describe ABM as delivering higher returns than any other marketing approach; half of those marketers cite significantly higher returns (ITSMA).

- On average, the number of people involved in a large technology purchase has increased from five to seven (IDC).

- For more than 90 percent of B2B buyers, the amount of their product research depends on the price of a purchase; as the price increases, the amount of research increases (Salesforce).

- Nearly 85 percent of marketers said ABM provided significant benefits to retain and expand existing client relationships (Marketo).

Measuring leads is no longer enough

Instead of trying to get new leads, focus on the best-fit accounts. Leads are ridiculously easy to get these days. Everyone already has a ton of contacts in their database. You can buy a list of leads, go to LinkedIn, or use tons of tools giving you the leads you want. Forget the leads; if they don't produce revenue, it doesn't matter how many leads you get.

REMEMBER

Salespeople don't close leads. They close accounts. It's the accounts that turn into customers for your company's Accounts Receivable ledger to bill for using your product or service. You don't get income from a lead. Your company makes revenue from an account.

Maximizing your marketing efforts

Marketing is an investment. Your company allocates time, money, and resources to marketing because it's an essential part of promoting your company's product or service and building your brand's presence. The purpose of marketing is to create new revenue opportunities. Account-based marketing takes your marketing efforts to a new level. You can track how much your marketing team invested per account, then report on the ROI associated with those accounts by associating your marketing efforts at the account level.

These strategies can maximize your marketing efforts using revenue as your primary metric:

>> **Aligning sales and marketing:** Before account-based marketing, the marketing team was focused on leads; the sales team was solely focused on revenue. With account-based marketing, the marketing and sales teams agree to find the right accounts that will grow revenue. This helps develop a strategy of marketing activities and campaigns that target those accounts. I talk about this in Chapter 3.

>> **Building credibility:** With lead-based marketing, often the leads generated were useless. As a marketer, I've heard the horror stories from salespeople about how the leads marketing gives them aren't worth anything. By shifting the marketing team's focus to the sales pipeline, you're increasing credibility with your sales team. The first step is to help the executive stakeholders in your company agree that something must fundamentally change.

>> **Creating business value:** In your company's annual financial statements, there isn't a line item for the number of leads generated. You only see financial information about the revenue and profitability of your company. Focusing on revenue as a key performance indicator (KPI) illustrates the marketing team's value to the business. Every CEO, CFO, and CSO understands that KPI. If you speak the same language, you have a seat at the table.

Starting the Conversation about ABM

Account-based marketing is a collaborative approach that engages multiple departments in your company including marketing, sales, and customer success. As with any new program or initiative at your company, starting up account-based marketing requires a kickoff conversation. The first step is to get your stakeholders together, and this section shows how you your company can start the conversation about account-based marketing.

Investing your resources the right way

The executives in your company care deeply about the amount of money marketing spends. Every dollar marketing spends is supposed to help with generating new revenue. Your marketing team has a problem if it is only generating new leads for sales and those leads can't be used to grow revenue. You have to take charge and put the right people from your team together to examine how to reallocate your resources the right way. These are the main resources you need for account-based marketing:

>> **People:** Your employees are the most essential resource you have at your company. For account-based marketing, your marketing and sales teams working together create a dream "smarketing" team. I tell you how to build your "smarketing" team in Chapter 3.

>> **Technology:** Account-based marketing is possible thanks to technology used to identify, target, and engage accounts. I discuss what software tools you need in Chapter 4.

>> **Money:** B2B marketers have a budget and track the amount they spend on various activities. With lead-based marketing, you look at how much you spent on each activity and how many new leads were generated. With account-based marketing, you track the amount you spent per campaign at the account level. I show you how to track these metrics in Part 6.

>> **Time:** This resource is one that there never seems to be enough of. With account-based marketing, you measure how much time you invest in each account (which is the best fit for your business) and how quickly it progresses through the stages towards a sale.

Supporting sales productivity

To support sales productivity, marketing's role is changing from lead generation to demand generation. Demand generation is the targeted marketing efforts to drive awareness of your company's product or service. Account-based marketing is all about generating demand within those best fit accounts to create velocity and get them down the pipeline faster, thus supporting sales productivity.

The productivity of a sales team is measured by its pipeline. The sales pipeline demonstrates how many revenue opportunities exist. An opportunity moves through the "buyer's journey" noted at different stages. With account-based marketing, activities are aligned at each stage to support sales. These are the stages of the buyer's journey, the marketing activities for supporting sales, and the associated success metrics:

1. **Demand generation:** New contacts or existing accounts are engaged. Your marketing team engages in activities to generate demand and promote your brand. These activities include

    - Attending events and tradeshows

    - Hosting webinars

    - Launching advertising campaigns

    - Named account targeting

    - Segmenting accounts into verticals

    The success metric for supporting demand generation activity is the number of revenue opportunities created for sales.

REMEMBER

    In the lead gen world, the success criteria for these activities could be vanity metrics, such as the number of content downloads, number of webinar attendees, and number of website visits. This completely ignores the quality, which further undermines the role of marketing in the eyes of sales. For demand gen, marketing focuses on one metric: potential revenue for each account.

2. **Opportunity:** At this stage, the account becomes a viable revenue opportunity. The contacts within the account are reviewing your platform, considering other options, and negotiating the contact. Marketing continues to support sales by "nurturing" these accounts. These are examples of nurturing campaigns:

    - Email campaign promoting a new whitepaper

    - Sharing a client case study or user story

    - Launching display advertising campaigns

    - Hosting a VIP dinner in the account's hometown

    The success metrics at the opportunity stage are the number of deals, and the size of the potential revenue, added to your company's pipeline.

REMEMBER

In a lead gen world, most B2B marketers don't do anything to help advance opportunities, because traditionally it's a sales activity at this stage. Marketers were only measuring the number of leads generated, not the most important result: revenue. With account-based marketing, your marketing and sales teams are collaborating together to help advance opportunities to the next stage.

3. **Closed/Won:** The final stage in the buyer's journey is when the account becomes a customer. The success metrics at the Closed/Won stage are the deal size and the number of deals closed.

   But marketing's work isn't over. Now it's time to turn those customers into advocates. This is when the buyer's journey ends, and the customer's journey begins. The marketing and sales teams must work closely with the customer success team on activities to retain this account.

REMEMBER

The four stages of the account-based marketing funnel are *Identify*, *Expand*, *Engage*, *Advocate*. It's the creation of customer advocates that helps your company organically expand its marketing efforts.

The sales pipeline may still look like a funnel because of how opportunities disappear. An opportunity can vanish for a number of reasons. Account-based marketing with the inverted funnel works together with the sales pipeline. Figure 2-1 compares the stages of the buyer's journey to the account-based marketing funnel.

FIGURE 2-1: Comparing the account-based marketing funnel with the buyer's journey.

IDENTIFY

EXPAND

ENGAGE

ADVOCATE

Target, discover, and spend wisely

Influencing customer sentiment

Advocacy is the most important stage of the new account-based marketing funnel. As a marketer, you know how to craft a message to create awareness for your product or service. You understand the importance of nurturing prospects with relevant content to help advance them through the sales pipeline. Account-based marketing requires you to continue nurturing your customers so they become raving fans and continue to renew their business.

You've probably heard the rule that 80 percent of your revenue comes from 20 percent of your customers. This is true for B2B marketing and sales. After the typical buyer's journey ends with a deal closing, the customer journey begins. Your marketing and sales teams worked together to close the deal. Now they engage with your customer success department to turn these customers into advocates. These are the stages of the customer's journey, the marketing activities for supporting customers, and the associated success metrics:

1. **Adoption:** Your accounts are officially customers. It's time for them to implement your product or service. This is where your customer success team takes over. Most B2B companies call their client services department *Customer Success* for this very reason, as it's all about empowering your clients to successfully adopt your technology. These are examples of activities to ensure successful adoption:

   - Product webinars

   - Implementation guides and checklists

   - "How to" videos

   - Customer or champion on-site training sessions

   The success metrics at the adoption stage are *usage* and *retention*.

WARNING

   The adoption stage is a pivotal moment in the customer's journey. If your customer can't adopt your technology or understand its ongoing benefits, then they're most likely to churn. I show how to prevent customer churn in the following section of this chapter.

2. **Upsell and cross-sell:** Many people often confuse cross-selling with upselling. Here's the difference:

   - A cross-sell is when you sell the same product to another business unit in the account that could be beneficial to the organization (this is important to note if you're selling to large, enterprise accounts).

   - An upsell is when you sell your customer an upgraded version of the same product; for example, a top-tier product that gives you unlimited access instead of a lower-tier product that only provides limited access.

REMEMBER

A cross-sell provides something new the customer didn't have before. An upsell gives your customer an additional benefit of the same product or service they already use.

With account-based marketing, you are continuously marketing to your current customers on additional features or benefits of your product. These marketing activities include

- Press releases announcing a new product feature
- Special pricing offers
- Infographics illustrating features of your product

The success metric in the upsell and cross-sell stage is new revenue from the same account. You will see new business and an increased deal size from your accounts, and increased engagement that can be monitored by the amount of communication and interaction your accounts have with customer success.

3. **Land and expand:** The idea of account-based marketing is to target all the contacts within an account, then engage them on their own channels with personalized marketing messages. In the land and expand stage, marketing focuses on looking for new opportunities to engage new contacts in the account to sell. As you've closed the initial deal and gone through the process of upselling and cross-selling your main contact within the account, you're learning more about their potential organizational needs. These marketing activities are necessary for landing and expanding within an existing account:

- Case studies and customer testimonials
- More detailed use cases, based on the industry or role for how different departments use your product
- Demonstrating your value proposition in every interaction
- Following through with your deliverables to your first customer contact within the account

REMEMBER

The success metrics in the land and expand stage are the same as the upsell and cross-sell stage: increasing revenue from your existing customer base.

Training your customer success team to look for new sales opportunities is essential. This can be done by coaching your customer success managers. I discuss how your customer success team can serve as an extension of sales and marketing in Part 5.

TIP

4. **"Always-on air cover":** This last stage of the customer journey is a bit like a war game. You've fought the battle to close a deal, and you won. You conquered new territory and further invested your stake through upselling, cross-selling, landing, and expanding. But the battle isn't over. The term *always-on air cover* means you continue to surround accounts with your

message. You never stop nurturing your clients. Even after they've made a purchase decision, you have to keep placing your marketing messages in front of the contacts in your customer accounts. These are a few ways to market to your customers and create customer advocates:

- Regular "town hall" webinars with your company's CEO

- Free training webinars for customers on product features

- Ongoing email communication from customer success

- Display advertising promoting content about your customers

- Monthly newsletter highlighting recent success and new content

- Regular meetups or a user conference

WARNING

These marketing activities only work when your company has a solid product offering. Your company's product must live up to your original value proposition and meet customer expectations. Your product must be easy to adopt and empower your customers. If your product fails, then no amount of marketing can improve the customer's experience.

Driving More Revenue from Account-Based Marketing

The bottom line for defining a company's success is revenue. Account-based marketing can help your company focus on revenue as it looks at the amount of money each account has the potential to bring in or currently is paying your company as a customer. Through account-based marketing, you are tracking revenue opportunities at the account level through data in your CRM. Figure 2-2 shows an example of an exported report from your CRM; it notes the annual recurring revenue (ARR) for each of your accounts.

TIP

If you're an early-stage B2B company with 100 clients or less, you should meet with your department heads each week in sales, marketing, customer success, and product to discuss how each account is doing. Are they happily using the product? Is there any opportunity to cross-sell or upsell? These conversations are essential to driving more revenue with account-based marketing. They help align your teams for the same goal: increasing revenue. How does a company keep or grow revenue? By closing new business to bring new revenue, while retaining the existing customer base.

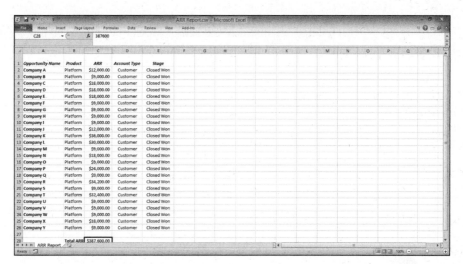

FIGURE 2-2:
Report showing your company's ARR by account.

Generating qualified opportunities

Part of the reason only 0.75 percent of leads ever became closed revenue is because there were no pre-qualification criteria for leads. New leads were gained through marketing activities, such as emailing your entire database of contacts and inviting them to attend your next webinar. Marketing had no idea when these leads would be a good fit. That's why the process of qualifying leads before handing them over to sales took place. It isn't hard to get a new lead in B2B marketing. It was hard to get the *right* lead.

REMEMBER

With account-based marketing, you no longer uses the terms marketing qualified leads (MQLs), sales accepted leads (SALs), or sales qualified leads (SQLs).

Traditional lead generation was all about quantity. Account-based marketing is all about quality. Before account-based marketing, most B2B marketers looked only at finding more leads. Now it's about connecting to the best contacts at accounts that can become opportunities. The ability for account-based marketing to qualify opportunities is a key deliverable to align your company with the same metric: revenue.

When you're looking to find qualified opportunities, you can use your marketing automation system. I show you how to use your marketing automation system for account-based marketing in Chapter 4.

Closing more new business

The focus for both sales and marketing must be on closing more new business. You can close more new business when you've created a list of target accounts, then determined which marketing messages need to be tailored for the account. When your team does this, you have much more success in generating new sales, and you further engage those accounts to create more energy and propel them through the pipeline faster.

By using account-based marketing and advertising to reach target sales accounts, marketing is positioning sales for more successful conversations with their buyers down the line. By the time sales reaches out to target accounts, buyers have been exposed to their company's messaging. This speeds up the sales process by cutting down on unnecessary sales introductions, and it sets the stage for a more personalized buying experience (increasing the likelihood that a lead will turn into a closed deal). ABM also ensures that you're focusing on the right leads from the start, so time and money aren't wasted chasing down dead-ends.

Preventing customer churn

According to Gartner Research, by demonstrating value proposition, B2B companies can expect more than two-thirds of their customers to be highly likely to buy more from them. If you aren't continuing to demonstrate your company's value proposition then it's likely your customer will walk away, or *churn*. If 80 percent of your company's revenue comes from 20 percent of your customers, then it's crucial for your organization to focus on preventing customer churn. If your customers aren't happy, you'll hear about it one way or another.

At the most basic level, account-based marketing is about the customer. In a time when B2B buyers crave more personalized selling experiences, ABM has surged to the forefront of marketing strategies as a way to improve the relevancy of sales and marketing messages. Buyers no longer are looking for a sales call or a marketing email to begin their research process.

What buyers want is relevant outreach that's personalized to meet their needs. That's exactly what ABM offers. Using targeted advertising, marketers can reach their buyers in an unobtrusive way on the channels that their buyers already use. Buyers can choose to engage with marketing messaging on their own terms.

Chapter 3

Aligning Sales and Marketing

W hen you've bought into the idea of launching account-based marketing for your B2B organization, it's time to move forward. As a marketer, I understand how important it is to give salespeople what they need immediately to be successful, whether it's a new piece of content or a new process for delivering qualified accounts.

For years, most companies have relied on the funnel to measure the number of new leads that came in each quarter, and monitored their progress through the funnel to become revenue opportunities and (eventually) closed deals. Marketing focused on generating more leads. Often, marketers don't ask their salespeople what they need because they're so focused on feeding leads into the funnel. Those days are over.

Account-based marketing (ABM) can breathe new life into your organization. ABM is all about flipping the traditional lead generation funnel on its head. No longer will marketing worry about reaching as many people as possible, increasing website traffic, or any other erroneous metrics.

Alas, you can't flip a switch and immediately make the transition from traditional lead generation to ABM: It is a process. Your current marketing and sales processes can't come to a complete halt, especially if they're currently generating revenue for your company. Ultimately, you will align your sales and marketing team members in a smarter, more effective way to both generate new revenue for your organization and retain and grow your existing customers.

In this chapter, I show you how to set the right goals that help your organization drive revenue. I discuss how to build your "A" team of players on your sales and marketing team to set realistic expectations of how ABM can grow revenue for your company.

Setting the Right Marketing Goals

I'll say it straight: How B2B marketers look at metrics is *awful*. As the field of marketing technology (MarTech) continues to grow, you can no longer look at B2B lead-based marketing as the be-all/end-all for driving revenue. An increase in leads at the top of the funnel may increase your engagement numbers, but it doesn't always lead to increased revenue for sales.

Ask yourself this question: "If Michael Jordan takes 1,000 shots and misses the basket every time, will anyone care how many shots he made?" Your answer probably is "No." The same thinking applies to lead-based marketing programs that don't result in revenue.

These are lead-based marketing metrics that I think are useless:

>> **Clicks:** When someone clicks on your banner ad, it feels great. But that pitch is useless when you reach the wrong people. Looking at total clicks is an insane way to determine whether your campaign was successful. What really matters is that the right person (who will actually buy your products or services) clicked on the link.

>> **Conversions:** The definition of a conversion varies company to company. In traditional lead-based marketing, a conversion is defined by a lead performing a desired action, such as clicking on your call-to-action (CTA) to download a piece of content. I'm always happy when I see that my email campaigns have a great open rate, and I'm even more excited when I see a ton of people clicked on the link that was included. But clicking a CTA doesn't mean they'll sign on the dotted line. It's crazy to think marketing celebrates "net new" conversions even when these aren't people who will actually make your company money.

>> **Page Views:** Another useless metric is how many times a person viewed a page. You can have a beautiful page packed with great content and optimized for SEO that is driving a ton of organic traffic to your website. On the flip side, that traffic can also be from your department's marketing intern who clicking

over and over again because she thinks it's important to increase page views. Oh, poor intern. What the marketing team should be doing is scrubbing this list of contacts who view your website against the list of people who are already in your database; this way, you can truly see how many new visitors are coming to your website.

» **Form Completions:** Does your company's revenue increase every time someone fills out a form? Mine doesn't. While some form fills might result in a discovery call or product demo that leads to closed business, I'd bet there are other factors that contributed to the sale beyond a simple name and email address.

One example here is how you might be excited when someone completes a form, even if that person only filled in two fields. And even when a form fill produces revenue, it is more often the exception than the rule. Marketers spend a lot of time looking at how many people converted after a form fill.

All of these marketing metrics add up to counting the number of leads. Leads are ridiculously easy to get these days. Everyone already has a ton of contacts in their database. You can buy a list of leads, go to LinkedIn, or use tons of tools giving you the leads you want.

TIP

Forget the leads. If they don't generate revenue, it doesn't matter how many leads you get.

This is why account-based marketing is catching fire: Leads from accounts that you care about are the leads that you want. Any lead that doesn't fit your ideal customer profile (ICP) doesn't really matter, does it?

Changing the B2B game

As digital marketing continues to evolve, we've seen *the rise of the buyers.* No matter your product or service, your buyers are more empowered and informed than ever before. Also, the number of stakeholders involved in a purchase decision is higher today (and will continue to grow in the future). This touches on one point that is very important to be successful with account-based marketing.

ABM is changing the B2B game because it helps sales and marketing teams become laser-focused. You don't ask a salesperson, "how many leads did you close this month?" you ask them "how many new accounts did you close?" Now, the two teams are working closely together with a selected list of targeted accounts. When both departments are involved, engaged, and have the same target, then you can increase the likelihood of success.

The game that's always been played in B2B is a numbers game: Count leads, webinars, ebooks, events, and other activities, not metrics that most matter for your company to grow revenue. In Chapter 1, I discuss the pitfalls with the traditional funnel and its limitations when marketing is focused only on generating demand and creating new leads. I presented a new model with a radical idea of flipping the sales funnel so you don't focus on lead marketing. Instead, you focus on finding your ideal customer, then engaging that account. This allows your organization to meet several goals:

>> A laser-focused sales and marketing strategy

>> A better customer experience

>> An improved sales-marketing relationship

>> More revenue

When marketing and sales are both incented to generate interest within and the right types of accounts and closing them, it creates alignment on the strategy and execution of this goal. It also saves resources from marketing and selling to leads that aren't a fit.

To be successful with account-based marketing, your sales and marketing teams must take a collaborative approach. Not only will input from sales increase the effectiveness of your ABM campaigns, but marketing can also provide air cover for sales by running targeted ads with relevant messaging that helps sales to create a more powerful dialogue with your potential buyers.

There's a challenge here: The status quo must be disrupted. Your marketing team can no longer take the easy route by blasting emails to as many leads as possible. The hard route requires a personalized message. This requires identifying your company's target accounts. Here's how you can start:

1. **Identify a list of target accounts.**

   Imagine a world with no more lead generation! With the flipped funnel, you're starting with a list of accounts. In Chapter 5, I discuss how to identify your target accounts and know who to sell by gaining a better understanding of your market segment.

2. **Expand your reach within the account.**

   When you connect with one contact who meets your persona criteria, the next step is to find more contacts within the account. In Chapter 8, you can read more about connecting with influencers and power sponsors to create velocity for sales.

3. **Engage the account.**

   Forget what you've traditionally done for nurturing leads and opportunities. With account-based marketing, you create tailored advertising messages and launch them on the channels your accounts are actively using, such as mobile, social, and video. You can read about this in Chapter 11.

4. **Grow the account's revenue.**

   Your sales win rates should be higher, because now you're going after the right account. After these accounts have closed, you can use account-based marketing to generate more sales from your existing customer base. Part 5 covers this in detail.

Most B2B marketers today don't think about revenue generation. With the traditional funnel, it's all about generating as many leads into the top of the funnel, with the hope that revenue comes out at the bottom. That old funnel is leaky and ineffective. Letting salespeople do all the hard work to close a deal no longer is an option. Marketing and sales must act as one team.

Creating a message that works for sales

Consider this scenario: Your marketing team determines it will target personas who are IT managers. You know that IT managers are key users of your product, and you have a customer case study or two about your company's success. But you're targeting IT managers who are in disparate industries (for example, gaming and manufacturing). You're adding another layer of segmentation.

The message can't be the same for an IT manager in both industries. Though their personas are the same, the gaming industry is very different from manufacturing. So your messages must be different. What you have to do from a sales process is understand what your contacts in account care about based on their stage in the buyer's journey. When you're creating a message that works for sales, gather both the marketing team and your salespeople in one room to ask your team these questions:

» Who is your ideal contact? How old is this person? Demographic information matters when you're creating a message.

» What gets them excited? What matters to them? Is it making their jobs easier, automating processes, or another motivation to resolve one of their pain points?

To create a message that works for individual personas by industry, you must personalize it. No single message works for every prospect. Marketing must collaborate with sales to create content and messages that resonate with each individual account.

Driving Revenue through Teamwork

Before you begin your account-based marketing campaigns, a conversation must occur between sales and marketing to identify those target accounts. This increases marketing's understanding of sales' goals, and reinforces marketing's position in the eyes of the sales team as an important part of the selling process. When marketing runs programs on the account level, sales sees how marketing can deliver on their target accounts. This eases tensions that the teams may have experienced over lead quality, while simultaneously bolstering marketing and sales effectiveness.

REMEMBER

You need to put a process in place to measure results. Account-based marketing is a very different approach than traditional lead-based marketing, so it requires new metrics.

"BIG 5 METRICS" FOR ACCOUNT-BASED MARKETING

Jon Miller (@jonmiller) is the CEO and founder of Engagio, an all-in-one account-based marketing platform that works to engage accounts and deepen the alignment between sales and marketing. As a co-founder and former CMO of Marketo, Jon has seen how the B2B industry requires a new, different mindset for how marketing and sales claim victory in ABM. Jon advocates that marketers embrace the "Big 5 Metrics" for account-based marketing:

- **Coverage:** Do you have sufficient data, contacts, and account plans for each target account?

- **Awareness:** Are the target accounts aware of your company and its solutions?

- **Engagement:** Are the right people at the account spending time with your company, and is that engagement going up over time?

- **Program Impact:** Are marketing programs reaching the target account, and are they having a long-term effect?

- **Influence:** Are the ABM activities improving sales outcomes, such as deal velocity, win rates, average contract values, and retention?

With ABM, marketing has a direct influence on the sales pipeline. Using these metrics, marketers can show how they influenced deals, created velocity to close new business, and helped the sales team win.

Selling the dream

Every dream is personal. You can't sell your own dream to others. You must empower them to achieve their dreams. This can be one of the biggest pitfalls in sales and marketing: Everyone tries to sell. Marketing tries to say how awesome its product is, not saying "Here's the problem we all face in the industry. If you agree with the problem, let's talk about our solution for it."

WARNING

It isn't about selling, it's about serving! If you tell your prospect why they should buy your product before you hear the problems your prospect faces, you'll never get anywhere.

REMEMBER

In the B2B sales process, don't sell the product. Instead, agree on the problem the contacts in your targeted accounts are currently facing. This will help provide you with a context on how your company can potentially provide a solution.

After the problem is agreed upon, then your company can present ways to solve it. Follow these steps:

1. **Agree on the problem.**

2. **Review ways to solve the problem.**

3. **Present your company's solution.**

At the most basic level, account-based marketing is about the customer. In a time when B2B buyers are craving more personalized selling experiences, ABM has moved the forefront of marketing strategies as a way to improve the relevancy of sales and marketing messages. Buyers no longer look for a sales call or a marketing email to kick off their research process.

According to CMO.com, 77 percent of B2B marketers believe real-time personalization is crucial. By using account-based marketing and advertising to reach target sales accounts, marketing is setting sales up for more successful conversations with their buyers. By the time sales reaches out to target accounts, buyers have been exposed to their company's messaging.

What they want is relevant outreach that's personalized to meet their needs — which is what ABM offers. Using targeted advertising, marketers can reach their buyers in an unobtrusive way on the channels that their buyers are already using, so buyers can choose to engage with marketing messaging on their own terms.

TIP

Keep this in mind when you're selling the dream to your targeted accounts: According to the Information Technology Services Marketing Association (ITSMA), 75 percent of executives will read unsolicited marketing materials that might contain content relevant to their business. If the content and message resonates with your target accounts, then you'll be one step closer to building a relationship.

These activities can help sell the dream:

>> List all the companies, personas, and roles in your ideal customer profile.

>> Meet with sales and your executive team to identify problems your prospects are trying to solve.

>> Create content that aligns with those problems, including

- Webinars

- Infographics

- White papers

- Blog posts

- Videos

- Events

- Press releases

- Social media

These are activities to reach your goal by surrounding your targeted accounts with content on the channels where they're active. This speeds up the sales process by reducing unnecessary sales introductions, and sets the stage for a more personalized buying experience (increasing the likelihood that a lead will turn into a closed deal). ABM also ensures that you're focusing on the right leads from the start, so time and money aren't wasted on dead ends.

As I've seen at my company, Terminus, successfully marketing to accounts starts with a conversation between marketing, sales, and other key stakeholders within your business. Effective ABM messaging requires an understanding of customer pain points. That insight comes from the sales reps who are having conversations with prospects every day. It isn't enough for marketing to set up an ABM program, then press "Go." Marketers need to work with sales to identify target accounts and a strategy to reach them.

Building your "A" team

To correctly execute account-based marketing, your sales and marketing teams must be aligned. For modern B2B organizations, it's no longer sales against marketing, but a single team: sales + marketing = "smarketing." Your new "smarketing" team has a common set of objectives:

TIP

Keep these goals top of mind for your "smarketing" team:

>> Target your ideal customers: your *accounts*.

>> Engage the contacts in your target accounts on the channels where they're active.

>> Advance those accounts quickly through the buying process by creating velocity through content and activities.

To be successful with your "smarketing" team, you have to put the right players in place. The good news is that you don't have to hire a bunch of new employees to be successful with account-based marketing.

These are the key roles in building your "A" team for account-based marketing:

>> **Business/sales development representative (BDR/SDR):** This individual is critical for the success of ABM. The development team must work in alignment with marketing on outbound and inbound efforts.

>> **Sales database administrator:** A data guru who updates the contact and account information in your CRM.

>> **Marketing operations/technology manager:** Someone to manage your marketing automation system; they align, the contacts with marketing activities, based on their stage in the purchase decision.

>> **Content manager:** This person works with marketing, sales, and customer success to supply collateral, activities, and digital media for every stage of the account's journey.

>> **Account executive:** The salesperson who will ultimately close the deal.

>> **Sales leader:** Team manager or director running the sales department.

>> **Customer success manager:** Client expert who will help turn your account into a customer advocate (described in Chapter 16).

>> **Executive stakeholder(s):** The leadership at your organization; depending on your size, the CMO, VP of Sales, or the CEO (or all of them) can have a stake in "smarketing."

Here's an example Craig Rosenberg (@funnelholic) presented on his blog about how to build a dream team to execute account-based marketing:

I spoke with the sales enablement team from a large technology company focused on the Fortune 50. They set up account teams with the account executives owning the account. Each team included a dedicated sales development rep, an account manager, a marketing manager, and an executive sponsor. These teams were accountable for driving business at this specific account and we are assigned various activities against specific prospects within the account. For example, the executive sponsor sent a series of personalized messages to target executives, marketing devised account-specific campaigns that were sent throughout the program, and the sales development rep drove meetings with manager-level contacts.

Who will sell the dream at your company? The future of B2B marketing is one team. Modern B2B organizations recognize that it's no longer sales or marketing who will sell the dream, it's sales and marketing: "Smarketing."

Renewing the Vows between Marketing and Sales

For years, sales and marketing have struggled to collaborate. Being in the B2B game for a while, I've heard complaints from both sides of the table:

>> Marketing creates campaigns and content to bring in tons of leads, then gripes when sales doesn't close a deal.

>> Sales says they can't close deals because marketing doesn't produce the right leads.

Does this sound familiar? To me, it sounds a bit like a bad marriage. Think about sales and marketing as a married couple. When they first met, they fell in love, with grand visions for their life together. They agreed to be in business together (after all, marriage is a contract). There's a mutual bank account now. They share in the good times celebrating their success.

Then things got tough with the business. Money doesn't come in as they thought it would. The bickering starts. Sales accuses marketing of not doing enough to support them. Marketing says that the team is doing everything it can to make things happen; sales is just lazy.

This misalignment happens when the goals are different between the two parties. There's something broken about this relationship. Using the family analogy, the same shared bank account pays the bills. It's the family bank account to which everyone is contributing. If you think about the sales and marketing teams within a company, it's the same thing. With account-based marketing, the "smarketing" team is focused on generating revenue (putting money into the same family bank account).

Connecting to marketing

Marketing must play a part in sales acceleration, and sales must play a part in marketing. Each account, and the marketing activities associated with it, is focused on ROI. It's time to renew those vows and reaffirm your commitment to succeeding as a modern, innovative B2B organization.

Like a marriage that's about to be saved, your sales and marketing teams can overcome any obstacle through

» **Talking to each other.** Keep communication open and positive. Utilize emails, phone calls, and weekly team meetings.

Better communication streamlines operational efficiency.

» **Sharing goals.** Create a strategic plan with the goal of growing revenue for your company.

Key performance indicator (KPI) metrics should monitor how soon accounts move through the pipeline (sales velocity).

» **Playing to your individual strengths.** By focusing on the strengths of individual contributors, then combining them as a team, you bring out the "A" game of your "smarketing" team.

Talking to your sales team

This formula will help your company succeed with account-based marketing. I recommend the following process for marketing and sales to create their first account plan to target a set of ideal customers:

1. **Gather marketing and sales in a room.**

   Include your sales and marketing team leaders, plus the executive stakeholder(s), for a "smarketing" brainstorming session.

2. **List companies that are current opportunities for your sales team.**

   There should be a list of 10 to 20 accounts for sales reps to close.

3. **Review the activity for each account.**

   Look at information in your CRM and marketing automation system for engagement history for your contacts in the target accounts. This helps in identifying the most useful content and activities (I discuss how to do this in Chapter 9).

4. **Review marketing campaigns.**

   If you've been running advertising, sending emails, or included these contacts in various campaigns, what has worked so far? This helps to create air cover for each contact throughout the buying journey.

5. **Develop a marketing plan for the next month.**

   Create a list of the activities, advertising, and content your marketing team will do for the next four weeks. Have a different activity or piece of content served up to your targeted contacts each week; this will help to determine whether any *velocity* was created to move the account further to a purchase decision. While marketing is running these air cover campaigns, the sales rep is calling on the account to check in.

Here's an example of an account marketing plan:

Week	Marketing	Sales
Week 1	Sends direct mail to primary contact in account	Calls the account after mail is delivered to check in
Week 2	Emails new whitepaper, case study, or ebook	Emails the account to see whether they have any questions about the content
Week 3	Runs display targeted advertising campaigns	Collaborates with marketing to see whether the account clicked on the ad
Week 4	Analyzes engagement metrics to see what's worked	Assesses next steps for moving forward

From there, you have a start for account-based marketing. This begins as a manual process; you look strategically at each contact within the account to see which types of activities are successful in driving engagement and creating velocity for sales. When your ABM program grows, you can leverage technology to execute account-based marketing at scale. I discuss this in Chapter 7.

Setting realistic expectations

I wish I could wave a magic wand and make dollars rain on the sales team. Sadly, that isn't how it works. You must set realistic expectations for your "smarketing" team, then convey those expectations to your executive stakeholders, your company's VP or C-level executive.

TIP

I recommend applying *SMART* guidelines to create goals for account-based marketing:

>> **Specific:** What will the goal accomplish?

For account-based marketing, the goal is to align sales and marketing into one "smarketing" team that

- Targets the best-fit potential customers to generate revenue.
- Turns your current customers into advocates.

>> **Measurable:** Which metrics determine whether the goal has been reached?

For ABM, the main metric is *revenue*. When "smarketing" works together on creating velocity to turn accounts into revenue, the proof arrives as dollar signs.

>> **Achievable:** Does your new "smarketing" team have the tools, talent, and resources to meet this goal?

Assign ownership roles to each member of your sales and marketing team, such as

- Creating content.
- Launching advertising campaigns to provide air cover for sales.
- Following up with emails.
- Engaging on social media.

>> **Result:** What is the primary benefit of accomplishing this goal?

The answer is *to generate revenue.* That's why I come to work every day: to make money doing something I'm passionate about. I get excited when I see my marketing and sales team working together to knock our quota out of the park, while delighting our customers.

>> **Timely:** How long will it take to achieve this goal?

The speed of your account-based marketing efforts may be influenced by company size. For example, a small company that doesn't have a contract to purchase will see the results of ABM much sooner than an enterprise organization that targets Fortune 500 companies.

Setting a SMART goal will help address potential roadblocks before you begin your "smarketing" team's first ABM campaign. List your important milestones, such as

>> Reducing spend

>> Increasing impressions

>> Expanding accounts

>> Increasing engagement

Playing to your strengths

In an effort to take your newly formed "smarketing" team to a new level, you must leverage each other's strengths. This helps each team member of the "smarketing" team take ownership of his or her contributions to revenue growth. The marketing team members have different strengths than salespeople. Marketing shouldn't think of itself as a seller. Instead, marketing *enables* sales. Marketing and sales bring these strengths to the "smarketing" team:

» Marketing engages targeted contacts on their terms, runs advertising campaigns, tailors personalized messaging, tracks engagement, and estimates ROI.

Marketers built incredible demand generation campaigns feeding inside sales. Using all these techniques, marketers can generate activity in the targeted accounts for sales.

» Sales identifies the maximum pain points of our customers, then helps marketers create the content. Your sales reps are on the front lines, calling and emailing their prospects. To provide content that presents a solution, it's essential for marketing to ask sales which problem those contacts are trying to solve. Instead of sending a case study to every prospect, marketing works with sales to customize content specifically addressing a problem, based on a contact's job role, seniority, and industry.

WARNING

It's hard abandoning the metrics that marketing has always focused on. ABM's main metric, revenue, is a significant change from pursuing lead-based marketing and focusing on the volume of leads.

Lead volume was the old way of doing business. The new metric is *revenue*. ABM isn't about lead generation. You don't want to give your sales team 2,000 leads that aren't worth anything. Using account-based marketing to target the right companies will produce better, qualified leads. This can tie into your goal of generating new leads if your executive team isn't ready to create a new KPI. Sales and marketing can produce big results with account-based marketing.

Chapter 4

Selecting Tools

B2B marketing and sales professionals have come to rely on technology to connect with their prospects and customers. Back in the day, it was all about "smiling and dialing" cold calling prospects to reach the right person on the phone. Thanks to technology, those days are over. Emails and the internet are making cold calls totally extinct. Today there are more software tools than ever that help to connect marketers with potential new clients.

Account-based marketing (ABM) is all about the intersection of marketing and technology. Marketing exists to help generate awareness and drive revenue for sales. Utilizing modern technology makes creating awareness of your company's product or service easier than it ever was before. By using technology, you can gather and store all the data on your customers. Thanks to software, you can design compelling content and distribute it to these same customers through targeted activities.

In this chapter, I discuss how changes in marketing technology (MarTech) are impacting the B2B marketing industry and the important trends you should note. I tell you what type of software is essential to include in your B2B MarTech stack that lets you harness the power of data, and how to use these tools for ABM to tie everything back to an account. This chapter gives you the types of marketing techniques and activities where you can apply technology to create awareness and interest from your prospects.

Understanding Marketing Technology

Marketing technology (MarTech) is the software that helps you execute your marketing activities. MarTech is the B2B marketing industry's term for applications that help you succeed with modern marketing activities. These marketing activities aren't just about sending emails to contacts in a database. They also apply that data to determine who should receive an email, what type of email to send, and the best time of day to send it.

MarTech is a rapidly growing category of software. The evolution of MarTech has given B2B marketing professionals many advantages. Because of the technology, that can execute marketing at scale. Scale means reaching your contacts and accounts in the hundreds and thousands without manual processes. The value this brings includes

>> **Speed:** Your marketing team saves time and money. With technology, you can quickly reach many people.

>> **Results:** You can see your success metrics for your marketing activities to identify what works and what doesn't. Depending on the technology tools you use, you can see these results in real time.

REMEMBER

The goal of account-based marketing is to generate revenue from your best-fit customers and prospects. Using technology allows your team to execute ABM at scale. MarTech offers a wide range of benefits for ABM at scale to reach hundreds or thousands of contacts, and at a personalized level.

Determining your MarTech needs

Your needs for MarTech are unique to your organization. For your sales and marketing ("smarketing") team to execute account-based marketing at scale, you need technology. But before you choose a solution, think about how you will use this technology.

The technology and tools you add should fulfill a need. As B2B marketing continues to shift away from traditional media (such as print, radio, and billboard advertising) to digital platforms (including online mobile, social, video, and display ads), marketers need a streamlined process to execute marketing activities at scale. This is where MarTech comes into play. These are the core needs that MarTech fulfills for B2B marketing activities:

>> **Create awareness:** Your prospects need to recognize your brand and logo. If they don't know you, they can't buy from you. MarTech gives you the ability to reach out to thousands of people without manual effort.

>> **Develop engaging content:** Using MarTech design software to build creative images and compelling content can help promote thought leadership for your category.

>> **Generate demand:** MarTech helps to extend the reach of your message by connecting with prospects looking for your product or service.

>> **Track engagement:** A central data repository shows the results of those activities.

>> **Manage revenue opportunities:** These activities will help generate potential deals for your company.

>> **Report on success metrics:** You can see which of these activities created revenue, and learn from those results.

REMEMBER

This is why the funnel was so popular with B2B sales and marketing teams, because prospects started with Awareness, Interest, Consideration, and Decision. During the decision-making process they would fall out of the funnel, making it skinny at the bottom. Figure 4-1 shows the buyer's journey with the traditional funnel.

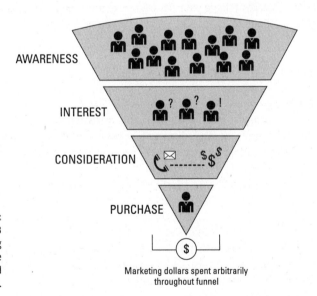

FIGURE 4-1:
The B2B
decision-making
process with the
lead-based
funnel.

AWARENESS

INTEREST

CONSIDERATION

PURCHASE

Marketing dollars spent arbitrarily
throughout funnel

With account-based marketing, you can flip the funnel on its head by using technology. You're starting by identifying the best-fit customers who represent potential buyers of your product or service. Before the evolution of MarTech, the "spray and pray" model was the predominant form of B2B marketing. Teams built lists of thousands of contacts to blast their message to, then hoped that one of those contacts might raise their hand to show interest. MarTech makes "spray and pray" null and void. Your company must get the data on those best-fit customers, then use tools and activities to reach out to them, and MarTech fulfills those needs.

Assessing your resources

It's important to note the resources you already have. These resources include

>> **People:** You're reading this book! Technology allows any marketer to become an army of one (especially for early-stage companies). If you're the head of a marketing team and you have employees who are specialized in various marketing roles, then you're even better equipped to execute account-based marketing.

>> **Processes:** You already have a process for marketing and sales. You should have a current method of capturing inbound leads on your website, tracking new prospects you met at an event, then following up with those contacts.

>> **Technology:** Your existing processes can be tailored with MarTech to execute ABM at scale. By training your people to use these new tools, you can create a highly skilled and operationally efficient marketing team.

Building a MarTech Stack

In the technology world, the term *stack* is used to describe the software, systems and tools that comprise your organization's infrastructure. In the B2B marketing world, you also have several different software platforms that make up your "stack." This technology is mostly web-based.

REMEMBER

Almost all MarTech software platforms and applications are web-based. This means your marketing and salespeople can access these tools anytime, anywhere.

WARNING

If you don't have a CRM and a marketing automation system, stop reading here. You can't execute account-based marketing at scale. ABM will be a time-consuming manual process for your team.

There are a few essential pieces you need to complete the B2B software puzzle. These software platforms *must* be in your MarTech stack:

>> **Customer Relationship Management (CRM) system:** Your company needs a centralized place to store and manage all of your customers' contact information. This includes both your current clients and prospects. A CRM is

the best place to store all of this information. The CRM serves as your central data repository. All of your data should be stored here instead of spread-sheets, as this can cause data silos. Data silos are a problem because they make it impossible for your team to access and update information in real time. The good news is that modern CRM platforms have a robust application programming interface (API). The API lets your systems "talk" to each other. I suggest using Salesforce because it integrates with almost every type of MarTech software in the marketplace. Salesforce is the 800 lb. gorilla, with more than 100,000 companies are using it, as there are options for small, mid-market, and enterprise-level organizations. Figure 4-2 shows an example of a contact in a CRM.

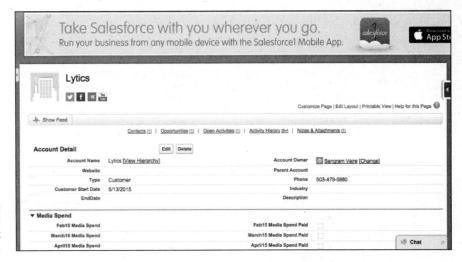

FIGURE 4-2: Using your CRM to store contact information.

>> **Marketing Automation:** The term *marketing automation* refers to using a single platform for tracking engagement with contacts in your CRM. A marketing automation platform gives you the tools to create activities then monitors the level of activity each contact is engaged in. Marketing automation is used for scoring the contacts created in your CRM. Whenever you add a new contact record to your CRM, the data is pulled into your marketing automation system through the API. Examples of marketing automation systems include Marketo, HubSpot, Eloqua, Salesfusion, and Pardot. Using a marketing automation tool, you can identify your customers, build lists, and send content. Figure 4-3 shows the home page of a marketing automation platform.

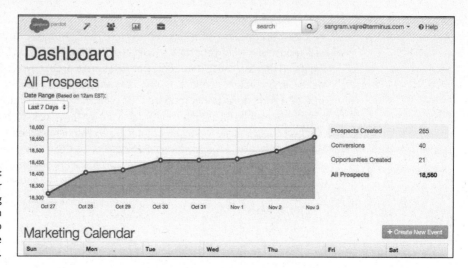

FIGURE 4-3:
Using your marketing automation system to streamline activities.

>> **Content Management System (CMS):** A CMS is the platform where you host your company's website. The most popular CMS on the market today is WordPress because of its easy-to-use functionality. All of the pages for your company's website are created and uploaded. The CMS also gives you a platform for posting blog content. Figure 4-4 shows the central dashboard of a CMS.

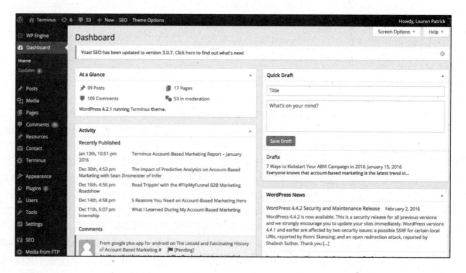

FIGURE 4-4:
Using a CMS to host your website and blog.

TIP

Thousands of templates are available for WordPress, some of which can be easily customized to reflect your business's brand standards.

WARNING

A custom CMS is more expensive than implementing a WordPress or Drupal platform. If you need customized development, prepared to invest thousands of dollars.

>> **Social media:** Modern B2B marketing and sales professionals *must* be engaged on social media platforms. There are two essential social media platforms:

- Twitter can be used to find individuals, companies, and trends using hashtags. Figure 4-5 shows an example of my Twitter profile.

- LinkedIn is used to search for individuals and companies. Figure 4-6 shows my LinkedIn profile.

FIGURE 4-5:
Example of a Twitter profile.

REMEMBER

Facebook is a powerful social media tool for advertising, but when it comes to engaging directly with contacts in your target accounts, stick to LinkedIn and Twitter.

>> **Account-based marketing (ABM):** You need to reach your best-fit accounts and the contacts within those accounts, then monitor engagement. An ABM platform lets you do this, while also controlling your advertising and the messages you're sending. Analytics capabilities are also included to see how successfully those campaigns target your prospects. The beauty of account-based marketing is you are engaging accounts on their terms through targeted advertising.

Combining these platforms builds your MarTech stack. Figure 4-7 shows an example of the MarTech stack I use.

FIGURE 4-6:
Example of a
LinkedIn profile.

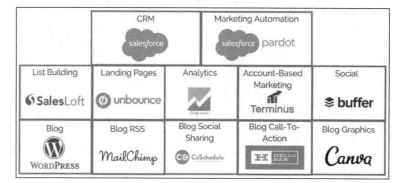

FIGURE 4-7:
Example of a
MarTech Stack.

MARTECH CATEGORIES ACCORDING TO @CHIEFMARTEC

Scott Brinker is the founder and thought leader at ChiefMarTec (`www.chiefmartec.com`). On Twitter (`@ChiefMarTec`), he's actively engaging with B2B marketing and sales thought leaders about the future of MarTech. Every year, he publishes a new infographic, "The Marketing Technology Landscape," demonstrating the growth of the MarTech category. There are more than 40 subcategories that Scott says make up the overall MarTech category. The "backbone" platforms (such as CRM, marketing automation, and your website) are the foundation of your MarTech stack. Your activities for account-based marketing rest on top of these "backbone" platforms. These are examples of products in the subcategories you'll need for ABM.

- Email marketing: Constant Contact, MailChimp

- Mobile marketing: Mobivity, AirPush, TapJoy

- Search and social ads: Kenshoo, AdProof, Adchemy, SearchForce, Sidecar, BrandNetworks

- Display ads: DataXO, Bizo, TruSignal, AdRocketFuel, NetMining, AdRolls, DoubleClick

- Video ads and marketing: Vimeo, Wistia, Brightcove

- Creative and design: Adobe Creative Cloud (InDesign, Photoshop), Canva

- Communities and reviews: Disqus, Jive, Telligent, Reevoo

- Social media marketing: Influitive, Attensity, Topsy, Wildfire, SproutSocial

- Events and webinars: Citrix, Cisco, EventBrite, Cvent

- Calls and call centers: Twillo, KeyMetric, LiveOps, CallRail

- Customer experience: Kana, Verint, Gainsight

- Loyalty and gamification: Badgeville, CrowdTwist, PunchTab

- Personalization: Terminus, DemandBase

- Testing and optimization: WebTrends, ion, Experiment.ly, Optimize.ly

- Marketing apps: Wizehive, Wufoo, Kontest, Woobox, SnapApp

- SEO (to gauge impact of keywords): BrightEdge, Yoast, plug into your WordPress

- Content marketing: Kapost, Visual.ly, Curata, Outbrain

- Sales enablement: Bloomfire, Contactually, Postwire, Cloze

- Marketing data: Dun & Bradstreet Netprospex, Data.com, ZoomInfo

- Channel/local marketing: Pica9, Balihoo, BrandMuscle

- Marketing resource management: Infor, NorthPlains, MarcomCentral

- Digital asset management: Widen, Bynder, Celum

- Agile and project management: Liquid, Atlassian, Asana, Clarizen

- Marketing analytics: Adometry, PivotLink, MarketShare

- Dashboards: Sizmek, Chart.io, Domo

- Web and mobile analytics: Bit.ly, Woopra, Clicky, Adobe Analytics

- Business intelligence: SAP, Oracle

Defining your digital presence

As a B2B marketer, your home is on the web. Across all of the digital platforms and tools in your MarTech stack, your brand must be aligned. By this I mean that your message, colors, content, creative, and all the other collateral you're using to engage prospects must be unified. Your digital presence and content should effectively communicate exactly what your company does. This is accomplished through online and offline marketing activities.

Setting Up Your Platforms

After you've selected your tools for account-based marketing, you need to implement them and train your team to use MarTech. Taking the time to correctly set up your MarTech platforms is worth its weight in gold. By integrating your CRM, marketing automation system, CMS, social media, and ABM platform, you can execute ABM at scale then accurately measure the results and watch your revenue grow.

Integrating your software

The platforms in your MarTech stack need to "talk" to each other. All of your applications are selected to build a comprehensive experience for marketing to your accounts.

TECHNICAL STUFF

This integration is accomplished through the application programming interface (API). The API allows your applications to connect and to prevent data silos.

When you connect your platforms, guides and instructions are available from your vendors. Figure 4-8 shows how you connect your CRM and marketing automation system.

After your backbone platforms are integrated, you can connect your CRM to your account-based marketing platform. You need to align the fields in your CRM with your criteria for executing targeted ads for account-based marketing. When you are using advertising as part of your account-based marketing plan, you drive your prospects to a landing page or microsite. Your ABM platform doesn't give you the ability to see these individual clicks. However, you can place tracking code on your website. Your marketing automation system will give you a unique tracking code to use. Figure 4-9 shows how you place tracking code on your website.

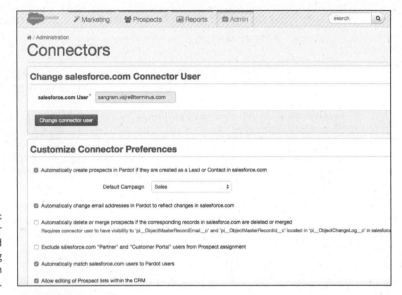

FIGURE 4-8:
Connecting your
CRM and
marketing
automation
system.

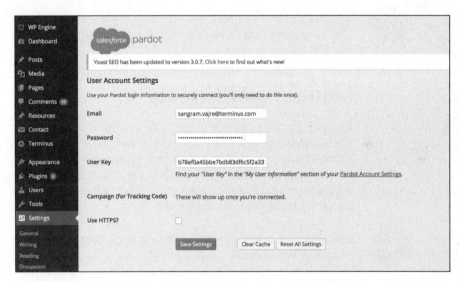

FIGURE 4-9:
Creating a
website tracking
code from your
marketing
automation
system.

You can also build landing pages for your account-based marketing campaigns. Using landing pages built in your marketing automation system, you can capture the contact information for your prospects. Figure 4-10 is an example of a landing page created in a marketing automation system, then used for an ABM campaign.

The Complete Guide To Targeted B2B Advertising

See everything you need to know to get engage accounts on their terms

Imagine if you could engage your key decision-makers on their terms --
the websites they are already visiting to do their job or the ones they use
to catch up on their social life. This helpful guide explains how to:

· **Determine if you are ready** for account-based advertising
· **Segment your target audience** to reach key decision-makers within
  the accounts you care most about
· **Create campaigns** your target accounts will love and engage with
· **Develop creative** that speaks to the pain points of your target
  accounts and peaks their interest
· **Measure and Optimize Results** to continually improve your
  campaigns and make you look like a marketing rockstar

THE COMPLETE GUIDE TO
Targeted **B2B** Advertising
EBOOK

Get Your Copy Of The eBook

Business Email *

Send it to me!

FIGURE 4-10:
Using landing
pages for ABM
campaigns.

**TECHNICAL
STUFF**

To measure the results of these activities, you see the results in your CRM. If your CRM can export data through an API, or even export as a .csv file, most ABM tool-sets and import your data.

Managing ABM tools

The term "marketing technologist" has only been around for a few years. With the rise of marketing automation, blogging, and social media, marketing has become an increasingly technical field. As your company adds software, tools, and applications to your technology stack, you must actively monitor your presence and activities across all of your platforms. This is where having an in-house marketing technologist becomes important.

TIP

It's important to assign ownership to your platforms. Here is how I structure my marketing department:

>> **Marketing technologist:** Perhaps you call this person your marketing operations, demand generation, or campaign manager. This person owns all of your tech operational process for both sales and marketing. These are the platforms for which they're responsible:

   ● *CRM:* Managing the database of your contacts, assigning tasks, and building workflows for how new prospects should come into your system from marketing automation.

- *Marketing automation:* Creating landing pages, code for calls-to-action (CTA) and other tracking code to measure the engagement from your marketing activities.

- *Account-based marketing:* Running advertising and campaigns, tracking ROI and cost-per-click (CPC).

- *Social media:* Loading tweets in such tools as HootSuite or Buffer to remove the manual process of writing a post.

>> **Marketing experience manager:** This person is commonly called the content or marketing communications (MarComm) manager. This person owns all of your digital content, media, and messages used to create awareness. These are the platforms for which they're responsible:

- *CMS:* Maintaining and uploading new content to your company's website and blog. All of the content on your company's website and blog should provide an experience and tell a story about your brand and the products/services you offer.

- *Content resources:* Creating whitepapers, ebooks, infographics, and customer case studies for downloading. Also responsible for running webinars and producing videos.

- *Design suite:* The tools you use to create content, such as whitepapers, infographics and ebooks. I cover this in the next section.

- *Communications:* Email newsletters, press releases, and collaborating for content in publications and third-party sites.

- *Social media:* Crafting content to post to social media, developing and writing posts for campaign, and cross-promoting content featured on other platforms.

TIP

Social media can fall under the responsibility of either the marketing technologist or the marketing content/communications manager. The marketing technologist may own the tools, then partner with the experience manager for the content to use in social media campaigns.

Tying everything back to an account

The reason you're using all of these digital tools is to streamline the activities and track them at the account level. Here's how the tools in your MarTech stack tie back to individual accounts:

>> **CRM:** Stores all the data on your accounts and contacts.

>> **Marketing automation:** Tracks how your *all* of your accounts engage.

>> **ABM platform:** Executing targeted advertising to your accounts.

Types of Marketing Activities

After you have your technology stack in place, you can determine the type of the activities you need to engage the contacts you have stored in your CRM and loaded into your marketing automation platform. There are several techniques that B2B marketers perform with technology to engage with prospects and customers. These activities are best practices for both B2B marketing and ABM.

Advertising

In the modern world, the digital and display advertising solutions available are evolving faster than ever. Unlike the *Mad Men* days of the 1950s, the advertising world moves at a lightning pace. Imagine what Don Draper would say when you told him he wouldn't have to wait for six months to receive the research that tells him whether his latest advertising is working. The modern marketer gets these real-time insights.

Advertising has become a scientific way of testing and refining your company's messages. You still go through similar motions as the mad men, but you're spending less money and less time.

The purpose of advertising is to build brand awareness. Especially if you're a new or early-stage company, the potential new customers you're trying to reach will not be familiar with your brand. Advertising helps to create awareness and name recognition. For the purposes of this book, I focus on four main types of advertising:

>> **Display:** You see these ads all over the web. Banner ads, pop ups, and creative pictures are trying to drive you to another link. This requires interaction when the end user clicks through to an additional landing page. *Impressions* are also a key metric; they count the number of times your ad was served up to an end user.

>> **Mobile:** Advertising on mobile devices continues proliferate. You've seen these ads while using applications on your mobile phone or while surfing on your internet browser.

>> **Video:** Video advertisements are gaining momentum. YouTube makes the user wait and watch a full video ad before allowing the user to view content.

>> **Social:** There are many social media platforms, with new platforms emerging every day. For B2B marketing teams, the two main social media applications for the most seamless advertising are LinkedIn and Twitter. The end user is already scrolling through social media feeds, timelines, and news articles. It's here where you can promote or "sponsor" updates and serve up advertising.

Social

Social media got its name because the platforms are designed to connect with other people. It's an easy way of engaging with the thought leaders who are posting about what you're interested in. You can either promote your own content, or insert yourself in conversations with hashtags.

Twitter has given you unprecedented If your prospects *like* you on Facebook or *follow* you on Twitter or LinkedIn, it shows they're engaged in your brand.

Using LinkedIn, you can target everyone based on profile information. LinkedIn lets you create ads based on industry, job role, seniority, and geographic location. For example, suppose you just published an ebook about how to be an awesome CMO. You can target CMOs on LinkedIn. If you have a list of companies, you can put your ads only in front of those companies.

Events

There are two main event categories for B2B marketers: tradeshows (or conferences hosted by someone else) and events you host yourself:

>> **Tradeshows and conferences:** There are tons of tradeshows and conferences. These industry events are a great way to bring people together.

You shouldn't attend every tradeshow in your industry. To determine what events you should attend, check for these important details:

- Look at list of other companies sponsoring the show. Are your competitors there? If so, how much presence do they have?

- Look at list of previous event attendees. Are they companies who are targeted accounts for your business?

- Search for specific associations or professional organizations. They often have one huge annual meeting or event.

If you opt to purchase a booth, make sure you also have a presence outside your booth (such as speaking at a breakout session or hosting a happy hour). You want to stand out so conference attendees remember your brand after the show ends.

REMEMBER

Before you travel to a tradeshow, it's important to know whether any of your prospects or customers are attending. Mine your database of contacts to prepare and send an email asking whether they'll be attending the same show too. Give them your booth number to find you and schedule a meeting.

>> **Roadshow**: Create your own event. Instead of attending events hosted by other people or organizations, you can host your own event where you live or where your company is headquartered. The goal for a roadshow isn't to have hundreds of people attend. The goal is to have the right group of people attend your event who are most likely to use your company's product or service. Here's how you can start planning your own roadshow:

1. Identify your prospects and customers in your CRM.

2. Create a list of who you want to attend using your marketing automation system.

3. Review the list for geographic locations where contacts are located to determine which cities might be the best fit for your show.

4. Further segment the list of contacts to determine which locations are closest to their hometown. Then start looking at a place within that city to host your awesome roadshow!

TIP

Make it fun! At an event I hosted, I had a team member who taught a Zumba class to our attendees during a break. The event management team brought in beach balls and a photography booth with silly costumes.

Direct mail

Direct mail is the new black. As a consumer, you get a ton of mail at home. How much mail do you receive at your office? You probably don't get as much. A lot of people appreciate when an interesting piece of mail arrives.

When it comes to B2B marketing, if you know which company you're targeting then consider engaging them by sending mail directly to their office. MarTech allows you to build a list of companies you want to send your mail to. Here's how to execute a direct mail piece:

1. **Identify your target list of companies (your accounts).**

   I discuss how to prepare a target account list in Chapter 5.

2. **Determine your message.**

   Because you've researched the company and determined that it's a viable prospect, you will know what they're interested in. You can then send them direct mail that talks about those specific interests.

3. **Come up with a clever mail piece.**

   At one company where I ran demand generation, our team found a cookie company that baked letter-shaped cookies spelling out our company's name. We sent these to our target account list and saw great (and delicious) results.

WARNING

Don't send anything related to your product. If you send product-related material, you will lose interest from that prospect. Direct mail is all about delighting the person you're sending mail. You want to make this customer feel good. You want to inspire them to reach back out to you.

Here are a few examples of creative direct mail:

>> **A book based on their interests.** I will send copies of this very book to my company's prospects (and will probably bookmark this page!)

>> **Swag.** This can be t-shirts, koozies, something branded with your company's logo to keep you top of mind.

>> **Something sweet.** Cookies with your company's name can really stand out. There are local delivery places that can customize your order; just search Google or Yelp.

>> **Something timely.** One of the best direct mail campaigns I've seen is from InsightSquared (`www.insightsquared.com`). They sell to B2B sales teams, so in Q4 they sent their prospects a can of an energy to drink to help them power through to the end of the year.

Using your marketing automation software, you can build out a separate list with the people you are mailing. You can then monitor their activity in real-time, knowing when the package is delivered, to see whether they came to your website and downloaded a piece of content. Marketing automation paired with direct mail will help track the effectiveness of this campaign.

Content

Content marketing makes it easier than ever for marketers to connect with their best-fit customers. B2B marketers are now creating content based on their ideal buyer persona. I tell you how to determine those best-fit customers in the Chapter 5, but you need digital marketing tools to create content.

REMEMBER

The two key components you need to remember for your content are

>> **Creative:** The design elements that make your content pretty.

>> **Copy:** The words and messaging paired with the design.

To create professional marketing materials, you have several options. You can execute this in-house if your marketing experience team (your MarComm or content manager) has design experience. The Adobe Design Suite, including Photoshop or Illustrator, lets you create graphics. Adobe InDesign is an excellent tool for laying out .pdf templates for whitepapers, ebooks, and infographics. Canva (www.canva.com) also helps to build your graphics.

If you don't want to execute your creative work in-house, you can hire a freelance designer. Some of my favorite sources for fast, inexpensive graphic are such websites as Fiverr (www.fiverr.com) and Guru (www.guru.com). These are online marketplaces for creative and professional services. You can list your projects, then have independent designers bid on them for the work. I've had a new logo designed for as $40. It looked great!

You will still need to write your copy (or message) to give to your graphic design team a baseline for creative design. I recommend Google Docs or Evernote. These web-based platforms are free and allow you to save all of your work and edits immediately. I am also a fan of the web-based app Grammar.ly, which works as a plug-in to proofread your work if you're writing online. Microsoft Word has a better spellcheck and grammar functionality for proofreading.

Here are the types of content you can create for your marketing activities:

>> **Whitepapers:** This long-form content is created in .pdf. The whitepaper got its name because of the use of white space in design. A whitepaper is at least six pages long and serves to promote thought leadership on a certain area of subject matter expertise.

>> **Ebooks:** An ebook is an even longer version of a whitepaper. Ebooks are at least ten pages, and incorporate more design elements to keep the content engaging throughout the length of the publication.

>> **Case Studies:** The most organic and powerful type of marketing is when your customers can connect directly with your potential buyers. Producing a case study gives you the opportunity to demonstrate how your company solved a pain point for your customers.

>> **Infographics:** Because the average adult's attention span is decreasing, infographics are an easy-to-digest collection of images and copy that tell a story. For example "10 reasons why you should use an infographic" would feature ten graphics explaining why you should use an infographic.

>> **Blog Posts:** In the world of new media, it's easy to write and publish your own articles on the web. Using WordPress gives you an easy platform to write and create your own blogs.

Always include at least one image and more than 400 words of copy when you write a blog post. Pay attention to the keywords in your blog post. Use a significant keyword, such as "blog," at least three times.

>> **Slide decks:** Microsoft PowerPoint presentations can be used in many different ways. The website SlideShare allows you to upload your slide presentations directly to the site, then share on social media.

>> **Videos:** This might be my favorite piece of content. I love to create videos, especially personalized videos. Creating your own video content lets your prospects and targeted accounts directly hear from you.

Webinars

A webinar is an online web broadcast produced by your company or a partner. There are many different platforms for hosting your webinar, such as GoToMeeting/GoToWebinar, Join.Me, WebEx, BrightTalk, and Google Hangout. The price depends on the number of "seats" for attendees.

There are two categories of webinars: thought leadership and product. Each category serves a different marketing purpose:

>> **Thought leadership:** You demonstrate your knowledge about a subject without making it a product pitch for your company. For example, a company focused on B2B marketing can host a webinar about doing webinars.

If your company is hosting the webinar, invite a non-employee thought leader to join the session. This reassures your webinar registrants that your webinar's content is unbiased, not a product pitch.

>> **Product:** This type of webinar showcases *how to* use your company's product or service. Using the B2B marketing company example, a product webinar shows marketers how to conduct a webinar focused on using webinar technology.

Prerecord your webinars. You can then edit the recording to remove any errors and replay these during your scheduled time so they appear to be live.

There is a time and place for each type of webinar. If you work for an early-stage company, you will want to create a thought-leadership webinar to demonstrate your industry knowledge and subject matter expertise. If you work for an established organization, you should continue doing thought leadership webinars on a regular basis (weekly, monthly, or quarterly), along with these product webinars.

Here's how to create a good webinar:

>> **Message:** The topic must be timely, focusing on industry trends or recent news developments. Here is one example of a successful webinar from my

colleagues at a company called Preparis (www.preparis.com) a B2B company that does business continuity planning and emergency preparedness. The marketing team decided to present a webinar about preparing for an active shooter. This was in 2013, right after the tragic shooting at Sandy Hook Elementary. The marketing team hired a former police officer who was trained by the Department of Homeland Security to host the webinar and educate businesses on how to prepare and respond to an active shooter at the office. That webinar had more than 800 registrants and 500 attendees listen live.

>> **Influencer:** Using the preceding example, the police officer was a great influencer to have on the webinar. He was able to provide an unbiased opinion of best practices that helped to promote thought leadership. If you're presenting a product webinar for your customers, include a senior executive or product specialist from your company who can demonstrate his or her knowledge and give exceptional guidance or training.

>> **Use cases:** Provide examples of how the topic you're discussing applies in everyday life.

>> **Content:** Should be less formal, more conversational, and present an agenda with a high-level overview.

>> **Q&A:** Leave at least 15 minutes at the end of your webinar to give your audience the opportunity to submit questions and have their answers discussed live on air.

>> **Send the recording:** Using your marketing automation tool, you can track your webinar registrants to create two different lists:

- Folks who listened in live.

- Folks who can be prompted to watch a replay.

REMEMBER

Always record your webinars. Before you go live on air, there is a record button in the webinar tool or dashboard. A webinar can be edited to create videos that you can then share. You can also replay the recording and transcribe your webinar. The transcription service Rev.com lets you upload your webinars then transcribes the recording at $1 per minute. You're then sent a Microsoft Word .doc with the full transcription of the session, so you can use all the great quotes for future whitepapers, ebooks, or blog posts.

Email

Emails are the easiest marketing technique of all. It's low cost, as it doesn't take much time to prepare and send an email. What does matter is the content of your email. B2B marketers use these metrics to determine whether an email was successful:

>> **Open rates:** The percentage of people who opened your email. This is a formula calculated by the dividing the number of emails opened/emails sent.

For example, if you sent an email to 10,000 people and 1,000 of those emails were opened, your open rate is 10 percent.

>> **Click-through rates:** The percentage of people who clicked on a link in your email. This is a formula calculated by dividing the number of emails sent/clicks to content in the email. For example, if you sent an email to 10,000 people and 100 of those people clicked on the link included, your click-through rate is 1 percent.

>> **Bounce rates:** The percentage of emails that are returned as undeliverable. A "bounce" happens when the email address doesn't exist or there is a typo. The formula for bounce rate is calculated by dividing the number of emails sent/ emails bounced.

For example, if you sent an email to 10,000 people and 200 of those emailed "bounced", your click-bounce rate is 2 percent. Your delivery rate is 98 percent.

TIP

Your marketing automation system will have a tool to provide you with open, click–through, and bounce rates.

A thoughtful email has the ability to produce higher open rates and increased click thru rates. Follow these steps for effective email marketing:

1. **Write compelling content.** Before you send your email, make sure it includes the following:

● *Compelling subject line:* Like the headline of a newspaper article of blog post, this should be catchy but not appear to be spam.

● *One central idea:* Your email should be short and sweet. A serving attitude should come through. It isn't about asking the person for something, but offering them something. Ask a question with intention of helping.

● *A clear call-to-action (CTA):* This is what you want the email recipient to do.

Examples of a CTA are to reply back to the email, download a piece of content, register for a webinar, or watch a video.

2. **Research the contact.** Know who exactly you are emailing. You hate receiving emails where the person sending it has no idea who you are and what you do? So do your prospects.

TIP

The most effective way of *getting* something is to *give*. Many B2B marketing and sales teams forget this rule. They ask prospects for their time without understanding what the prospects need and want.

With account-based marketing, you're taking the steps to build a relationship with the contacts in the account. An email can start building the foundation of the relationship.

Calls

Making a successful marketing phone call is extremely hard. "Dial and smile" is dying. You shouldn't waste your time doing a cold call. The calls you make should be based on qualification. You're establishing a relationship on trust, value, and mutual interest. It isn't "Hey, I'm going to call you because my boss says I need to make this many calls a day to meet my quota." Instead, it should be "Thank you for attending our recent webinar." These are examples of how to start building the relationship before you pick up the phone:

>> **Meet them at an event:** If you're at an event, asking for that business card, ask when would be the best time to connect after the show.

>> **Follow on social:** By reaching out to someone on Twitter, you can tweet to them with content before ever picking up the phone.

>> **Connect on LinkedIn:** More than any other platform, LinkedIn has contributed to the death of the cold call. You can find out exactly who a person is, and their role within the company.

WARNING

Sending them a message asking to connect is the first step, but don't ask for the call in that first message. LinkedIn doesn't let you include links in an introductory message, so start by explaining who you are, and why you want to connect before asking for time for a phone call.

2

Identifying Accounts for Marketing

IN THIS PART . . .

Targeting the best-fit accounts based on ideal customer profile (ICP) and persona criteria

Creating a tiered list of accounts to prioritize your marketing activities and efforts

Using data in your CRM to discover accounts that fit your ICP

Adding data for new accounts and appending contact data

Defining criteria, such as BANT, to qualify revenue opportunities

Progressing accounts to the next stage of the buyer's journey

Chapter 5

Targeting Your Best-Fit Accounts

Your ideal list of target accounts is the foundation for account-based marketing (ABM). The most basic level of B2B marketing is knowing your target audience. You must know the right companies, and the right people in those companies, who best fit your product or service. Many companies neglected this rule with traditional lead-based marketing efforts. The marketing team would blast an email to 10,000 people without taking the time to identify who from those thousands of contacts is the best fit.

Identifying the best-fit prospects to target is essential for success. With ABM, you start the buyer's journey by identifying your prospects for marketing. These prospects are determined by a number of criteria, such as the industry they work in, the companies they work for, and their roles and responsibilities within those organizations.

This chapter shows how to identify the right businesses to engage with your message. (That's why it's called B2B marketing!) I show you how to use your existing customer data to identify the right industries and companies, then leverage persona criteria to identify the roles of people within those organizations. You can use these persona features for your marketing materials to create a meaningful message that illustrates why your prospects should hire your company. Then, I explain how to build lists of accounts to target based on how well they fit within your defined criteria.

Focusing on the Right Market

How can you know which companies and which industries are the best fit for your product or service? Unless you're a new company that has never sold a deal, this is a valid question. If you have a handful of customers, or even 50 or 100 clients, then you have a starting point. Using your existing customer data, you can profile your existing customers. Analyze the data to find which companies are your best-fit customers today. You can determine whether they are the best-fit by the following criteria:

>> **Amount the customer pays your company:** The total annual recurring revenue (ARR) or monthly recurring revenue (MRR) is a starting point for all of your customers. There's the mantra that 80 percent of your revenue comes from 20 percent of your customers, and unless you're a purely transactional organization, the amount of revenue matters. The deal size of your current customer is a starting point for the deals you hope to close in the future.

>> **Time needed to service the customers:** If a customer doesn't pay your company much revenue and requires lots of attention, they probably aren't an ideal fit for your business. Holding a certain customer's hand all the time prevents your team from servicing other customers. This problem is magnified when the problem child doesn't pay much revenue to your company.

>> **Problem you solve for your customer:** Why your customer wanted to buy from your company in the first place. Your client decided to purchase from your company because your product or service addresses a pain point. This problem is answered by your business solution. Understanding that original need will help you find the other industries and companies that can benefit from your solution.

When you review these features within your existing customer database, you find a baseline of the types of customers that are a good fit with your business. From there, you can identify the industry in which they are categorized.

Specifying the industry

Identifying the right industry is different for every B2B marketing team. The most important part of this process is understanding which industries, or categories, will benefit the most from your business solution. There are two common ways that B2B marketers specify which industry they want to target using verticals and segments within those verticals.

>> **Verticals:** This refers to the market. A vertical market is the type of industry. Examples of vertical markets include financial services, commercial real estate, fashion merchandising, retail stores, and gaming.

>> **Segments:** Within those verticals there are segments. Segments are largely based on the size of companies within those verticals. I show how to categorize company size in the next section.

REMEMBER

Identifying the industry you're targeting is important. Your marketing message needs to be tailored. You need different vocabularies to target a gaming company and a large financial services organization.

Sizing the company

After you've determined which industries you want to target, you need to understand the size of the companies in those verticals that are the best fit for your product or service. Two main numbers define the size of a company:

>> **Revenue:** your customer or prospect's annual recurring revenue (ARR)

>> **Size:** the number of people that your customer or prospect employs.

Your sales process depends on the size of the companies you target. According to Gartner's research, companies fit into three main categories by size:

>> **Small to mid-size business (SMB):** These SMB companies are defined by the number of employees, (typically fewer than 100 employees). SMBs usually have less than $50 million in ARR. The number of stakeholders in an SMB purchase decision is smaller because of the smaller number of employees.

>> **Mid-size:** These larger companies typically have 100 to 999 employees. They have more than $50 million in ARR, but less than $1 billion. Mid-size companies can vary in organizational structure; the departmental hierarchy depends on how many people are in the company. The buying cycle gets longer when you're selling to mid-size companies, because there are more stakeholders in the purchase decision.

>> **Enterprise:** These billion-dollar companies have more than 1,000 employees. Because these organizations are very large, the deal size is larger, and your sales cycle is more complex. A strategy must be created to target all of the stakeholders in this purchase decision. I discuss this in Part 3.

Segmenting by industry and company size

After you identify your industry vertical and company size, you know which segment of the market you want to target. Segmenting is essential for account-based marketing. Your product or service may not be a fit for a certain type of organization. For example, an SMB client may require more hand holding for less revenue because the customer lacks the internal resources needed to succeed with your product. It could also be true that SMB companies are more self-starting and low maintenance, because employees have more autonomy and are less risk averse. Less red tape sometimes means they can pull the trigger to buy faster with less help in the buying process.

Price is a key component to determine the type of organization you should sell to:

>> When your pricing structure is more transactional (such as an online ordering form instead of a lengthy contract), you're a good fit for SMB companies.

>> When you have a more complex sales cycle that relies heavily on an inside sales team trying to set appointments, with no face-to-face interactions needed, you can go target mid-market organizations.

>> When your product is expensive and needs a lengthy contract, don't waste time targeting smaller companies. Focus on top-tier enterprise organizations.

The value here is maximizing your operational efficiency. By knowing the company size that can pay your price, you get the most bang for your buck. The sales cycle for SMB can be less than a week. For Enterprise, your deals are much longer in time and larger in size.

SMB and Mid-Market companies require similar sales tactics, which is mostly because of the scope of the sale. This depends on the pricing of your product, and whether a contract is required. Another factor is the contacts within these organizations who you will ultimately work with during the purchase decision.

Creating an Ideal Customer Profile

Finding the ideal customer isn't like trying to find a needle in a haystack. You can build a magnet to make all of the needles jump out of the hay! (Please wear eye protection.)

After you've determined the industry and company size of your best-fit customers, you can reach a deeper level by writing your ideal customer profile (ICP). Here's how.

Determining your ICP

Knowing who you should be selling to helps immensely in account-based marketing. For your ICP, consider the following features to identify the best-fit customers. Here is an example of an ICP:

>> **Industry:** The vertical channel you're targeting.

In this example, I use the financial services industry.

>> **Company Size:** SMB. In my example, the ideal companies I want to work with have about 50 employees and less than $10 million in ARR.

>> **Department:** Marketing. I know that marketing professionals in the financial services industry can benefit from my product.

>> **Responsibilities:** The marketing department's team members who are tasked with doing display advertising on various channels, such as mobile ads, social media, and video.

>> **Role:** These marketing professionals fit various levels within the organization. They have titles from coordinator, associate manager, manager, and director up to the vice president or CMO. Because I'm targeting SMB companies, the titles vary according to the number of team members in the marketing department.

TIP

Examine your CRM to see the titles of the contacts who are your current customers. Knowing the titles of your existing customers who have proven to be successful with your product is helpful when creating your ICP.

Your ICP becomes the qualification criteria for identifying the best-fit contacts for account-based marketing. Figure 5-1 shows what your ideal customer profile looks like as an ID card.

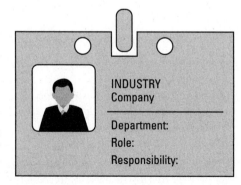

FIGURE 5-1:
Ideal Customer
Profile as
an ID card.

At my company, Terminus, we referred to this process as "Finding Nikki." Nikki is our marketing technologist. She's responsible for managing all of the marketing operations tools from the CRM and marketing automation systems to social media platforms. Nikki helps discover and purchase these tools that help drive the success of our marketing activities. If your business needs to reach Nikki, you need to know her role and responsibility within the company to find whether she fits your ICP.

Crafting personas

After you've built your ICP, you add a layer that defines your personas. The persona details can be very specific, including demographic information.

TIP

Some companies choose to even include specific television shows, celebrities, or other pop culture information that your persona might care about in order to get more creative with the types of marketing activities for these personas. It's fun, but not always necessary for crafting personas.

For account-based marketing, you need to know some important details for your persona:

>> **Who is your persona?** Take your ICP with industry, company size, department, responsibilities, and role. For "Nikki," she is a technology operations manager in the marketing department of an SMB company that sells B2B marketing software. She's responsible for managing all the marketing technology (MarTech) tools.

>> **What does your persona care about?** Knowing Nikki's role in the marketing department, think about what her pain points might be. She has so many systems that she needs on system of record to store all of her data. She needs a tool for identifying who to target for marketing. Nikki also needs the capability to report the measurements and metrics of what marketing activities are working and what are not.

Nikki needs products and solutions that make her job easier.

REMEMBER

>> **How does your product or service help?** The solution for alleviating Nikki's pain points would be a combined MarTech stack of a CRM (single system of record), marketing automation for reporting activities, and an account-based marketing platform for measuring ROI on all of the marketing activities for the companies that she's targeting with her marketing.

Because this is a B2B purchase decision, you know Nikki isn't the only persona you'll have to sell to. She reports to a VP or CMO. Nikki may also have someone reporting to her, such as a marketing coordinator. The CMO persona will have different responsibilities than Nikki, and the marketing coordinator also plays a different role. It's important for you to create different use cases for how each of these personas will benefit from working with your business. Figure 5-2 shows how you these three different personas would use a new product.

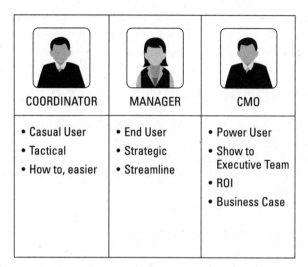

FIGURE 5-2:
Persona chart of
use cases.

Understanding personas' motivations

By taking the time to understand each of your personas motivations, you can have more effective conversations. When you know what motivates these personas, you can address these points with your marketing messaging. These are the most important considerations for understanding your personas' motivations:

>> **Wants:** Using "Nikki" as our example, she wants to be an innovative MarTech manager who contributes to her marketing team's success through the use of marketing tools and software applications.

>> **Needs:** Nikki needs technology that makes it easier to do her job. Your product should make Nikki's job easier, not harder. Otherwise, it's a bad product. Nikki doesn't need a bad product.

>> **Pains:** Nikki's biggest pain is that she doesn't have enough time to do everything she wants to do, or what her executive team has tasked her with.

>> **Fears:** What keeps Nikki up at night? The stress from her job. Because Nikki is a high-achiever, she wants to win and is afraid of failing.

When you understand what motivates each of your personas, you're positioned for success with your marketing messages.

Making a Value Proposition

When you've taken the steps to determine your best-fit customers who fit your ICP, and then to identify those personas within that ideal company, you're in a good position to create a value proposition. Commonly referred to as a *value prop*, a value proposition calls attention to the features and capabilities of a product, service, or feature. In B2B marketing, providing your prospect a value proposition demonstrates the benefit of doing business with your company.

Differentiating value based on roles

Because you've taken the time to identify personas with whom you want to do business, you can address a value proposition to their individual responsibilities. To create a value proposition based on roles, you will need to consider the challenge each of your personas is faced with, and the solution for overcoming those challenges.

Tailoring your message

Your message must be personalized for each of your personas. Each of your personas has specific wants, needs, pains, and fears. Here's an example of a value proposition for why a B2B marketing professional would want to use account-based marketing.

Account-based marketing gives you the ability to accelerate your sales pipeline. Because you are laser-focused on the best-fit accounts for your business, you engage only qualified prospects. For your marketing team, this allows you to better target the contacts which match personas in your ICP accounts. Better targeting eliminates the process of typical lead generation. You're providing additional air-cover for sales by using a combination of content marketing activities in addition to targeting display advertising at these best-fit accounts. For your sales team, this shortens the deal cycle and increases your win rate.

Remembering everyone is different

Acknowledging that no persona is like another is important. Personalized messages based on your persona's unique motivations will resonate much more than a blanket message that screams "You should buy my product!" Remember these key points for personalizing your marketing activities to each of your personas.

>> **Who:** The person behind the persona. "Nikki" is a real live human being! Treat Nikki as a person, not just a data point.

>> **What:** The tasks and responsibilities this human must take care of every day. Nikki has a lot on her plate.

>> **Where:** The place or channel you should try to engage with Nikki. Most days, she's probably chained to her desk working. But maybe Nikki gets to go to an annual conference.

>> **When:** If Nikki is busy at work, then the best time to reach her may be after regular business hours. If Nikki goes to an annual tradeshow, find out when that is.

>> **Why:** Engaging Nikki on her own terms, at the right time and place, is much more effective than continuing to blast her with emails.

>> **How:** This is the premise of account-based marketing. You're using a combination of the right marketing activities to engage with Nikki.

Building Your List of Target Accounts

The point of account-based marketing is to target your best-fit accounts. What are the best companies you can do business with? If you've created your ICP and drafted personas within that ICP, then you know which types of companies and buyers you want to target. These are your target accounts. From there, your marketing and sales ("smarketing") team works together to build your list of target accounts in order of priority. Prioritizing your target accounts is commonly referred to as *tiering* your targets.

Starting with a tiered list of companies

By having a structured list of target accounts, you will know which companies to focus your time, energy, and resources for account-based marketing. There are typically three tiers of companies: 1, 2, 3, or A, B, C. These are based on priority. The point is to use your energy and resources to focus on your Tier A accounts. These best-fits *must* have demonstrated interest (intent) that they want to do business with your company. Intent is shown through activity, such as visiting your website, downloading content, or registering for your events. To be on any of your tier lists, these companies should meet at least some of your ICP criteria. Here is how you should tier your target accounts:

>> **Tier A:** These accounts are an absolute best-fit. Your Tier A accounts perfectly meet your ICP criteria. In a perfect world, you would have a universe of Tier A accounts that's never-ending. New prospects continue to find your business

on the web, social media, at events, and through other marketing activities. You also have your Tier A list of your best customers that you have potential to cross-sell and upsell with additional products or upgrades.

>> **Tier B:** Accounts that meet most of your ICP criteria. In an ideal world, your prospects and customers would meet all of the criteria for your perfect account, but that isn't the case. Your Tier B accounts are companies that fit most of your ICP. Thinking about such ICP criteria as company size and industry, a Tier B account can be in the right industry you're targeting, but larger or smaller than your ideal company size in revenue or employees.

>> **Tier C:** Accounts that meet *some* of your ICP and have demonstrated intent. You will always have people come to your website or download content (this demonstrates intent). You will have to look at those individuals and the companies they work for through the lens of your ICP and personas. They may only meet one of your ICP criteria, such as industry, but they can be considered a low-priority target, or Tier C account, because they have shown intent.

Here's an example: Your business is targeting financial services companies in North America. Your ideal customer is a company in the Fortune 500 group, but smaller companies have also found success with your product. Here is how you apply a tier structure to your universe of target accounts.

>> **Tier A:** Fortune 500 financial services companies

>> **Tier B:** Fortune 501-1000 financial services companies

>> **Tier C:** Any other company in the financial services industry

REMEMBER

Your Tier A, B, and C accounts on your tiered account list should have demonstrated intent . If they haven't demonstrated intent, these accounts should remain on your email nurturing campaigns or "drip" marketing. Your marketing activities continue using technology in your marketing automation or account-based marketing campaigns to provide "air cover" through such campaigns as emails or display advertising. This keeps your business top-of-mind without investing too much in your resources. If intent hasn't been shown, don't waste your sales development team's time by having them call or directly email these accounts.

Applying your ICP to the company list

You should align your ideal company profile to your list of accounts to determine which tier they fall into. Looking at this from the context of a strategy, your list of target accounts is used as a starting point. These are the accounts you want to do business with. It lends itself to using different strategies for your different tiers. Here is an example of how I use an ICP to tier accounts:

>> **B2B or B2C Company:** To be on any of my tiered account list, the company must be a B2B organization. I know B2C companies aren't a good fit for my product.

>> **Industry:** For my company, I target B2B companies in the technology industry, selling software-as-a-service (SaaS). If the account isn't a technology company, they aren't a good fit.

>> **Size:** The size is most often the company's annual recurring revenue (ARR) and number of employees. Depending on your industry, this could change. These are a few examples of other size factors for B2B companies:

- *Healthcare:* The number of beds in a hospital.

- *Financial services:* The amount of capital, or millions/billions of dollars in assets.

- *Commercial real estate:* The number of properties, buildings, or amount of square feet in the portfolio.

>> **Using a CRM:** The companies who want to use my product need to have a CRM in place. If they don't have a CRM, they can't use my product; it ties directly into a CRM.

>> **Using a marketing automation tool**: My ICP already has a marketing automation platform, such as Marketo, Eloqua, Pardot, HubSpot, or Act-On. If they're using a lesser-known marketing automation system, they may not be a good fit for my product. That could put them on the Tier B or C account list.

>> **Using advertising technology:** This is a huge consideration, and can move a target account to the Tier A list. Because this account already is familiar with advertising technology, I know the company can be successful with my platform. If they aren't using advertising technology, I may put them on the Tier B list.

REMEMBER

There is no "one size fits all" rule for your ICP. This must be unique for your own organization, based on your products and services, and the types of companies that are most successful partnering with your business.

The account executives at my company know that when they find a prospect that meets all of these criteria, it's a Tier A account. After you find someone who doesn't fit all of these, they're a Tier B account. The account may use Salesforce and marketing automation, but has never previously used any digital advertising. My sales team may be able to close them, but the odds are worse. I have customers who don't fit all of these qualifications, but still are a good fit. How you should structure your tiered account list is based on best-fit. Tier A fits all your criteria, Tier B is missing one or two of your ICP criteria, and Tier C is missing two or more criteria.

Laser-focusing on best-fit

The goal of account-based marketing is to engage the right companies, your target accounts, so you're no longer wasting your resources on lead generation for companies that aren't a great fit. You need to know your ICP to know whether the account meets all the ideal criteria. Through engagement and marketing activities, you move these accounts from a prospect to opportunity in your pipeline, then turn these accounts into customer revenue. If a company doesn't meet your ICP, that doesn't mean you should ignore them completely.

WARNING

Don't delete a company from your database if they aren't a good fit. Instead, create a separate list for marketing to them in a nurturing campaign. You can make them a fan of your marketing, and develop them into a potential reference. I discuss this in Part 4.

Prospecting within accounts

With B2B marketing, it's about connecting with other businesses to build a partnership. Account-based marketing adds another layer by defining the ideal customers who you believe will be most successful with your business. However, you don't market to another business; you target the people in the business who will make the purchase decision. Those people are called *prospects*. In Chapter 6, I show how to get the data you need to prospect within your target accounts.

Chapter 6

Fueling the Account-Based Marketing Engine

There's the saying "garbage in, garbage out." According to DataWarehouse, bad data costs U.S. businesses more than $600 billion in annually wasted resources. You need good data to make the right decisions. Without good data, you can barely do marketing, let alone account-based marketing (ABM). Having the right data is essential. Revenue opportunities are missed when you don't have the proper insights. You need data on your target accounts: who you are selling to, the companies they work for, how to reach them, and what their responsibilities are within their individual business units. This will give you a baseline of understanding to begin engagement through targeted marketing activities.

The more you know about your accounts, the faster you can rev up the ABM engine to grow your campaigns. ABM's foundation is to target the *right* accounts with a message that speaks to their interests, pain points, and addresses a business problem for which your company can provide a solution. The beautiful thing about today's technology is you have the ability to obtain the data on your ideal customers from your CRM.

In this chapter, I show you how to decide whether you have the right data for ABM. I discuss the importance of regularly updating and maintaining your CRM with accurate information about your contacts, then tying those contacts to accounts. I cover how to determine whether your data is incomplete and how to fill in those missing elements. I also tell you how to use predictive analytics software to find data on your accounts to ensure those companies fit in your ideal customer profile (ICP).

Managing Your Existing CRM Data

The customer relationship management (CRM) system is the primary data warehouse for any marketing and sales team. Your CRM is where all the information about your customers and prospects lives. This data is the lifeblood of your business. Bad data includes missing or incomplete information. If you have bad data in your CRM, you can't execute your best marketing efforts. Making sense of all the data points currently available to your marketing team will help give you a foundation for account-based marketing. The starting point is to look in your CRM at your existing data.

Leveraging your customer data

Contact information about your accounts is the main type of data stored in your CRM. Unless you're a brand new company, the existing data in your CRM will help serve as a baseline for starting account-based marketing.

WARNING

Your data shouldn't live in spreadsheets. If you are currently managing your data in Microsoft Access or Excel, or just a notebook on your salesperson's desk, stop reading this book now. You can't execute ABM with spreadsheets. If you have already purchased a license for a CRM, then keep reading.

Unless you're in the very early stages of your company, you have customer accounts. The account data on your current customers (or customers who are no longer doing business with you) will help you in determining if these are the types of accounts you want to target in the future. The existing data in your CRM should include all of your accounts, both customers and prospects. The information fields on these accounts are called data points. These are the data points of information in your CRM:

>> **Lead:** A prospect or person who has expressed interest. You've discovered a new person through any of your marketing activities, such as meeting someone new at a tradeshow who wasn't in your database before, a prospect who came across your website, or a prospect who discovered your company on social media.

>> **Account:** A company the prospect/customer works for. The type of information needed to build a complete profile of the account includes the company name, website, revenue, and employee count. You need to discover all the contacts who could play a role in helping make this account a revenue-generating customer.

>> **Contact:** You added this prospect to your database creating a new contact. You add in the person's name, title, company, email address, and phone number. If the company previously wasn't in your database, you create a new account.

>> **Opportunity:** A potential deal. The value of the opportunity should represent the amount of revenue they will pay your company monthly and/or annually.

>> **Current revenue:** How much your existing customers will pay your company for your product or service.

Figure 6-1 shows a snapshot of existing customer data.

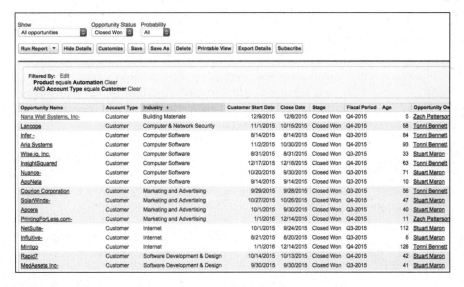

FIGURE 6-1: Using data already in your CRM.

REMEMBER

According to the vocabulary of CRM vendors, an account can technically also be a partner, vendor, or any company you have to manage a relationship with. For the purpose of account-based marketing, I use the term account only for prospects or customers.

Comparing customers with your ICP

To determine your ideal customer profile (ICP), you start by looking at your existing customer data. Your current customers will give you an idea of the types of organizations that have been most successful with your product and service. Here is how you take the ICP you created and examine your customers:

>> **Pull your list of customer accounts**: Prepare a spreadsheet of all the customers you're doing business with, including the following information:

- Company size (revenue and/or employees)

- Deal size (how much revenue they're currently paying you)

- Time to service (look at activity in the CRM to see how often you're interacting with the customers)

>> **Compare with your ICP:** Based on the company sizes, the amount they're paying your business in MRR/ARR, and the time it takes to service the account, you can determine who from your current customers meets your ICP.

Figuring out what you can use

You will discover during this process something you probably already knew: Some of your current customers *aren't* the best fit for your business. You'll see how much your customer is paying you in revenue compared to the amount of work and time it takes to service the account.

WARNING

You shouldn't release a customer because they don't fit your ICP. The customer is still paying your business. It is, however, a point to be cognizant of as you continue your relationship, especially if this not-so-great fit is a demanding customer who takes a lot of your time and resources.

TIP

Put your customers who best fit your ICP on a champion or VIP list. These are the customers you want to invest in to create customer advocates. They can be used for marketing resources, such as case studies, user conferences, referrals, or references. I explain more about how to create customer advocates in Part 5.

Obtaining New Data on Target Accounts

Assuming you have created your ICP and personas, and you know from your existing customer data the types of companies who are the best fit for your product or service, the next step is to find more companies who meet your ideal account profile. Some of this data may already exist in your CRM on your current prospects and opportunities. You will need to make sure you have clean, current data in your CRM on the right accounts, then add data for better segmentation, targeting, and tracking. Without good data, you can't do ABM.

Gathering the right data

The data you need in your CRM for account-based marketing rightfully focuses first on accounts. Having the right account data helps to make the marketing process seamless and better measure the results of your account-based marketing campaigns. These are the starting data points you need on companies to execute account-based marketing:

>> **Company name:** The name of the business that is the name of the account.

>> **Company description:** What they do, or their product/service offering.

>> **Company website:** The URL/domain.

>> **Industry:** To confirm the company fits in your ICP.

>> **Size:** Annual revenue and/or number of employees to ensure it fits in your ICP.

>> **Technology:** The products and services the company utilizes.

Acquiring correct company information

There are tons of sources to find this data on companies for your target accounts. These are a few vendors I have found to be useful to obtain company data for account-based marketing:

TIP

>> **Dun & Bradstreet (www.dnb.com):** Dun & Bradstreet maintains information on more than 250 million companies worldwide. Dun & Bradstreet assigns a D-U-N-S Number, which is a unique nine-digit number on which a Dun & Bradstreet Credit Report has been generated. Dun & Bradstreet does this to maintain the world's largest database of B2B company and revenue information. After the D-U-N-S number is assigned to a business, this unique identifier can never belong to another company. It stays with a business forever.

The D-U-N-S Number can be used to ensure a company is only listed in your CRM once.

>> **Salesforce Data.com (www.salesforce.com/data):** Salesforce Data.com allows you to both clean your existing Salesforce data and easily add verified account and contact records within your CRM. They partner with Dun & Bradstreet to offer more than 80 fields of account data, including corporate

linkage through the D-U-N-S number. The D-U-N-S number automatically is matched to your existing accounts in your CRM, or will create new accounts based on your ICP criteria you entered to find new company information. The dataset also includes Standard Industrial Classification (SIC) and the North American Industry Classification System (NAICS) industry codes for categories such as manufacturing, finance, and retail. This account information will be useful, as it can then transfer into a campaign in your account-based marketing platform. After the campaign, you can measure the results for account-level attribution because you have accurate company information, name, domain, and geographic location.

>> **DataFox (`www.datafox.com`):** This software uses algorithms and natural language processing to gather, organize, and present sales triggers for companies you're targeting for account-based marketing. Using the platform's filtering system, you can find companies that fit your ICP criteria, such as size, industry sector (and sub-sector), funding, and geographic location.

>> **Mattermark (`http://mattermark.com`):** This platform is used for advanced search and data enrichment. Mattermark looks up companies and helps you stay on top of daily funding events from anywhere (which is important if you're targeting accounts that are early-stage companies). There is also a mobile app allowing you to search for companies, plus an extension with Google Chrome that lets you see company information from the targeted account's website.

>> **CrunchBase (`www.crunchbase.com`):** If you're a B2B organization that is targeting companies that are involved in venture capital, investing, or funding, then you must read CrunchBase. This site presents up-to-the-minute news about which accounts have raised a strategic round of funding, and provides contact information for executive-level employees.

TECHNICAL
STUFF

These data sources sync with Salesforce through the API to import company information directly into your CRM, marketing automation, and account-based marketing platforms, thereby avoiding the process of manual data entry.

Part of your ICP may include the type of technology the company is using. If you're selling your product with a channel partner, then knowing which companies are using your partner's technology is an essential part of your marketing and sales process. These vendors are helpful in identifying the technology and software your target accounts utilize:

>> **BuiltWith (`http://builtwith.com`):** The name does as it implies. BuiltWith tell you what kind of technology the company is using. The value is that you can see whether the company fits in your ICP based on their technology. If you know your product or service requires a specific platform software, such

as a particular CRM, then BuiltWith will tell you whether there is a match. The company has more than 14,000 web technologies and over 250 million websites in its database.

>> **Bombora** (`http://bombora.com/data`): An aggregator of B2B intent data that tracks over 2,500 B2B topics across such actions as specific internet searches, webinars, event signups, video, and social. Bombora then aggregates users into more than 60 scalable predictive segments. This predictive data helps show whether the contacts in your target accounts are looking for a particular product or service that you sell.

>> **Datanyze** (`www.datanyze.com`): Search companies to create a list of accounts that meet your ICP criteria. Choose the technology providers you want to track, and Datanyze will show you which of your accounts have started or stopped using a particular technology each day. The Chrome extension allows you to view such data points as revenue, employees, and technology partners to quickly qualify accounts. The information can be synced directly to any CRM or marketing automation platform to enrich, score and append technology and company data. The email finder tool helps you find your contact's correct email address in two clicks. You can also export prospects from popular online directories to Datanyze or into your CRM.

>> **Ghostery** (`www.ghostery.com`): This application is an extension of your Internet browser, such as Google Chrome or Firefox. When you go to your account's website, Ghostery pops up a window that shows you all the apps running a java script, pixel, and all the technology the website or company is using. If you're selling marketing automation software, Ghostery you look at their website to see whether this prospect is already using a marketing automation platform.

Finding the right people in those companies

A true ABM campaign will include the persona criteria you created. You will need data that matches these personas to find all the people involved in the account's purchase decision. Data will help give you the knowledge of how to reach your contacts in your targeted accounts. These are the people you will prospect with marketing activities. All of this information is stored in your CRM. These data sources will help you with obtaining the right contact data on your personas:

>> First and last name

>> Job title

>> Seniority

>> Physical office address

>> Phone number

>> Email address

The account detail page in your CRM will show you all of the data related to an account. I've found these data sources most useful for obtaining contact information:

>> **LinkedIn (`www.linkedin.com`):** The LinkedIn Navigator tool gives you recommendations for which contacts you should connect with, then syncs daily with your CRM. You have free access to more than 380 million professional profiles.

   Here's an example: You're targeting engineers within an IT department. You created an ad on LinkedIn that targets that job profile and industry. You have the contact for this engineer in your CRM. Now, you need to add in the manager, director, and VP of the engineer's company, because they all have a stake in the decision to purchase from your company.

>> **NetProspex (`www.netprospex.com`):** This tool was recently acquired by Dun & Bradstreet, and is designed specifically for marketing data management. It allows you to add new targeted contacts, expand visibility, and enable ABM using titles and look-alike profiles. The SalesProspex tool tracks more than 2,800 technologies at more than two million companies, so you can quickly add lists of companies to your CRM and append data on existing contacts and accounts.

>> **Salesforce Data.com Connect (`www.data.com/connect`):** This crowd-sourced community provides more than 45 million complete business contacts and is available integrated into the Data.com Prospector offering within Salesforce. Customers can search for contacts and decision makers at specific accounts, by industry, location, function, level, and more, right within their instance of Salesforce. Individuals can also join the Data.com Connect community to contribute and earn, or purchase, credits to find new leads.

>> **DiscoverOrg (`http://discoverorg.com`):** Datasets are updated at least every 90 days profiling every company to include an organizational chart for the department, a list of installed technology, and even current or planned projects. This data can be targeted towards job titles or company financial information, including specifics for the Fortune 1000, Forbes 400, and S&P 500 companies.

>> **ZoomInfo (`www.zoominfo.com`):** The platform provides profiles and contact information for more than 135 million people. It integrates directly into your CRM to import detailed profiles at the contact and account-level. Emails, phone numbers, job titles, companies, and other data are compared in your

TIP

CRM to identify any mismatches. The Enhance feature fills in missing fields to help build out a full contact record. This helps to improve segmentation when you create lists of contacts and accounts.

These data providers help you find contact data on types of personas within an account will let you filter by company name. This makes it easy to find the right people in your target accounts.

Utilizing predictive analytics

Now you have a list of companies and contacts you should target. If you only have one salesperson and a list of 100 companies, it's a daunting task to reach out to all those accounts. What if the list were even bigger, with 1,000 companies, or 10,000, that fit these criteria? With account-based marketing, what you're looking for is who from that massive list of prospects is the best fit to buy your product. Predictive analytics software shows you who to target, based on intent data. Intent data can show you which companies are researching particular topics of interest.

Predictive analytics works to examine companies that are your current customers to find similar companies you currently have in your CRM that would also be a good fit. Imagine if you're an established company with 2,000 current customers. You closed 1,000 of those customers within the last year. A predictive analytics tool works to find all the other companies currently in your CRM that are open leads or opportunities that match the same criteria. This is called *historical back-testing.* Predictive analytics takes your data to analyze similarities from your current customer data and your ideal customers. I've found these tools useful:

>> **6Sense** (`https://6sense.com`): 6sense is a B2B predictive intelligence engine for sales and marketing. Using its private network of billions of time-sensitive intent interactions, 6sense uncovers net-new prospects at every stage of the funnel and determines which existing prospects are in market to buy. 6sense predicts what products prospects will buy, how much they will buy, and when. 6sense is the central nervous system that powers every part of B2B marketing and sales.

>> **EverString** (`www.everstring.com`): EverString allows you to build pipeline and increase conversion rates with the only account-based, full-funnel predictive analytics solution for sales and marketing. EverString Decision Platform provides a complete, simple, and transparent SaaS offering for lead scoring and predictive demand generation. It's an intelligence layer that enables the predictive generation of marketing.

>> **Infer** (`www.infer.com`): Infer's predictive models analyze thousands of internal and external buying signals and use proven data science to predict which prospects will go on to be great customers. Its technology uses

historical data from your CRM app, as well as activity data and signals from the web – (such as website traffic, relevant job postings, patent filings, social presence, and the technology vendors a company uses) to determine which contacts and accounts are most likely to convert. In addition, Infer's Prospect Management platform goes further by helping businesses identify high-value segments, review and act on intelligent recommendations, and automate next-best actions.

» **Lattice Engines (`http://lattice-engines.com`):** The platform allows you to search for contacts based on job title and seniority (or "level") to create high-quality lists of contacts and accounts that match your ICP and personas. With Lattice, companies can

- Find net-new contacts that have expressed intent on external sites but not yet engaged with your company.

  Identify accounts that look similar to your existing customers or ICP.

- Revive "dead" prospects from your existing database.

  This activity helps with reinforcing and adding to your list of Tier A, B, or C accounts.

» **Mintigo (`www.mintigo.com`):** Mintigo's Predictive Marketing Platform evaluates every account and assigns a predictive score according to your "CustomerDNA™". This enables you to quickly identify accounts that are most likely to purchase your product. By using predictive scoring along with Mintigo's data attributes such as technologies used and purchase intent that make up the score, you can target the right prospects with the right message. Mintigo will also help you identify net new target accounts that match your CustomerDNA™ as well as leads and contacts for those accounts.

Figure 6-2 shows you how to import this new data into your CRM.

FIGURE 6-2: Importing data feeds into your CRM.

PRESCRIPTIVE ANALYTICS

Like a doctor writing a prescription for an illness, prescriptive analytics tools tell you how to reach your contacts. You've invested in predictive analytics tools to obtain data on your contacts, now you need to know what activities to use to reach them.

Based on data, prescriptive analytics tells you how to market and sell to those contacts. You don't have to think. For example, if 50 percent of your Closed/Won deals came to a webinar, then prescriptive analytics will tell you to conduct more webinars. Another prescription would be to use your account-based marketing platform to serve ads to those targeted accounts on Facebook, or to direct mail.

These analytics tools prescribe what you should do on a roadmap to grow your revenue through account and contact-specific activities. While there aren't any products in the marketplace yet for prescriptive analytics, both prescriptive and predictive analytics tools represent the future of account-based marketing.

Creating New Accounts

An account is created any time a new company is entered into your CRM. With traditional B2B marketing, a lead came in through an inbound or outbound marketing activity, then the lead became a contact in your CRM. The contact would become an account, with the account representing the company you would do business with.

Some B2B companies only use lead-to-account distinctions in their CRM. Most companies today don't create an account until there's an opportunity. Every marketer is different. What remains the same for every marketing team though is that revenue opportunities are associated with a parent account.

For account-based marketing, you should *always* create accounts in your CRM. Accounts are created when

>> You import a list of accounts and/or contacts from a data provider.

>> Automatically from an inbound prospect who

  • Downloaded a piece of content (such as an ebook, whitepaper, or case study).

  • Visited your website that had tracking code from your marketing automation system, integrated with your CRM.

- Completed a form on a landing page that was created with your marketing automation system.

>> Manually added by a member of your "smarketing" team from an outbound activity such as a call, email, or meeting at a tradeshow.

Completing a full profile

Your account needs a fully completed profile. You need these data points to complete a full profile:

>> Company name

>> Company office address

>> Company website

>> Industry

>> Size

>> First and last name

>> Job title

>> Seniority

>> Phone number

>> Email address

Figure 6-3 shows a profile of an account in your CRM.

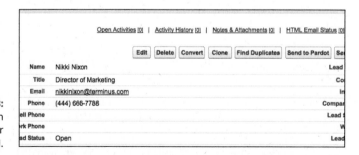

FIGURE 6-3:
A full profile of an account in your CRM.

Avoiding duplicate accounts

It's an awful situation where you have the same company listed as two different accounts. This can happen if you aren't using a unique identification number, and one of your team members enters "ACME" and another team member enters

"ACME Inc." Acme is the same company but it has a duplicate account. Figure 6-4 shows how to use data tools to manually check and verify that the account isn't a duplicate in your CRM.

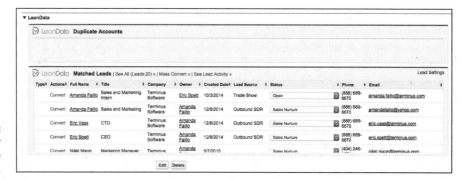

FIGURE 6-4:
Checking your
CRM for duplicate
accounts.

There are additional software tools you can use to check to see whether there are duplicate accounts in your CRM.

>> **Cloudingo** (http://cloudingo.com) works to clean and "de-dupe" accounts in your CRM. The customizable dashboard allows you to view all your data on one screen, including the number and types of duplicates that exist. Cloudingo finds duplicates by matching records on certain criteria within fields such as e-mail address, last name, and company name across your contacts and accounts.

>> **Dun & Bradstreet Optimizer** (www.dnb.com/sales-marketing/list-cleaning.html): The Optimizer from Dun & Bradstreet has a patented "Entity Match" technology to identify duplicates and correct company data using its D-U-N-S unique identification number.

>> **RingLead** (www.ringlead.com): The company offers a suite of tools for analyzing and cleaning your data. The Dupe Dive tool scans your CRM records and provides business intelligence on the state of your data quality, and includes a duplicates dashboard. RingLead's Deduplication Bundle includes running your data through a validation process, identifying the number of duplicates you have in your CRM, and using Data Cleanse to remove duplicates until none remain.

>> **Salesforce Data.com Clean:** This tool cleans and enriches your existing data to make sure you have complete, up-to-date information on accounts and contacts. Data.com Clean provides a number of ways to keep your Salesforce CRM records up to date. It removes the potential human error of manual data entry, reducing duplicates, and links to its verified database of accounts and contacts for automatic updating as the data changes. You can also use the

Clean button to manually update and enrich records as needed. With the Data.com Clean service, you get metrics and analytics that are useful for gauging your data health overall, and knowing where you need to focus data improvement efforts in order to ensure complete, reliable and insightful data for your account-based marketing initiatives.

>> **LeanData (`www.leandatainc.com`):** The platform helps you identify duplicate accounts and contacts. LeanData runs in your CRM and acts as your ABM platform. If you get a new inbound lead from your website, it syncs the record to your CRM, LeanData then enriches the lead with account-level information. LeanData can be configured to match new leads to the proper account and auto-convert that lead into a new contact if business rules dictate.

Assigning new accounts to owners

When you create new accounts, you can assign accounts to owners in your "smarketing" team either manually or automatically:

>> **Manually:** You type the account and its associated fields into your CRM, then assign an owner based on the stage of the purchase decision.

>> **Automatically:** Because your CRM is integrated with your CMS, marketing automation, and ABM platform, if a new lead comes in then you can create a workflow to assign new accounts to owners. These accounts can be assigned by territory, price, size, or any metric you want that best suits the structure of your sales team.

REMEMBER

Not all CRMs have automatic workflow options. In some cases, users may need to upgrade their CRM packages to gain access to workflow features.

There will always be an owner of an account in your CRM. The account owner should represent where the account is in the buyer's journey or customer experience. These are examples of account owners:

>> **Marketing:** The marketing team owns accounts that are currently in nurturing programs, or recently added after an event. These could also be Tier C accounts who match some of your ICP criteria but aren't the best fit. Marketing should transfer ownership of an account to the sales team when there appear to be intent or buying signals.

>> **Sales/Business Development Representative:** Owns accounts in the prospect stage. These are accounts that have been qualified as a Tier A or B account and are currently engaged in a cadence of outbound marketing activities such as calls and email campaigns.

>> **Sales Account Executive:** These are accounts that have an associated revenue opportunity. Sales will own accounts until they're closed. There are two types of closed accounts:

- *Closed/Lost:* The account was an opportunity that decided against buying from your company.

- *Closed/Won:* The account decided to purchase from your company and became a customer.

>> **Customer Success:** After the deal is done, the account is transferred to a customer success manager (CSM). The CSM is responsible for managing the relationship with your customer, renewing their annual contract (if there is one) and identifying potential opportunities to cross-sell or upsell the account. Figure 6-5 shows an example of who owns an account in your CRM.

Account Name	Opportunity Name	Close Date	Fiscal Period	Age	Opportunity Owner
Stage: Negotiation/Review (12 records)					
				avg 57.5	
Stonebranch	Stonebranch 12	12/31/2015	Q4-2015	8	Tonni Bennett
Lockheed Martin	Lockheed Martin	12/31/2015	Q4-2015	12	Tonni Bennett
Wrike	Wrike	12/31/2015	Q4-2015	60	Tonni Bennett
greenlight.guru	greenlight.guru-	12/31/2015	Q4-2015	42	Tonni Bennett
Parstream	Parstream	12/31/2015	Q4-2015	47	Tonni Bennett
AlterG	AlterG	12/31/2015	Q4-2015	48	Tonni Bennett
Aviso	Aviso	12/26/2015	Q4-2015	67	Tonni Bennett
EarthLink	EarthLink-	11/30/2015	Q4-2015	110	Tonni Bennett
Visible Equity	Visible Equity	11/30/2015	Q4-2015	83	Tonni Bennett
Business.com	Business.com	11/30/2015	Q4-2015	89	Tonni Bennett
eFolder	eFolder-	11/27/2015	Q4-2015	63	Tonni Bennett
Transpay	Transpay	11/27/2015	Q4-2015	61	Tonni Bennett
Stage: Awaiting Signature (2 records)					
				avg 102.5	
NPS	Matt Squarzoni	11/30/2015	Q4-2015	73	Tonni Bennett
Revjet	Revjet-	11/30/2015	Q4-2015	132	Tonni Bennett
Grand Totals (14 records)					

FIGURE 6-5: Showing who from your "smarketing" team owns the account.

Protecting Data Quality

According to Dun & Bradstreet's Worldwide Database, B2B data decays at least 30 percent each year. The data decay is caused by your contacts in the accounts changing jobs, leaving companies, or other factors. If your CRM is more than two years old, a lot of the data within it may be inaccurate or outdated. These are the main areas to be concerned with for protecting your data quality:

>> **Clean:** Correct and accurate. You don't have duplicates or typos in your account's information.

>> **Organized:** You don't have an orphan contact that isn't tied to an account. A full profile of an account and it contacts has been completed.

>> **Updated:** If you're actively working an account, regularly updating the data will help to ensure you have all the right information.

>> **Appended:** You aren't relying on one salesperson or a form completion. Appending data means you're finding more high-quality data to append your contact and account information. Using the data partners I mentioned earlier in this chapter will help you with appending data to create a full profile of an account.

Profiling your data records

According to InsightSquared, data quality best practices increase revenue by an average of 66 percent for B2B organizations. Data profiling is all about under-standing your data. This will help you determine whether you have a full story of all the data for your contacts in your target accounts. These software tools are useful for data profiling:

>> **LeanData (`www.leandatainc.com`):** The platform helps you identify the proper accounts for new leads and enriches them with account-level informa-tion. Many companies spend a lot of money to update their account informa-tion, but don't make that good data actionable for leads. LeanData uses your existing information to update leads in your system to ensure your good data is available in other systems.

>> **Leadspace (`www.leadspace.com`):** Leadspace is a predictive analytics platform for B2B demand creation, with unique capabilities for account-based marketing. Leadspace brings together predictive scoring, B2B data enrich-ment, and the ability to identify net-new prospects by social and other buying intent signals, at both the company and individual level. Leadspace lead-to-account matching connects people to accounts to understand the relation-ships among them, overcoming one of the main ABM roadblocks. Integrated with major CRM and marketing automation platforms, Leadspace discovers net-new prospects, scores individuals and companies, and performs real-time database enrichment and segmentation for outbound and account-based marketing, as well as identifying cross-sell and upsell opportunities.

>> **Salesforce Data.com Assessment App (`https://appexchange.salesforce.com`):** Available on the Salesforce AppExchange, the Data.com Assessment App gives you overall health scores for your CRM data, shows you match rates for your contact, lead, and account records to Data.com source data, and gives a data field-level read out of where the data could be improved. There are also report packages available on the AppExchange for Data.com customers that provide dashboards and reporting on your data quality and performance.

>> **Social123 (**`http://social123.com`**):** This Data-as-a-Service (DaaS) platform is a social-sourced B2B data provider with a global contact database that is always refreshing in real time. Customers benefit from the origination of net-new contact information to full-service data appends. Social123 offers a reliable data solution on the market due to the self-reported nature of the data. The platform identifies inaccurate records within its clients' databases, correct and replace them, and then layers on up to 45 fields of self-reported information, such as groups, skills, titles, and even a validated email address (tested within the proprietary email validation software).

TIP

Make a checklist for the data in your CRM. Whoever is entering data in your CRM, whether your database administrator or your sales account executive, should follow these rules and guidelines to ensure your data is as accurate as possible. Here is an example checklist for your CRM data:

>> **Who:** Name, title, company name, company size, revenue.

>> **Where:** Office address and website (the company's digital home).

>> **How:** The best way to reach the person, phone number, email address, and social media. CRMs now include a field for Twitter and LinkedIn.

TIP

Invite your accounts to connect on LinkedIn. Connecting with your contacts on LinkedIn will help on many levels. First, you can engage them in social selling. Secondly, if the contact has a job change, you're alerted and can remove that contact from the account in your CRM.

Determining whether your data is bad

I'll go ahead and say it: a lot of the data in your CRM is junk. According to HubSpot, your data can go bad at a rate up to 25 percent in less than one year. The devil is truly in the details when it comes to managing your CRM. These are a few ways to know whether your data is incomplete or inaccurate:

>> **Missing information:** Any field that isn't completed for a contact in your account, such as omitting a phone number or email address.

>> **Incorrect:** You may have the right company but the wrong contact. As you build out contacts in your CRM and tie them to an account, you may discover that a contact should no longer be tied to an account. John Smith may have left his position at Acme Corporation, and therefore should be removed and possibly recreated with his new company's account.

>> **Misspelled:** A typo in an email address, and your contact will never receive your communication.

TIP

Looking at bounce rates or undeliverable emails in your marketing automation platform will help you discover whether there's a potential error in the email address.

Bad data is bad for your business. Maintaining your CRM requires vigilance, which is why many B2B organizations have a dedicated database administrator of marketing operations person who is tasked with managing the data. This person is also responsible for being vigilant on contact and account opportunities.

There are several beasts you will have to face now that you've chosen to revolutionize your marketing efforts with ABM. Now that you have all this data in your CRM, it can be a beast:

>> **Ghosts in your data**: Contacts you thought existed, but actually are just bad data for contacts who don't actually belong to your target accounts.

>> **Multi-headed monsters**: You're trying to market to several decision makers, and after you've targeted one, three more contacts raise their hand to have a say in the purchase decision.

>> **Giants:** Huge, hard to manage accounts with lots of contacts you have to ensure are assigned correctly.

>> **Disparate:** A contact separated from an account tied to a revenue opportunity. Accounts are supposed to bring together the fragmented pieces of data.

Updating account information

To keep it clean and up to date, your data should identify your potential customers. It should be segmented so that not everyone who downloads content from your website is turned over to sales. Everyone's CRM is set up differently. If anything changes with the contact, or something happens in the company such as an acquisition or merger, the account should be updated.

TIP

Checking sources such as LinkedIn (www.LinkedIn.com) to connect with the contacts in an account will alert you of any changes within the organization.

Chapter 7

Qualifying Your Target Accounts

The Corporate Executive Board (CEB) stated that, by 2017, as much of 90 percent of the account's journey to making a purchase decision will be complete before they first connect with your company. Salespeople will evolve into order-takers, closing new revenue from accounts that already know they want to buy from your business. Based on these statistics, it's clear how marketing has an integral role to play in education, because marketing will be solely responsible for bringing in new customers. This is part of the reason I'm such a fan of the term "smarketing" to show sales and marketing alignment.

Traditionally, marketing has lived in a world of leads. Marketing owned all the leads, then turned them over to sales after they were qualified. Now, with account-based marketing, the "smarketing" team starts by determining whether your accounts fit your ideal customer profile (ICP) and whether contacts in those accounts align with the personas you created for your best-fit users. After marketing qualifies these accounts, it's up to sales to determine whether the accounts are ready to do business with your company.

In this chapter, I tell you how to ask the right qualification questions to determine whether your accounts are ready to move to the next stage of the purchase decision. I discuss ways to look for "triggers," or buying signals, that an account is progressing to an opportunity, then how to determine whether multiple revenue opportunities exist within the account.

Gauging Interest

Your target list of accounts may have 500 companies listed. From the 500 accounts, how many people in those accounts are actively engaging with your company? Contacts in accounts demonstrate their interest through activities that fall into the categories of either inbound or outbound marketing.

Comparing inbound and outbound activities

The first stage when a contact in an account begins the buyer's journey is awareness. This prospect is becoming aware of your product or service, and is engaging in your marketing activities. These activities are either *inbound* or *outbound*:

>> **Inbound**: Your prospects are taking the action; you aren't. The prospect is checking out your website and downloading content (such as an ebook, whitepaper, or case study). You're notified about these inbound activities by your marketing automation system.

>> **Outbound:** You've determined that this prospect meets your ICP and is on your list of target accounts. Your business or sales development representative (BDR/SDR) is engaged in a cadence of calls and emails to engage this prospect.

The next step is to connect to the prospect on a "discovery" call. This is when your BDR/SDR has an initial conversation with the prospect. In this call, your team begins the process of qualification to determine how much interest exists for making a purchase decision.

REMEMBER

Depending on your sales process, a prospect may want to go straight into a trial or purchase of your product without a discovery call.

Discovering BANT

There's no gray area with account-based marketing. Either an account is interested in purchasing from your company, or it isn't. This is the phase to find whether there is an opportunity to generate revenue for your company.

To qualify an opportunity, you need a set of rules. There is a list for qualifying, called *BANT*:

>> **Budget:** The contact said there is money approved to make a purchase decision. The budget has been set by the higher-ups at the account you're working.

If there is no budget, or the budget is too small for your product or service, you should walk away.

>> **Authority:** Your contact either said they have the power to make a purchase decision, or they do not.

Your contact can be the influencer or ultimate user of your company's product or service, but they aren't the ultimate decision maker. See Chapter 3 for a list of the stakeholders who have authority in a buying decision.

>> **Need:** The contact stated there is a business need that your product or service can help meet.

Often, you need a discovery call with the contact, or multiple stakeholders within the account, to discover the need. After the need is determined, you can align marketing content to help educate your contacts on the purchase decision; for example, a case study of how your business helped a client fulfill that same need.

>> **Time:** Your potential customer stated that there is a timeline for making a decision.

Avoid wasting your money or energy marketing to an account that doesn't have a target date for making a purchase.

When a contact meets all of the BANT criteria, it's a significant revenue opportunity. It's time to build out the account in your CRM and deliver it to sales.

Asking the right qualification questions

The qualification questions are asked during the discovery call. On the discovery call, you should have a script for your BDR/SDR. A great way to do this is to say "Most of our customers today see one of these pain points," then give examples of common problems your existing clients had. You can also say "What we've seen across our industry is that people are struggling with. . .," then fill in a pain point that your product/service alleviates. Next, ask, "Does that ring true to you at all?" These questions can help determine whether the prospect is intending to buy.

TIP

Before the discovery call, review your prospect's profile on LinkedIn. If you see a "manager" title, usually they need approval from their supervisor. Your prospect may be the ultimate user of your product, but must present a business case for the purchase decision to the higher-ups.

BANT OR CHAMP?

InsightSquared (www.insightsquared.com) released a great blog post, "Don't BANT. Just CHAMP." Like BANT, CHAMP is an acronym for qualification questions: *CHallenges, Authority, Money,* and *Prioritization:*

- **Challenges:** Your prospect buys things because they have a challenge. Ask them "What challenges is your business facing?" or "What problems do you need to solve?" If you have a solution for the challenges that your prospect and their company are facing, then you have a real beginning of an "Opportunity," and some potential to sell to this prospect and account. Asking "What made you decide to solve this problem now?" will also give you an idea of how quickly they're looking to make a purchase decision.

- **Authority:** Many sales reps believe that "Authority" means you should disqualify leads with low-influencing contacts. That isn't the case! "Authority" means you must ask your prospect questions that help you map out that company's organizational structure. Ask them such questions as "In addition to yourself, who else is involved in making this solution happen at your company?" and "Would it make sense for us to schedule a call with your team to answer any questions they may have?"

- **Money:** After you've qualified their challenges and needs, it's time to find their expectations for the investment they need to make to fulfill these needs. Price and budget are critical factors in any buying decision. If your prospect can't afford your product or service, you can't sell to them. Ask them "Do you have a portion of your budget allocated to solving this problem?" or "Is your finance team or CFO involved in approving this?

  While this can come off as an "Authority" type of qualifying question, it is equally indicative of how the budget approval process works at the company (depending on the prospect's answer).

- **Prioritization:** BANT calls this "Timing." Ask your prospect, "Is it a top priority for this quarter, or is it a goal they want to solve at some point before the end of the fiscal year?" or "When were you planning on starting the implementation?" If they don't need a solution until the end of the year, that means it's in a queue of other priorities. Find those priorities to get an idea of your prospect's business plan.

REMEMBER

B2B purchase decisions rarely involve one person. According to CEB, an average of 5.4 people are involved in today's B2B purchase decisions.

The purpose of the discovery call is to identify the problem that needs solving, and everyone who is involved in the purchase decision. You should create your own qualification questions that show how your solution answers a problem. These are examples of questions to ask to determine whether BANT exists:

>> **Budget:** Do you have this line item approved? Has money been allocated?

>> **Authority:** What's the purchase approval process? Who are the decision makers on your team?

>> **Need:** Why are you looking to purchase? What pain must be solved?

>> **Timing:** When are you looking to implement/go live with a solution?

TIP

During the discovery calls from the qualification process, take detailed notes. It's important to note all the stakeholders in the purchase decision. "I know you're interested in buying. What is the process? Who else will I need to talk to? What does the procurement or approval process look like?" This helps you understand all the hoops you need to jump through to get the deal done.

Intending to buy

The purpose of BANT questions, qualification criteria, and the discovery call is to gauge whether the prospect intends to buy. The questions you ask should be specific, and geared towards your product or service. It's okay to ask "Is this a problem you need to solve now? Can you fill me in on the details?"

WARNING

This process of discovery may resemble the traditional B2B funnel, but it is not. You're receiving new accounts, then analyzing these prospects to determine whether there is intent.

You have to be specific to find whether the prospect is ready to move forward. I've found it to be effective to say "Clearly, you're really involved in this process. You would be a great fit for our service. I'm glad we started with you. Who else do we need to be involved to make this happen?"

Here are the next steps, based on whether the prospect is ready to buy:

>> **Intending to buy:** The prospect is turned over to sales. The account represents a significant revenue opportunity.

>> **Not ready to buy:** Note the responses in your CRM about why they weren't ready to buy, then place the prospect in a "nurturing" marketing campaign.

Converting Accounts to Opportunities

Not all accounts become opportunities immediately. You are either nurturing an account that isn't ready to buy, or converting accounts that can bring in new revenue for your business.

Nurturing or converting

If the account is ready to buy, it's converted to an opportunity. If the account doesn't meet BANT criteria and isn't ready to buy, it shouldn't be pursued. However, you should continue marketing to these accounts, so your company stays top of mind. The account may buy later. This is why marketing should continue to "nurture" these accounts. These are types of marketing nurture campaigns:

>> Establish an email program of drips.

 A drip email is set up through marketing automation. These emails contain links to blog posts or relevant content. They continue promoting thought leadership.

>> Invite them to attend your upcoming webinars.

>> Send emails with new content, such as whitepapers, ebooks, and case studies. These should be based on the job role and industry vertical of the account you're targeting.

WARNING

When creating opportunities with account-based marketing, your marketing shouldn't hand off just one contact to sales. What marketing should deliver to sales is a complete account with multiple contacts.

Monitoring activities for buying signals

According to SiriusDecisions, 70 percent of the buyer's journey is already complete before the prospect connects with a salesperson. This percentage will continue to increase because marketing technology (MarTech) tools and are evolving at a rapid place. As more new media channels continue to emerge (such as social, mobile, display, and video) your buyers will become even more savvy about your company's products and services before they consider committing to an investment.

Your prospects within an account will want to engage in different ways. Some of your potential customers first will want to talk directly to a salesperson. Others will want to watch a video. Different marketing activities can signal whether an account is ready to buy. This is why it's important to have a system in place that monitors your prospects' activities. This system is your marketing automation platform.

In your marketing automation system, you can load files for your content, such as ebooks, whitepapers, case studies, webinar recordings, or any file you want to use or publish in your resource library. Marketing automation systems also let you put tracking code on your website. When prospects come to your website or download a file, it's recorded in your marketing automation system and synced with your CRM through the API connector.

REMEMBER

The tracking code installed on your website only captures whether a visitor hit a specific page. It may not help log more specific events like a file download. Marketing automation users may need to use tracked redirect links or host their content in a marketing automation system in order to report on more specific activity.

Triggering at the right time

A beautiful thing about MarTech is the ability to see what's happening with your prospect and customer accounts in real-time. Marketing automation platforms can show you in real-time who is on your site. If you can see your prospect in real-time on your site, then you can alert your sales team. The sales team, whether your business or sales development rep (BDR/SDR), can then follow up. These responses can be triggered by your prospect's activities:

>> **Call:** It's a bold and modern tactic to say "Hi (name)! (Your name) calling from (your company). I saw you were on our website and I just wanted to check in to see whether I can help with anything."

  If you have the prospect's voicemail, leave a voicemail with similar content.

>> **Email:** Send an email to follow up. "Hi (name)! Hope you're having a good week. I just left you a voicemail and wanted to follow up through email. We saw you (downloaded content) from our website. Is there anything I can do to help?"

WARNING

Asking an account whether they're ready to buy may scare them off. You don't want to inundate your prospect. You should reach out very professionally. Tweeting "Hey @JohnSmith are you ready to talk again?" *isn't* a best practice for sales.

If the prospect emails you back and says "I'm not ready, just reading," or something along those lines, then let him or her continue their own process of discovery. If the prospect says "Yes, I want to see a demo," or asks for pricing, it's time to turn the account over to sales.

Communicating with your accounts

It's important to communicate clearly and directly with your accounts. Providing your prospect with a list of next steps or follow-up actions will help to make the buyer's journey smooth and successful. There should be a process within your sales team for transitioning inbound/outbound prospects who became accounts.

When the account is ready to move the next stage of the purchase decision (to see a demo or to obtain pricing), then the business/sales development rep transitions the account to a sales account executive. Here is how you should communicate with accounts when converting them:

>> Provide the first and last name of the account executive.

>> Tell the prospect what the account executive is responsible for, such as setting up a demo or providing pricing.

>> List the next steps. "My colleague (Name) will work with you to find a time to take you on a product tour."

>> Ask the prospect whether there's anyone else who must be involved from his or her company.

REMEMBER

You need to know whether your prospect is the ultimate decision-maker. You may have discovered this during the BANT qualification process when you asked about "authority." If not, ask again; these additional people are stakeholders in the purchase decision.

Qualifying a Revenue Opportunity

The qualification process for a prospect requires an investment in time and resources from your marketing team.

With account-based marketing, I calling this qualification process the account's journey. I'm also doing away with the traditional acronyms of MQL, SAL and SQL, and using these criteria:

>> **MQA:** Marketing qualified accounts who meet your ICP. Because you are no longer focusing on leads, the term "MQL" for marketing qualified leads is erroneous.

>> **SQA:** Sales qualifies the account.

I'm discarding the term "sales accepted lead" (SAL). Sales doesn't close leads, they acquire accounts. After all, your salespeople are called "Account Executives," not "Lead Executives".

>> **Opportunity:** A potential revenue deal within the account.

REMEMBER

In the #FlipMyFunnel model for ABM, there are stages: Identify, Expand, Engage, and Advocate. This fourth stage involves turning your customers into advocates. This is the reason I'm calling it the account's journey is because the account lifecycle goes beyond the typical B2B buyer's journey into a customer experience. Marketing will continue to engage with accounts after the opportunity becomes a Closed/Won deal.

Examining the account's journey

You're getting out of the qualification process for leads. Your prospect accounts came in through either inbound or outbound marketing activities. Here is the journey your accounts have taken thus far during the identify stage to determine whether they're the best fit for your company.

>> **Inbound:** A prospect came in organically through your website or downloading content:

- The prospect's activity was captured in marketing automation, then synced with your CRM.

- If the prospect wasn't originally in your CRM, it was captured as a new lead, becoming a contact and a new account.

- You analyzed the account against your ICP to determine whether they meet your requirements for a Tier A, B, or C account.

- If they met your ICP, the account is assigned to a BDR/SDR to begin emailing or calling the account.

- A discovery call happens to determine whether the account meets BANT or your own internal qualification criteria.

- If the account meets BANT, then it's turned over to sales.

- An opportunity is created after the demo.

>> **Outbound:** The account is a "named" account, identified by marketing as a best fit for meeting your ICP criteria:

- The account is assigned to a BDR/SDR to begin emailing and calling the account.

- The SDR is the one who qualifies them on the call for meeting BANT criteria.

- If the account meets BANT criteria, a demo is scheduled and turned over to sales.

ACCOUNT-BASED SALES DEVELOPMENT WITH SALESLOFT

One of my favorite tools used by my BDRs is SalesLoft's Cadence. This SaaS product syncs with your CRM, pulling in contact data about your named accounts. From there, you create emails that you want to send automatically, interchanging a strategy of calls and emails to connect with the accounts you have identified. This pattern of emails and calls is called a cadence, hence the name of the product. You can structure your cadence out over multiple days or weeks, allowing you to measure the number of "touches" needed to get the account to agree to move forward with a discovery call.

Agreeing on sales-ready opportunities

All of your stakeholders for your company's revenue should agree about what a revenue opportunity looks like. An opportunity will be added to your pipeline of potential new revenue. This pipeline is the lifeline of your business, helping your company to grow.

REMEMBER

It's important for marketing and sales to be aligned as one "smarketing" team. Using ABM, you will see a growth in marketing-sourced pipeline. Because of Mar-Tech tools, "smarketing" team members can look at the pipeline and say "This opportunity was on our Tier (A, B, or C) list," then examine the steps taken to turn this account into an opportunity. It provides your "smarketing" team with a road-map to create future opportunities.

A sales-ready opportunity goes on your Tier A list. Marketing will need to continue supporting sales to help close the deal.

Here are the steps your "smarketing" team should take to agree on sales-ready opportunities:

>> Fit in your ICP acceptable range.

>> Met BANT.

>> Had an initial discovery call.

>> Prospect requested demo and/or pricing.

Figure 7-1 shows how an account is turned into opportunity in your CRM.

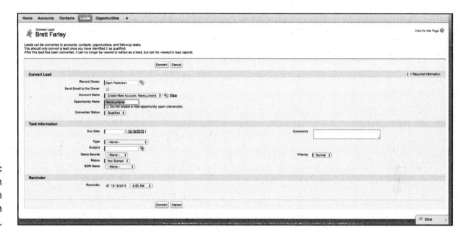

FIGURE 7-1:
Turning an account into an opportunity in your CRM.

TIP

Organize a weekly meeting with your "smarketing" team. At my company, I gather my BDRs, marketers, and salespeople into one room to talk about opportunities or potential roadblocks.

Building a full view of an account

Having a holistic view of your account is important. As you move into the next stage of the account-based marketing funnel, "Expand," you will expand your marketing efforts by adding more contacts to the account. B2B platforms usually have more than one user, and all these users become contacts under the account in your CRM. It's important to market to every contact who may be involved in the purchase decision.

Your initial prospect came in through inbound or outbound marketing, which you made into an account in your CRM. This contact in the account is the contact who is associated with a revenue opportunity.

Finding multiple opportunities within one account

An account can represent multiple opportunities for revenue, especially when your business offers a suite of products. If you're targeting large, enterprise organizations, the different departments or business units present the chance to sell to different people. This is why it's important to build a relationship with all the stakeholders involved.

In the Identify stage of the funnel, you identify the accounts that can present an opportunity. If this is a brand new account in your CRM, then you'll be starting with one initial contact to whom you might be able to sell. If this is an existing account, the increase in marketing activities may signal an opportunity to upsell with another product or service.

3

Expanding Contacts Into Accounts

IN THIS PART . . .

Taking the personas you created to find contacts in the account

Building an account-specific plan for reaching contacts across all buying centers

Combining your marketing automation system with your ABM strategy

Learning how a "smarketing" team works together throughout the account's journey

Chapter 8

Reaching the Right People in Target Accounts

The second stage in account-based marketing (ABM) is Expand. It's absolutely critical for B2B marketers to think of the Expand stage as the reason why ABM exists. The decision process in most B2B companies is done by more than just one person. That's why B2B stands for "business-to-business." The purchase decision won't come from just a single lead who completed a form on your website. It's a group decision.

This chapter tells you how to connect with more people in the opportunity account. I discuss the types of contacts in your target accounts involved in the purchase decision, and how to use an organizational chart to recognize all of the relevant stakeholders. I also tell you how to look for potential buying centers across the organization.

Preparing Your Account-Specific Plan

To progress the opportunity into a Closed/Won deal, you need an account-specific plan. An account plan is the strategy and tactics for targeting a contact. Your opportunity accounts may require tailoring your ABM efforts to multiple contacts. These contacts should align with your personas (as shown in Chapter 5).

Because you've done the leg work to identify your personas, you know the contacts in the account have different roles. You need a plan to engage all of those contacts according to their responsibilities; their wants and needs will impact the purchase decision.

Consider these roles in your account-specific plan:

>> **Stakeholder:** The stakeholder is accountable for the success of your project if/when the deal is done. The stakeholder is the user of your product or service. There can be multiple stakeholders, depending on the number of users.

>> **Champion:** The person who is your voice in the purchase decision. Your champion is the "super user" of your product or services, and therefore the primary stakeholder.

>> **Decision-maker:** In larger B2B organizations, your champion may not be the decision-maker. The decision-maker is the one contact who gives approval for the purchase. This contact also is the person who signs the contract, if needed.

>> **Power sponsor:** In mid-market or enterprise companies, the power sponsor is the person who presents the purchase request or contract to the decision-maker. The power sponsor is the executive stakeholder in the team or department that will use your product or service.

REMEMBER

Depending on the size of the organization, these roles can be the same contact in the account. You will have stakeholders and decision-makers; these aren't necessarily the same people. This is why it's important to have an account-specific plan for the roles you're targeting.

Finding the right stakeholders

According to Gartner's research, an average of seven to ten stakeholders participate in a B2B purchase decision. While there can be multiple stakeholders, there is only one ultimate decision-maker who will give the green light whether to purchase or not.

A stakeholder can be any person in the company you are trying to sell. Stakeholders are individual contributors who usually don't have any direct reports. Individual contributors report to a team manager or department director. Examples of individual contributors are

>> A marketing and/or sales coordinator

>> An administrative assistant

>> BDR/SDRs or your sales enablement team members

>> Sales account executives

>> Marketing managers who don't have direct reports

These stakeholders can all voice an opinion to the decision-maker. This is commonly called a *sphere of influence* surrounding the decision-maker. Figure 8-1 shows a sphere of influence from the individual stakeholders.

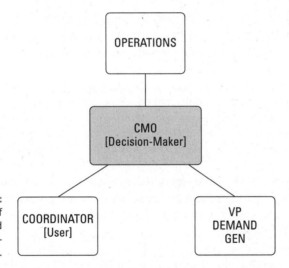

OPERATIONS

CMO
[Decision-Maker]

COORDINATOR
[User]

VP
DEMAND
GEN

FIGURE 8-1:
The sphere of influence around the decision-maker.

REMEMBER

The number of influencers, stakeholders, or other individual contributors within an account depends on the size of the company you're targeting.

Consider these guidelines for identifying your stakeholders, according to company size:

>> **SMB:** If you're targeting small, early-stage companies, then you may only have one stakeholder. This stakeholder may also the decision-maker, especially when your sales process is transactional and doesn't require a contract.

However, when you require a contract and you're targeting manager-level personas, then this manager within an SMB will have to present the contract to a higher-up (such as a director or executive). That person is the decision-maker with final approval.

>> **Mid-Market:** You find more than one stakeholder. Even when you don't require a contract, expect to address multiple influencers in the purchase decision. The primary stakeholder is your champion to empower throughout the buying process. Your champion is the person who presents the contract or purchase decision to his or her power sponsor (the executive stakeholder, who could also be the decision-maker).

>> **Enterprise:** You may have more than ten stakeholders, including a C-level executive who is the power sponsor and/or decision-maker. You'll have an estimate on the type of stakeholders based on your ICP. Because you've identified your product/service is ideal for enterprise companies, you will identify all the potential users. These users are individual influencers or contributors who can impact the purchase decision.

REMEMBER

This is why it's important to identify all of your personas. By understanding the job titles, roles, and responsibilities of people involved in the purchase decision, you can identify all the potential contacts in the account.

In the Expand stage of ABM, you're expanding the target account with as much data as possible about the additional contacts in the account. It's about finding quality data to append your existing accounts. You want to find as much good data about the contacts in your target accounts; this will improve your marketing efforts by knowing who exactly you need to reach in each account.

Your CRM allows you to roll up all of those contacts at the account level. You will need a plan to target all of these contacts. Using personas, you can identify potential stakeholders. If you sell a SaaS platform to B2B companies, these are personas who can be stakeholders:

>> **C-level executive:** The Chief Marketing Officer (CMO) is the executive stakeholder who must justify the purchase to fellow executives in the C-suite, such as the Chief Executive Officer (CEO), Chief Financial Officer (CFO), Chief Operating Officer (COO), or Chief Revenue Officer (CRO, a title that's becoming more popular for the C-level executive in charge of sales and customer retention).

>> **Vice President (VP) or Executive Vice President (EVP):** If you're targeting larger mid-market or enterprise companies, the VP is the person in charge of the department (or a team within a department); the VP reports to an executive officer. The VP is a stakeholder and power sponsor because she

impacts the performance of the entire department within the organization. He or she can also be the decision-maker who will sign off on the purchase.

>> **Director or Senior Director:** In SMB or mid-market companies, the Director of Marketing could be the head of marketing and report directly to the CEO. In a larger enterprise company, the director may oversee an individual unit and report to a VP or C-level executive.

>> **Manager:** Many B2B technology companies recognize the manager-level titles as the ultimate users of their platform or service. These are the users who have been proven to be the most successful. The manager is your champion; the manager advocates to his or her director, VP, or C-level executive why the purchase is justified.

>> **Individual Contributor:** Commonly called an administrator, coordinator, representative, or account executive, these individual contributors can be influencers or stakeholders in the buying process.

Enabling your champion

Your champion is your VIP. This is the contact you want to enable with information, empowering him or her to turn your opportunity into a Closed/Won deal. In your CRM, the champion is the contact within the account to whom an opportunity is assigned. Under an opportunity, you have all the contacts associated with it (as an opportunity is tied to an account) but there, is a *primary* contact on an opportunity. This primary contact is your champion.

TIP

Using the notes section of your CRM, you can discuss why this person is your champion according to their propensity to become a power user of your product or service.

The champion may also be the person who will become your VIP when the deal is done. Your Customer Champion is the person who gets trained to adopt your product.

REMEMBER

With account-based marketing, nurturing continues long after the deal has been signed. It's important to start training your customers from the initial point of contact.

You should enable your champion throughout the entire lifecycle, or the account's journey. When your champion is first identified, supply them with content that's personalized for their specific use. If the champion is an IT manager, you should be armed with a whitepaper illustrating the benefits of how your solution solves a larger problem facing the IT industry. A blog post from your company also is an easy way for the IT manager to read about your thought leadership position, then share the link with his or her executive or other stakeholders in the organization.

Pointing out potential detractors

The purchase decision isn't always smooth. When you targeting accounts in larger enterprise companies, there are more contacts and stakeholders involved in the buying process. It's likely you'll encounter a "naysayer" or detractor who can impact the purchase. Because you're taking the time to add more contacts to your accounts in your CRM, you can note contacts who may present a roadblock to closing the deal.

Watch for these objections to spot potential detractors:

>> **Competition:** The detractor may ask your point blank "How do you compare with Acme Company?" This person may have created a request for proposal (RFP) with a potential competitor of yours in mind.

>> **Functionality:** The naysayer will ask lots of questions about how your product or service works. They want to see how it compares to the technology your team already has in place, or benchmark you against your competition.

>> **Price:** Be alert to haggling over price by line. The more you're prepared to justify your costs, or offer a potential price break, the better you can placate this detractor.

TIP

The detractor can end up becoming your champion. This contact may just need more coaching to illustrate the benefits of your product or service.

Discovering your power sponsor

Your power sponsor has the final decision, or has power to influence the purchase. This may be the person who is presenting a business case to their boss, executive stakeholder, or board of directors to receive purchase approval. The power sponsor is the one who will sign off, or present the business case to the executive who will sign your deal. When you go through the qualification process during a demo or discovery call, asking the BANT questions about authority will help. These are examples of questions to ask to discover the power sponsor:

>> Who from your team will we be engaged with?

>> How many users will we have and to whom do they report?

>> Who must be in the approval process?

>> Who must be looped into our conversation to get you started quickly with our platform?

Using Tools for Expansion

There is a whole subcategory of marketing technology (MarTech) dedicated to expanding your reach. The more contacts you capture in your CRM for your target accounts, the more opportunities there are to engage potential stakeholders. It's important for you to build relationships with the account's contacts as you continue to work with the account through the purchase decision. The good news is that you can use software and technology to help connect with every contact in an account.

Selecting the right software

The account-based marketing subcategory of MarTech is rapidly growing. Thanks to the evolution of MarTech, B2B "smarketing" professionals have a bevy of options for connecting with more contacts in their target accounts. One of the primary methods of connecting with these contacts is through display advertising. Using an ABM platform, you can

>> Target the contacts you want to engage in an account.

>> Load your own advertising and content for campaigns.

>> Set a budget for how much you want to spend for each campaign.

>> Measure the results at the account level.

Depending on the amount of resources you want to invest in your B2B account-based advertising, there are many different platforms. Consider these software providers to help expand the reach of your marketing messages:

>> **Azalead** (`http://azalead.com`): This mobile app and B2B sales platform for ABM identifies your anonymous web visitors and provides customized alerts to sales teams. Azalead lets its users see which accounts viewed a certain product or service on your website. You can search the name of an account to see what web pages, emails, and ads they have responded to.

>> **Demandbase** (`www.demandbase.com`): The B2B Marketing Cloud from Demandbase offers real-time identification service bridges the gap between known and anonymous web visitors by identifying and segmenting website visitors. Demandbase's comprehensive web-based platform includes advertising, personalization for campaigns, conversion solutions, and tools to measure performance across your marketing activities at the account level.

- » **Engagio** (`www.engagio.com`): Founded by Marketo co-founder Jon Miller, Engagio is an account-based outbound marketing platform for B2B companies with complex, enterprise sales. Engagio's ABM platform complements marketing automation platforms like Marketo with account-centric capabilities, so it helps companies to engage target accounts, expand customer relationships, and deepen sales-and-marketing alignment. The company's first solution integrates with marketing automation and Salesforce to streamline account-based reporting and analytics.

    By matching leads to accounts, the solution helps companies know which marketing investments work best to reach target accounts and accelerate deals, understand which accounts have the best engagement and opportunity for growth, and measure the impact and ROI of your ABM programs (all without spending tons of time in Excel).

- » **Terminus** (`www.terminus.com`): The first self-service ABM platform that enables marketers to execute ABM at scale. With more than 200 million data points, you can target your best-fit accounts with your ICP and persona criteria, then launch your campaigns in less than 30 minutes. The dashboard-style reporting provides metrics at the account level to provide metrics on campaign performance.

- » **Vendemore** (`www.vendemore.com`): Built with the Fortune 500 companies in mind, the company's goal is to be the SAP of the account-based marketing world. Vendemore provides targeted digital content advertising to complex selling B2B companies to increase sales pipeline, lower percentage of lost sales, and increase revenue on existing clients. Vendemore uses predictive analytics and personalized advertising to allow its users to engage contacts within a target account.

THE FIRST-EVER ABM CATEGORY

G2 Crowd (`www.g2crowd.com`) is the world's leading business software review platform, leveraging over 50,000 user reviews read by nearly 400,000 software buyers each month to help them make better purchasing decisions. It's a go-to source for B2B professionals to gain better insight and understanding for the technology and solutions to satisfy business needs.

The categories in G2 Crowd include everything a company needs in its technology infrastructure (or "stack"), such as Customer Success, Finance, HR, IT, and (of course) Marketing. In 2015, G2 Crowd announced the first-ever Account-Based Marketing subcategory under Marketing. You can view a complete listing at `www.g2crowd.com/categories/account-based-marketing/products`.

Avoiding manual data entry

There are tools that can automatically upload information on all the contacts in an account. If you're starting account-based marketing in the Identify stage, you may have purchased a list of contacts from such a source as Social123 or ZoomInfo (see Chapter 6 for more information on potential data providers). Don't waste your time on the administrative work of manually inputting the information into your CRM.

WARNING

You need to add these contacts to an existing account. The account should be associated with an opportunity that's already been created.

Continuing to expand accounts

The saying goes that it costs more to bring on a new customer than to keep an existing one. This is true with ABM. Expanding your relationship with an existing account is much less expensive than acquiring data on new accounts. While the cost of data acquisition is decreasing (it's cheaper to buy lists of data than ever before), the cost to find information on your target accounts will increase because your account list will continue to grow as your business evolves.

REMEMBER

This is why it's important to have a tiered list of accounts: Tier A, Tier B, and Tier C. It's important to prioritize the accounts by the best fit within your ICP, personas, and BANT or qualification criteria. Your "smarketing" team has a set amount of time, money, and resources dedicated to first identifying your target accounts, then expanding and appending those accounts with as much data as impossible.

TIP

Focus on expanding your reach in your Tier A accounts first. Your Tier A accounts are the best fit for your business.

Adding Contacts to an Account

With account-based marketing, there is an ongoing process of expansion, but it's about quality, not quantity. You targeted your best-fit accounts with your ICP to determine whether they're Tier A, B, or C accounts. Next, you will continue to expand your reach within an account by adding more contacts and their information. It's important to use your personas to identify the contacts you need to add to an account. These personas are the people you determined are the users of your product or service.

Appending more contact data to accounts

Appending data means adding more information. This additional data for your contacts should append to your targeted accounts in your CRM. It's about gathering more quality data for your best-fit accounts, not every company listed in your CRM. It's about focusing on quality instead of quantity for appending data. This data includes

>> **Contact information:** First/last name, phone number, email, social media.

>> **Role profile:** Job title, department.

These contacts should be the stakeholders for the purchase decision. You don't need to add a contact for every person you encounter who works for the company you're targeting.

Writing out your organizational chart

Your target accounts have specific departments that make up the company. These departments are called *buying centers.* When you wrote out your personas, you listed which department or responsibilities they have in those buying centers. If you were selling a product to a marketing department, your personas have different roles and reasons for how they would use your product. This is called a *use case.* Figure 8-2 shows an example of an organizational chart.

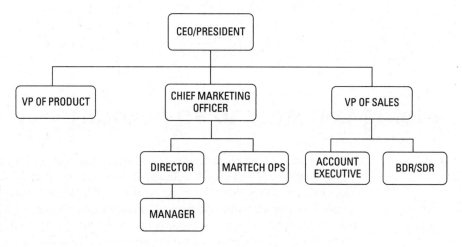

FIGURE 8-2:
Example of an organizational chart.

Working with new contacts during the sales process

Additional people will raise their hand during the purchase decision. You need to qualify them the same way that you qualified the original contact in the account during the first stage, Identify. You used a set of qualification criteria (commonly referred to as BANT questions, for *Budget, Authority, Need,* and *Timeline*). This is important, because you want to understand whether these new contacts have authority. The new contact can actually be the power sponsor or the ultimate decision-maker for your opportunity.

REMEMBER

When you get into the BANT conversation, you shouldn't be asking these contacts information for you already know. Because you've already built out the account, you should know such information as company size, industry, and the type of technology they're using.

TIP

Research the new contacts on LinkedIn before engaging with them. Find out how long your contact has been with the company so you can ask them specific questions about their roles and responsibilities. These conversations should be valuable. Start the conversation with, "Hi (name), I saw you've been (role) at (company) for (length of time). Can you tell me a bit about what you've been working on?" This is a good way to start the conversation with your new contact.

Identifying buying centers

You may discover that your product or service is used by additional departments in your target account. These additional departments are called buying centers. A buying center has the same stakeholder structure with a primary user or "champion" who can also become a customer.

TIP

Using your personas, you can know from the start of the account's journey that there are opportunities to sell your product or service to other buying centers. This is more common for B2B "smarketing" teams that target enterprise companies.

REMEMBER

Knowing all of the potential buying centers is important for the account-based marketing model. After you close your first deal with your target account, you invest more resources in training for adoption to create your customer advocate. Turning your customers into fans helps generate potential new opportunities to grow revenue. You can cross-sell to another buying center within the account.

IN THIS CHAPTER

Automating all your marketing activities

Scoring and grading based on BANT

Aligning your marketing automation and CRM system

Chapter 9

Using Marketing Automation for Your Account Strategy

arketing automation is a relatively new product category. The first major players in the marketing automation space, (including Marketo, HubSpot, Pardo, Eloqua, and Act-On) are less than ten years old. In the past decade, the amount of activity for digital marketing has grown so quickly that marketers needed a way to streamline all of their programs.

Marketing automation allows for modern marketers to manage and measure all of your activities and campaigns in a single place. It's integrated with your CRM to capture all your contact data. The power of good data is what energizes a marketing automation system. Having the data and insights about all of your prospects and customers is essential for account-based marketing (ABM). Without a marketing automation system, account-based marketing would be an impossible task.

According to Mathew Sweezey, author of *Marketing Automation For Dummies,* more than a quarter of all B2B Fortune 500 companies are already using marketing automation, along with 76 percent of the world's largest software-as-a-service (SaaS) companies. You can use marketing automation to reach contacts and create activity. By expanding your marketing efforts to all the contacts in the account, you will create a more powerful presence to accelerate your opportunities.

In this chapter, I tell you how to expand your reach using marketing automation. I discuss how you can segment your accounts according to different profile criteria, then measure the success of your marketing activities with scoring and grading to understand which content and messaging is the most effective for engaging your targeted contacts.

Strategizing Your Expansion Tactics

Marketing automation software platforms were designed for marketing teams to more effectively market across multiple digital channels, removing the manual work. Instead of copying and pasting the same email to 100 contacts, your marketing automation system lets you draft the email and send it to thousands of people; your message is personalized for each contact. Your ABM programs will mix such activities as emails, advertising, sharing content, and engaging on social media according to the type of companies and people you want to do business with.

You'll use a variety of marketing tactics to help build a relationship with the contacts in your target accounts. Next, you can see how your relationship is progressing with your accounts using marketing automation. Your marketing automation will show you which activities and strategies are working to progress accounts to the next stage of the buyer's journey.

REMEMBER

Technology can't do it all. You need an account plan for how you'll expand your reach to connect with all the contacts in an account that will help to keep your company top of mind.

Nurturing for inbound vs. outbound

There are two ways you initially connect with your accounts: They reach out to you, or you reach out to them. This is called *inbound* or *outbound* marketing. Your marketing automation system tracks both inbound and outbound activities. These activities are commonly called "nurturing," as they help to nurture an account to increase its likelihood of purchasing from your company. Depending on whether you're doing inbound or outbound marketing, different activities and content are needed for nurturing your contacts.

Inbound

According to Demand Gen Report, 90 percent of buyers say that when they're ready to buy, they will find you. Your buyers are looking for a solution to a problem. It's the marketing team's job to make sure your company's solution is easy to find. The organic way your prospects find you is called *inbound marketing*. These inbound marketing activities are accomplished through your marketing automation platform:

>> **Forms:** A form should be placed on your website for prospects to fill out. This makes it easy for prospects to indicate their interest in your product offering, or at least in a particular piece of content. A form gives the prospect an opportunity to request more information or to be contacted by your team. Forms capture such contact information as the prospect's name, company, email address, and phone number. A basic form, such as "Contact Us," is found in the navigation bar of almost every B2B company. Every marketer is familiar with the "hot lead" who just filled out a form wanting to see a demo.

TIP

The term *gated* is used for protecting content with a form. You *gate* your content in your resource library to ensure that you can follow up with the prospects who download a piece of content, such as a whitepaper. Progressive profiling is a type of gating. It uses a gated form that dynamically updates form fields to only ask for data that you don't already have about your prospect.

The information completed on the form goes directly into your marketing automation system. "Un-gated" content, such as infographic, doesn't have a form; it's placed on a landing page. Un-gated links should be used when you're sending emails promoting new content. An un-gated strategy should also be used when you already have the prospect's information or use a progressive profiling strategy that allows you to collect more, new information each time a prospect downloads a new asset.

>> **Landing Pages:** A landing page is the site where the prospect goes to download content, such as whitepapers, case studies, or ebooks (after completing the "gated" form), or to view infographics or other "un-gated" content. When you're running a paid advertising campaign, the landing page is where your prospect goes after clicking on an advertisement.

>> **Search Engine Optimization (SEO):** Your potential customers are beginning their search for a solution online. The keywords they're entering in their organic searches drive traffic to your website. SEO is used for creating keywords on your website to help people find you. You should create content with keywords focused on the types of accounts you want to attract. For example, if your goal is to attract more video marketing accounts, you could create a series of blogs on different ways to use video marketing, and make sure they're optimized for SEO.

>> **Social Media:** Your company's presence on social media platforms, such as LinkedIn, Twitter, and Facebook. Some marketing automation tools integrate directly with social media so you can post content directly to these platforms. When your prospects click on a link from these social sites, this interaction is captured within marketing automation. You could also include custom redirect links or tracked links to promote content on a social media tool; it logs that activity back into your marketing automation system.

>> **Website:** Your company's website and blog are inbound marketing channels. It's here where the great content exists that's optimized with the keywords describing your company's product or service. Some landing pages or forms may be hosted outside of the website or marketing site's CMS by the marketing automation provider. If you're using a CMS to manage your website, you could create a post that's a landing page, but it's more likely that you'll either add links to external landing pages and forms, or embed forms onto existing pages on your site. Your marketing automation system will also provide you with tracking code to place in your website's CMS to monitor which individual pages your contacts visit.

>> **Webinars:** Almost all marketing automation systems integrate with webinar platforms, such as GoToWebinar, WebEx, and BrightTalk. When you send an email inviting prospects to register, and they click on the link, this activity is recorded in marketing automation. If they attend the live session or replay the recording, this activity also is captured.

>> **Events:** Setting up events as a campaign in marketing automation is important. When you attend a tradeshow, you add the new contacts you met at the show to this campaign to watch their progression. You should set up campaigns for in-person events (such as conferences and VIP dinners) and virtual events (webinars) to record how these prospects move from the outbound activity to additional engagement.

>> **Video:** Your marketing automation tool integrates with video marketing services, such as Wistia or Vidyard, that monitor the activity of the contact viewing your video. You can see whether a prospect clicked on the video link and the number of minutes they watched the content.

Outbound

Outbound marketing means proactively reaching out to potential prospects within your target accounts to tell them about your company's solution. Not all prospects will come to you, so you need to create an outbound marketing strategy to get in front of them. If you have your list of target accounts, your outbound activities are meant to reach out and engage the contacts in those accounts. Examples of outbound marketing activities are

>> **Advertising:** Targeted advertising through Google Ads or an account-based marketing platform, tailored for your contacts.

With an ABM advertising platform, you build a list of contacts to target from the data in your CRM, then present customized advertising on digital channels (such as mobile, social, and video). You can see whether your targeted contacts clicked on any of your advertisements, giving you account-level attribution. This data is captured in both your marketing automation system and CRM.

>> **Search Engine Marketing (SEM)**: Paid keyword promotion on search engines, such as Google. When someone searches "account-based marketing," I want my company to appear at the top of the results.

>> **Email:** Your marketing automation system has several types of emails you can send. Every marketing automation platform comes with email templates to make it easy for your marketing team to plug in content and send emails.

The types of emails you send include

TIP

- *Drip/nurture emails:* These highly personalized emails are set up to send on a schedule. They "drip" to your prospects to nurture them from the prospect stage into potential opportunities. Drip emails contain a link to content, such as a recent blog post, whitepaper, or ebook, to help increase the awareness of your company's solution.

  Drip emails should be updated regularly to keep your content fresh. Don't send a whitepaper that was published more than a year ago to a new contact in an account.

- *Sharing new content:* List emails promoting a new piece of content are a great way to promote your company's thought leadership.

- *Event invitations:* Inviting your prospects and customer accounts to attend an upcoming webinar, sending the link to register, or visit your booth at a trade show.

>> **Direct Mail:** Even though direct mail is an offline activity (you're physically sending your prospects something in the mail), you should set this up as a campaign in marketing automation. This helps you monitor what happened after you sent the mail, and whether the contacts in the account became an opportunity.

>> **Video:** Your marketing automation tool integrates with video marketing services, such as Wistia or Vidyard, that monitor the activity of the contact viewing your video. With outbound marketing, you're tracking whether someone watches a video a BDR sends them instead of whether they watched a video they "discovered" on a landing page or website.

Monitoring marketing activities

You need know where your prospects are most active, and whether this is on inbound or outbound channels. Sending prospects content and engaging them helps to create activity, ultimately bringing them closer to revenue, but you need to specifically know what's working. Using your marketing automation system, you can monitor the activities that try to connect with your contacts. You monitor the engagement level of your contacts in accounts through reports. By using reports, you can see which reports are generating the most interest. Figure 9-1 shows an example of the reports available in your marketing automation system.

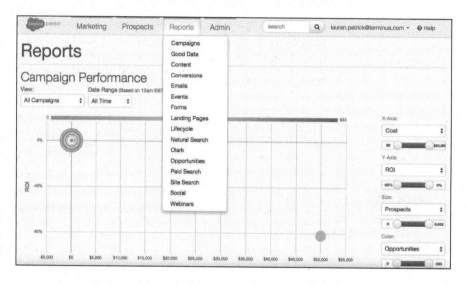

FIGURE 9-1:
Viewing reports on your activities in marketing automation.

You can drill down in these reports to see which campaigns are most effective for your contacts in accounts. Figure 9-2 shows a snapshot of activity at the contact-level with applicable scores.

TECHNICAL STUFF

You can set up rules in your marketing automation system. Rules are if/then statements predicated on specific activities.

Here is an example of a rule: If an opportunity is created, then those people are removed from an inbound nurture program, such as a drip email. Because your contact in the account is progressing to an opportunity, the contact needs different types of marketing. Your messaging, advertising, and content need to be specific to each stage.

TIP

You can get advanced with a nurture track for each stage of the account's journey: prospect, opportunity, and customer. When the contacts get transferred will depend on which stage they are in the purchase decision.

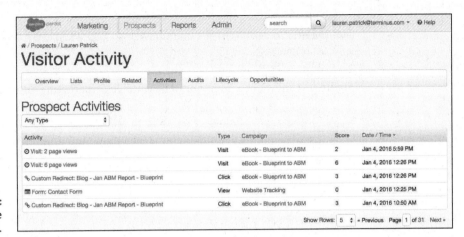

FIGURE 9-2:
Activities at the
contact level.

REMEMBER

The first person who came in through inbound marketing will become the primary contact in the account associated with the opportunity. As you expand your marketing efforts to other contacts in the account, you need to make sure they're all tied to the same revenue opportunity. If not, those contacts would continue to receive nurture email drips because they're still listed in the prospect stage. There are two ways to set this up correctly to ensure all contacts tied to the account receive the same stage–based content:

>> The sales account executive who owns the account should update the stage of contacts associated in the account in your CRM to change the messaging for the entire account.

>> If the contact has been investigating your website, and is not yet associated with a revenue opportunity, leave the other contacts in the account in the prospect stage so they continue to receive introductory content. These nurturing activities help to "warm up" all the contacts in the account.

Filtering for the right contacts

When you're executing inbound or outbound marketing activities, there are times when you need to import lists of contact data into your marketing automation system. You need to import these new lists when you partner with a third party for such marketing activities as

>> **Webinars:** A webinar you co-hosted or served as a panelist was hosted on another company's webinar platform, and they emailed you the .csv list of attendees.

>> **Events:** You exhibited at a tradeshow or sponsored an event and received a list of contacts.

Figure 9-3 shows how to import a list into your marketing automation system.

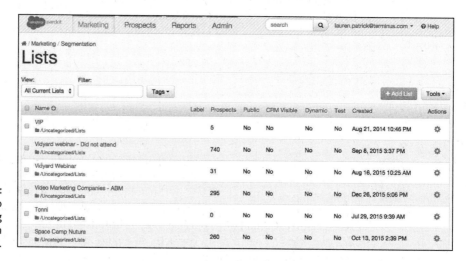

FIGURE 9-3:
Import a list into
your marketing
automation
system.

What's also important is that you have tiered accounts, ranked by your most important companies where you want to generate revenue. If you want to target large enterprises, you can divide your sales team to focus on the top accounts.

You have your list of accounts. Now you need to create a segmented list of who you want to reach. Create a list of accounts to prospect. You can filter by

>> Industry

>> Company

>> Geographic location

>> Job titles

Figure 9-4 shows contacts filtered by persona criteria, such as the financial services industry.

From there, you create a list of prospect accounts in your marketing automation system. When you have a list of named accounts, you can create a dynamic list that adds contacts when they meet certain criteria. When you upload a list of contacts, you can have your marketing automation system add them to a list. If they're older contacts already in your marketing automation system, you can run a segmentation rule to add them to a list. Figure 9-5 shows a list of prospect accounts.

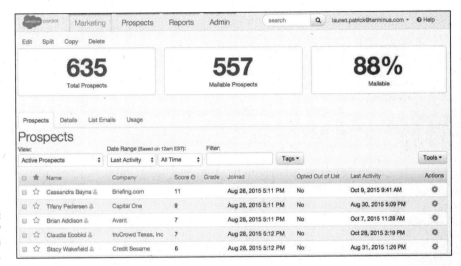

FIGURE 9-4: Filtering by ICP and persona criteria.

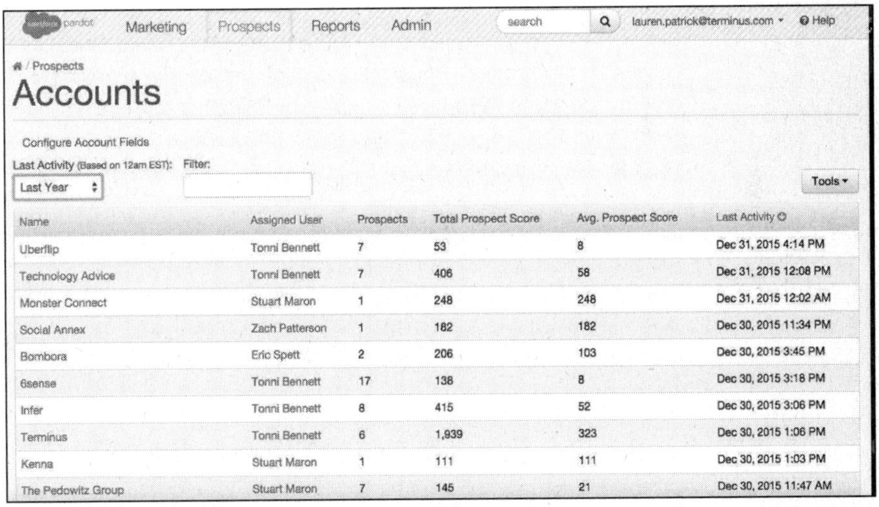

FIGURE 9-5: A list of prospect accounts.

Advancing from initial touch to account nurture

As your ramp up your marketing activities, new prospects you may never have heard of before will pop up. These new prospects may be contacts for an existing account, or they can be totally new to your universe of "named" accounts.

REMEMBER

You want to know which contacts from these companies participated in one of your marketing activities, such as attending an event. Check these metrics:

>> Who from the account came to the event?

>> Did the account become an opportunity?

Figure 9-6 shows an inbound lead being added as a new account in your marketing automation system.

THE FIRST MARKETING AUTOMATION EVANGELIST: MATHEW SWEEZEY

Before I saw the light about account-based marketing, I was Head of Marketing at Pardot. This incredible company was one of the first major players in the marketing automation scene. Pardot was acquired by ExactTarget for $95 million in 2012, then ExactTarget was acquired by Salesforce for $2.5 billion in 2013. The world's largest CRM provider clearly saw the value in owning a marketing automation system.

One of the assets that contributed to our success at Pardot was our *evangelist*. Mathew Sweezey (@msweezey) saw the potential for marketing automation to be a game changer for B2B marketing and sales. He wrote the first book about marketing automation, *Marketing Automation For Dummies*. Mathew continues to write about the importance of marketing automation across various blogs and websites, in addition to social media.

If you're new to marketing automation systems, I recommend *Marketing Automation For Dummies*. It will put you in a fantastic position to accelerate your marketing campaigns and become a savvy marketing technologist.

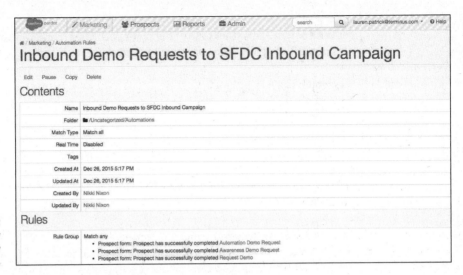

FIGURE 9-6:
Automatically
adding a new
account.

Learning the Fundamentals of Scoring and Grading

Before the internet, the buyer and seller relationship was skewed. Buyers had to trust marketing messages. The internet became the great equalizer. Sellers had to become more transparent about their products than ever. The buying process has rapidly evolved in the last decade because of the internet and the evolution of web-based marketing technology (MarTech). There is so much information available for buyers.

Marketing automation comes into play as it gives you, the seller, insights into what your buyer is looking at. It levels the playing field. Marketing automation removes the manual process of trying to determine whether your accounts are ready to move to the next phase of the purchase decision. Using data from their activities, you know whether your accounts are ready to buy. You know this through scoring and grading.

Scoring based on activities

Marketing automation has a tool to gauge the level of engagement for each of your contacts. This is called giving the contact a score. Scoring is done by assigning points to each of your marketing activities. Each marketing activity is worth a certain amount of points. You set scores to see how interested your contact is in certain content. This tracks buyer behavior with your marketing activities. Examples of marketing activities to score include

>> Time viewing your site

>> Pages viewed

>> Email opens

>> Clicks to content

>> Content downloads (completing a form to download a whitepaper, ebook, or case study)

There's a scoring system in your marketing automation system. Your "smarketing" team should agree on how many points are associated with each marketing activity. With scoring, you can track levels of engagement for all the contacts and accounts in your CRM, because it is integrated with your marketing automation platform. Figure 9-7 shows scoring rules.

	Marketing	Prospects	Reports	Admin

Scoring Rules

Edit Scoring Rules

Scoring Rules

Custom Redirect Click	3 points
Email Open	0 points
Event Checked In	0 points
Event Registered	0 points
File Access	3 points
Form Error	-5 points
Form Handler Error	-5 points
Form Handler Submission	50 points
Form Submission	50 points
Landing Page Error	-5 points
Landing Page Success	50 points
Olark Chat	10 points
Opportunity Created	50 points
Opportunity Lost	-100 points

FIGURE 9-7: Scoring rules in marketing automation.

Scoring degradation

Negative points are associated with some activities. This is called *scoring degradation*. Score degradation is the process of lowering someone's score to make sure it's correctly portraying whether the account is ready to move forward. If the contact isn't ready to buy, you can downgrade their score in your marketing automation system to give them a negative score. If they're inactive for a certain period of time, you can also reduce their score in the MA system so you are only nurturing the most active contacts in your target accounts.

Using a negative score helps to ensure these accounts don't get forwarded as sales qualified accounts (SQA). If, for example, your SDR has just completed an initial discovery score with a marketing qualified account (MQA), and the contact wasn't ready to move forward, the SDR can downgrade the contact's score to remove them from future marketing activities.

Combining scores for a single account

With traditional lead-based marketing, you would look at the score of a single contact to see whether he or she was ready to move forward in the purchase decision. In account-based marketing, you're recognizing that more than one contact is involved in the purchase, so you need to look at scores for *all* the contacts in your target account.

You take these individual contacts' scores and aggregate them into a comprehensive score. If you were selling to other B2B marketers, you would look for scores in marketing job roles in the account. By adding up the scores for all the contacts in the marketing team, you can see engagement within the whole account.

Figure 9-8 shows the scores of multiple contacts in an account.

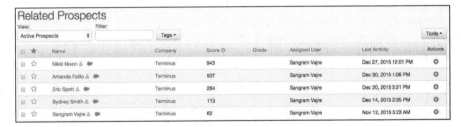

FIGURE 9-8:
Scoring multiple contacts in an account.

Grading based on best fit

Scoring and grading are easily confused. A score lets you know whether the contact is ready for sales but the grade is used to determine how well the contact fits within your ICP and persona criteria. Grading criteria include

>> Company size (employees and revenue)

>> Industry (outside your vertical)

>> Job title (role and responsibilities)

>> Technology used

Giving a contact the grade of A means they're a perfect fit. Giving them a grade of D or below means you won't want them.

REMEMBER

You have a list of Tier A, B, or C accounts. While the Tier B or C accounts technically aren't a perfect fit with your ICP criteria, if the score is high and they're demonstrating interest in your product or service, you can still attempt to do business with them.

TIP

Set up grading rules for specific personas. You created personas to identify the qualities of your best-fit users. You can match your persona criteria to determine what would qualify as a contact within a Tier A account. These contacts automatically would be added to a drip email program when they come to your site.

If you're using an account-based marketing platform for targeted advertising to your contacts, you can draw these personas into a specific landing page. Set your rule from there to add them to the email nurture program.

TIP

You can set up these rules so your competition can't access your content. "Block anyone from ACME Corporation from downloading the whitepaper." After you identify these competing companies, you should create a list and give all the contacts in these companies a grade of an F, because you know they will never purchase from your company.

Flowing Data Back into Your CRM

In theory, targeting the right accounts is easy. In action, this can present many challenges. Because most marketing teams were created for lead-based marketing, the most popular software solutions also are lead-based.

This may surprise you, but your CRM and marketing automation system weren't initially set up for account-based marketing. By default, these software platforms were designed for lead-based marketing. Your CRM was built to manage contacts, then marketing automation is used to engage the contacts in activities and track the metrics. Activity was measured at the contact level. Marketers and salespeople haven't been able to report at the account level. The reports would include lists of leads, or opportunities, and engagement on those contacts. To get to the account-level engagement, you have to manually design the necessary reports.

Today, CRM systems don't directly report on opportunities at the account level. Your CEO may ask you, "How many accounts that came to a marketing event have closed as a direct result?" There's no way to run a report for this data. You can import your lists of contacts who attended this event into your CRM under a campaign.

WARNING

If you were asked to pull a report in your CRM of accounts in the opportunity stage, you couldn't automatically run this report. You can run a report to find the list of contacts associated with an opportunity.

Integrating your platforms

Integration is accomplished by the application programming interface (API). Your marketing automation system pings or calls the API to transfer information back into the CRM.

TECHNICAL
STUFF

Depending on your marketing automation provider, the number of API calls may be limited.

WARNING

If your API calls are limited, you won't have real-time insights into your campaigns from the CRM. If you sent out a list email, you could see the open rates, but not who is opening them.

You need to view this as an account. Did the account come to the event? Who from the account? That's the conversation you need to have with your marketing team, and the type of reporting your sales team should care about. Unfortunately, none of the software available in the market generates this type of report today. It's all at the contact level.

This is a huge opportunity. Multiple marketing technology (MarTech) platforms, when combined with your CRM and marketing automation system, allow you to execute account-based marketing. You need tools that can measure account-based performance.

WARNING

Your CRM doesn't produce account reports. You can run reports on contacts and open opportunities, but you can't get a holistic view of what is happening within your Tier A, B, or C accounts.

Assigning tasks and follow-up

If you have set up a rule correctly, you will automatically create new contacts and accounts in the CRM when they engage with content in your marketing automation system. You will need to execute the qualification process again to determine whether the account meets your ICP criteria and undergo the same vetting process.

If someone downloads a piece of content after completing a form, you've triggered this in marketing automation to also create a new contact/account in your CRM. Alerting your sales account executives and BDR/SDRs through email that says a new person has been assigned to them:

CRM tasks: If you run your sales development process through your CRM, use tasks to indicate a new contact has been assigned.

Email notification: If you use a sales development platform, such as SalesLoft's Cadence, you can import the notification, view in CRM, and import into Cadence. Now they're on your list of follow-ups.

Determining the next steps

The concept of using MarTech for ABM is simple but it's a huge change in the status quo. The whole team must be on board with this plan for connecting with contacts in accounts who have achieved a minimum score. Management must have bought in to be on the same page with next steps.

Internally, your "smarketing" team should sit down together to review the process for using marketing automation. Because you're using the MA for various activities and sending content, each team member needs to know the next steps, based on certain activities. To determine the next steps, ask these questions:

» If a form is completed, who from the sales development team should respond? Which ICP and persona criteria should be used to qualify inbound form completions?

» Who from marketing owns drip emails? Which content is included in the drips? How often should this be refreshed?

» Which rules are created for adding contacts automatically to your CRM? Who owns creating these rules?

» When should marketing and sales review account scores together to determine whether there's an uptick in engagement among targeted accounts?

Chapter 10

Distilling the Key Roles of "Smarketing"

The importance of bringing your sales and marketing teams together to create one "smarketing" team can't be overstated. For too long in the B2B world, marketing has focused on lead generation to provide sales with tons of leads. Salespeople aren't called "lead executives." Salespeople are called account executives because they close *accounts*.

In fact, we don't even call the people responsible for answering inbound and outbound leads "lead executives." These people are business or sales development representatives (BDRs or SDRs), depending on your company. Marketers shouldn't want to give random leads that came in from your website to an account executive whose mission is to close new deals and grow revenue for the company.

In this chapter, I review why marketing should remember that their number 1 internal client is sales. Working together, your "smarketing" team should structure a tiered account list that's aligned with the qualified sales opportunities to generate more revenue.

Making Sales Your Marketing Team's Number 1 Customer

Before account-based marketing, sales did all the heavy lifting. Marketing could qualify leads and flip them over to sales, from there leaving sales to do a demo. Sales had to create an opportunity. Maybe marketing would supply a few pieces of content to help nurture these opportunities, such as a case study or a webinar, but it was sales' mission to close the deal.

A modern B2B marketing team must share the workload and take ownership of accounts that will grow revenue for the company.

Reestablishing marketing's mission

Marketing's mission has always been to increase brand awareness. It was the awareness created by marketing activities that generated leads to help sales grow. But when you asked a marketer, "What leads will turn into opportunities this quarter?" he or she probably can't tell you. On the flip side, when you asked the sales team, "What is marketing doing this quarter to help you close deals?" they can't name all of the activities marketing was doing to generate revenue.

The mission of the marketing team has changed. Marketing is directly focused on growing revenue in accounts, not on leads. The sales development team and account executives have a mission to grow revenue by selling into these accounts. Marketing must support the sales team every step of the way.

Account-based marketing aligns sales and marketing as one "smarketing" team. Now, as a unified "smarketing" team, marketing and sales work collaboratively to create content and execute activities for the target list of accounts. Marketing takes more ownership of accounts, which leads to revenue. Here are the ways marketing helps the sales team achieve its goals:

» **Focusing on priority accounts.** Ask a salesperson, "Which accounts may close this quarter?" Or "What accounts are you working on?" He or she will start listing off companies they're targeting to close. Marketing helps by focusing on this list of companies.

» **Building a repeatable model for growing revenue.** Ask any account executive, "What do you do for a living?" His or her answer will discuss how they close deals with a certain type of business or industry. Marketing takes ownership of ensuring these accounts get closed by sharing the same success metric: new revenue.

- >> **Measuring success.** After helping sales close a targeted account, marketing can look at the metrics associated with the activities used to turn this account into a customer. What content was sent to the contacts in the account? Did they attend an event? Knowing which tactics worked to bring on new revenue is an essential part of marketing's mission.

- >> **Providing a better customer experience.** After all of this work is done to capture an account, marketing must focus on retaining this customer. With account-based marketing, the "smarketing" team is aligned with the customer success team to focus on a target list of accounts to turn into customer advocates.

The mission of the marketing team expands across the organization to capture new accounts, and keep them, to maintain and increase revenue.

Finding urgency among your accounts

In a perfect world, every time a prospect or opportunity is ready to buy, they pick up the phone to call a salesperson and let them know. The direct phone call doesn't happen very often. According to SiriusDecisions, 70 percent of the buyer's journey is completed before they ever reach out to a company. So how does a marketer identify the right time to reach out to an account that's ready to buy? The answer is marketing automation.

REMEMBER

You must have a marketing automation system to execute account-based marketing at scale. Without marketing automation, ABM is an entirely manual process.

Using marketing automation for account-based marketing, you can look for buying signals that demonstrate urgency. Your marketing automation platform monitors the activities for all the contacts associated with an account in your CRM. When you see several people from the same company engaging with activities, it's a strong indicator the account is ready to move forward. The buying signals can include

- >> **Visiting your website.** Repeat visits to certain pages on your website (such as your pricing page, customers, and blog posts) demonstrate interest from the account.

- >> **Downloading content.** Your marketing automation system alerts you any time a piece of content is downloaded. Assigning scores to each of these content pieces (such as 30 points for downloading a whitepaper) will add up to a higher score for the account.

>> **Attending webinars.** Contacts who attend every webinar you host (especially contacts in the opportunity stage) are showing strong interest.

>> **Form completion.** Contacts who complete a form (inbound) show more urgency than when an SDR cold calls or emails (outbound).

WARNING

You still need to qualify any inbound contacts who have submitted a form. Showing urgency doesn't mean they're the best fit for your business.

REMEMBER

Having a sales account executive or SDR repeatedly call an account or send emails won't nurture accounts, and it won't create urgency.

Urgency within accounts can also be shown through emails. Sometimes, you'll get lucky. A contact replies directly to an email sent by marketing or sales. These types of email responses include

>> **Webinar invitations.** I've seen emails come through from contacts stating "let's talk before this webinar" wanting to learn more.

>> **Drip emails.** One of the main reasons marketing sends a recurring pattern of emails to "nurture" accounts is in the hope that contacts will raise their hand and say they're ready to move forward.

>> **Direct emails to sales.** It's always exciting for the salesperson to receive the email that the account is ready to move forward.

REMEMBER

Marketing is sending webinar invitations, drip, and nurture emails through marketing automation, so this activity is recorded in your CRM. However, your salespeople should record such activity as these one-off email responses by logging them in the notes section of the CRM. This helps to maintain a complete history of interactions the sales rep has with contacts in the account.

Providing air cover throughout the sales process

Like a military campaign, marketing's mission is to support sales as they're battling for a deal. Sales is in the trenches, engaging the multiple contacts in the account to sell the benefits of your solution. The sales account executive is working on all the people in the account who can influence the purchase decision, plus the ultimate decision-maker. As sales is doing battle for a deal, marketing must provide air cover.

Marketing provides air cover by supplying sales with ammunition for each contact in the target account. By providing air cover for sales, the account executive can focus his or her efforts on overcoming objections, negotiating pricing, and other closing activities. The type of ammunition marketing gives sales during this time includes

>> **Webinars:** While marketing owns the content and production of webinars, an upcoming webinar is a tool that SDRs and AEs can use to invite a prospect or opportunity. They can personally send an email stating, "Hi (first name), I wanted to be sure you saw this upcoming webinar about (topic) as I think it can be useful based on our discussions," then list the reasons why.

>> **Events:** Marketing owns the event calendar and determines which events the company should participate in. During calls with prospects and opportunities, SDRs and AEs should ask which events their contacts are attending. This helps identify any industry trade shows or events to attend where marketing can helps sales expand their reach.

>> **Nurturing emails:** Marketing should have a program running to regularly send emails (or "drips") with new content to prospects and opportunities depending on their stages. This helps because each week your contacts receive new information, which keeps your company top of mind during the sales process.

TIP

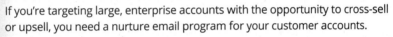

If you're targeting large, enterprise accounts with the opportunity to cross-sell or upsell, you need a nurture email program for your customer accounts.

>> **Regular email newsletter:** Each month or quarter, marketing should send an email newsletter with links to recent content. This content should include different types of content, such as

- Blog post
- Webinar recording
- New infographic, ebook, or whitepaper
- Invitation to an event

>> **Social media:** Salespeople should be connecting with contacts in the account on LinkedIn and following them on Twitter. Marketing should sponsor posts and updates targeted to these accounts to provide air cover.

>> **Direct mail:** Marketing should send items in the mail to sales prospects and opportunities. Items like "swag" with pens, t-shirts, or koozies are a great way to surprise potential customers.

>> **Advertising:** Run digital advertising campaigns (on such channels as social media, mobile, display, and video) targeted to sales' contacts, depending on the stage and industry.

TIP

This can be managed through your ABM platform to record attribute metrics at the account level.

Surrounding accounts with your message creates a "halo effect." A halo effect helps your message to resonate across multiple channels. This increases velocity within an account, moving the account faster through the buyer's journey to make a purchase decision.

Benefitting from "Smarketing" Alignment

Every team member plays a unique and key role for growing revenue for your B2B sales organization. My own marketing team has joked that I should become the "Chief Smarketing Officer," because I regularly join sales calls and meetings to help move opportunities further down the pipeline to becoming our customers.

Going for your goals together

When you've done the work to define your ideal customer profile (ICP) and created your personas for the types of people you need to connect with, then obtained the right data on those contacts to expand them into accounts, you can begin engaging those accounts. When you have all of these pieces in place, you can use marketing automation to further understand the account's engagement with your various sales and marketing activities.

REMEMBER

Your have to know who is going to manage each of these individual parts of your "smarketing" machine.

The goal of the "smarketing" team is to generate revenue. Each person on the "smarketing" team has individual goals to reach the company's revenue goal. Whether you're an independent business owner, a small business with less than 25 employees and only one marketing person and a few account executives, or a large company with hundreds of marketing and salespeople, the roles you need to fill to be successful with ABM remain the same. Here are the roles and goals for each "smarketing" team member:

>> **Business/Sales Development Representative (BDR/SDR):** The goal of sales development is to warm up accounts to set appointments and product demos for sales. There are two ways this is accomplished:

- *Inbound* by answering form completions to download content or "contact us" forms, then qualifying those accounts

- *Outbound* by identifying contacts in your CRM, or from a new list, who fit your ICP and personas

The sales/business development team is building interest, educating, and getting contacts in accounts excited to attend a demo with sales. During this process, contacts should be added to email drips and nurture campaigns.

TIP

In your CRM, there should be a dropdown for adding contacts to a list for an email nurture campaign. When a BDR completes a conversation where the account isn't ready to buy, the contact can be added to an email campaign, then receive emails for next 90 days to warm up the account.

>> **Sales database administrator:** This person can be a dedicated or sales admin, or this responsibility could fall to marketing; ultimately, one "smarketing" team member needs to maintain the cleanest CRM possible. Your CRM should have complete profiles built for your targeted accounts with contact data. A clean CRM with good data will help to reach your company's revenue goals. Additional responsibilities for this role can be fielding technical questions, looking at new tech vendors, and watching competitive products to find how much of your targeted market is adopting this new technology.

>> **Marketing operations manager:** The goal of marketing operations is to streamline the processes and activities for identifying accounts and engaging them with activities. Marketing ops owns the technology and tools in your marketing technology (MarTech) "stack", especially marketing automation. The marketing ops person is tasked with such responsibilities as

- Segmenting lists for email nurtures, drips, and event invitations.

- Applying engagement scoring/grading.

- Measuring (identifying whether your efforts in a campaign are working).

TIP

Marketing ops should automate a report to find when a contact hasn't been connected in 90 days. The contact can be added to an email drip program in your marketing automation system.

>> **Marketing communications (MarComm) manager:** The goal of this person is providing content supporting sales and providing air cover. The content supplied in the sales process helps to generate velocity and accelerate opportunities through the sales pipeline. MarComm should collaborate with sales to come up with campaigns. The success of those campaigns is measured in marketing automation by whether the right accounts are downloading content or responding to activities.

REMEMBER

With ABM, the purpose of content marketing isn't to drive inbound leads; it's to reach the targeted contacts in your account. The marketing content should be made for the exact audience you need to.

>> **Sales account executive:** The sole goal of an AE is to bring in revenue. This is done by completing demos set by the SDRs, following up after appointments, then using negotiation strategies for closing business. With account-based marketing, the AE must be sure he or she is bringing the *right* accounts in the door that fit your ICP and persona.

REMEMBER

The AE should build relationships with these accounts. The information an AE learns about the account will help, especially when the deal is won. When the new customer account is transitioned to customer success, the AE should provide customer success with all the right information.

>> **Sales leader:** A Director or VP of Sales is responsible for ensuring the sales team meets the company's revenue goal each quarter. This is accomplished through supporting and enabling the sales team of AEs and BDR/SDRs. The sales leader should also have a targeted list of accounts, tiered by accounts they want to close in the next 30, 60 or 90 days. Having a plan for how to achieve this revenue goal helps win more revenue faster. The sales leader also is tasked with defining the ICP and positioning the product for each persona.

>> **Account manager:** When your company targets large, enterprise organizations, an account management team is tasked with renewing contracts and looking for opportunities to upsell and cross-sell in the account. Customer success is responsible for ensuring that the account is using your product or service, and the goal of account management is to maintain or grow revenue from your clients.

>> **Executive stakeholders:** Your executive or C-level leaders are part of the "smarketing" team; their goals are growing the business through revenue generation, reducing customer churn, and providing an overall strategic vision for your organization.

TIP

In some marketing companies, marketing employees are awarded bonuses for individual performance for hitting quarterly success metrics. Consider giving bonuses to marketing for helping sales meet their revenue goals, to push marketing's focus from a lead-based to a revenue-generating mindset.

Targeting accounts across all stages

Each of your accounts is in a different stage of making a purchase decision. With account-based marketing, marketing and sales teams share ownership of accounts according to their stage of the buyer's journey. ABM elevates the buyer's journey by looking at it as an *account's journey*. Here are the stages of the account's journey to making a purchase decision:

» **New:** The contact is entered into your CRM, through either an inbound form completion or content download. An account also can be entered into your system through a data acquisition import, or manually added by an SDR/BDR. These are the roles sales and marketing plays during this phase:

- For sales, the SDR/BDR is qualifying the account to ensure it fits within your ICP and persona.

- Marketing automatically syncs the new contact's information in the CRM with marketing automation and adds the account to an email nurture campaign.

» **Marketing Qualified Account (MQA):** The account meets your ICP and persona criteria. It's a fit for your business:

- The sales development team begins a cadence of calls and emails to learn whether BANT, or other qualification criteria, exists. If so, sales creates an appointment with a sales AE.

- Marketing supports sales by providing content, targeting the account with advertising, and inviting the contacts in an account to webinars or in-person events.

» **Sales Qualified Account (SQA):** The account demonstrates intent after the appointment with the account executive and expresses a need for your product or service:

- For sales, the BDR/SDR sets the appointment for a demo then transitions the account to an account executive. The AE completes a demo with the prospect and determines whether there is a revenue opportunity.

- Marketing supports the stage-progression by supplying case studies, use cases, and customer video testimonials to show how clients have found success with your company. Recent blog posts or webinar recordings also can be sent by sales through email.

» **Opportunity:** The account has asked for pricing or a contract detailing the service agreement. In your CRM, a monetary revenue opportunity is entered by the AE and added to the sales pipeline:

- Sales continues to engage contacts in the account, answering questions, sending follow-up emails, and negotiating pricing.

- Marketing continues supplying content, such as implementation guides, competitive analysis, or an ROI calculator showing the value of your product or service. Direct mail campaigns with cookies, swag, or other items help with progression.

>> **Customer:** The deal has been won. The opportunity is converted to a Closed/Won account:

- Sales ensures that the contract is signed and payment terms are provided. The account is transitioned to the implementation or customer success team

- Marketing provides checklists, how to videos, or other training materials to support the on-boarding process.

In many organizations these types of resources may fall under the Customer Success team, which should be tightly aligned with marketing.

REMEMBER

>> **Closed/Lost:** when the opportunity didn't come through and the deal didn't close, the account is marked in your CRM as "Closed/Lost":

- Sales documents in the notes section of your CRM why the account failed to become a customer

- Marketing adds the account to a "Do not market" or "Closed/Lost" list in your marketing automation system so resources aren't wasted marketing to this account in the future.

Lining up your pipeline

Your pipeline is all the potential revenue associated with opportunities. The C-level executives in a B2B company monitor pipeline activity closely; it's the lifeblood of their organization. The term *pipeline marketing* is a precursor to ABM. Pipeline marketing refers to marketing to accounts in your pipeline, depending on the stage. What's important with account-based marketing is that marketing is contributing directly to opportunities in the pipeline. This is called *marketing sourced pipeline*.

Banking on Your Strengths

Every person has different strengths. This is especially true for marketing and salespeople. Marketing's strengths are in creating content, campaigns, and generating awareness for a B2B company's brand. Marketing supplies the creative content to drive interest, creating leads for sales to pursue (opportunities). Sales' strengths are in the tactical know-how and training to turn those opportunities into Closed/Won deals. If you ask a marketing operations or content manager to get on the phone and close a deal, he or she probably can't do it. At the same time, you wouldn't ask a salesperson to write a 10-page whitepaper or produce a webinar. This is why it's important for your "smarketing" team to bank on each other's strengths and collaborate on campaigns for all stages of the account's journey.

Creating a sustainable process

Working together, your "smarketing" team should create a process that is repeatable for each stage of the account's journey. This helps execute account-based marketing at scale. A sustainable process for your "smarketing" team should be both repeatable and scalable.

The stages of the account's journey from New, Prospect, and Opportunity to Customer should align with the flipped funnel when creating a sustainable process. Your company's account-based marketing activities should be a scalable, repeatable set of strategies. The goal of aligning all these activities is to have a model for growing revenue. Here are the steps "smarketing" should undertake for creating a sustainable ABM process.

Identify

The goal is to get the accounts you identified on a discovery call and/or to agree to a sales demo. Accounts are identified with either inbound or outbound marketing.

When inbound, the new prospect is identified when they download content or complete a form, thus being added to your CRM and synched with your marketing automation system. An alert is sent to the BDR/SDR. They follow up with a cadence of calls and emails, sending supporting content created by marketing (such as recent blog posts, infographics, and whitepapers). The accounts are added to an email nurture or drip.

When the account was identified in your CRM, and the BDR/SDR is working to connect with them, it's outbound marketing.

Expand

The goal is to connect with as many contacts as possible in your target accounts. By expanding your reach within an account to connect with more people, you better identify the influencers and decision-makers in the account. At this stage, the BDR/SDR or sales administrator should be adding more contact data to the account to build a full profile in your CRM. Marketing should assist by adding these contacts to segmented lists in marketing automation, adding them to email nurture programs, and confirming that they're receiving invitations to applicable online and offline events.

Engage

This goal is to connect with the contacts in your accounts who influence the purchase decision. This activity creates energy and velocity to advance accounts into the next stage of the journey. Here are the next stages of progression and associated activities:

>> **New account to qualified prospect:** BDR/SDR is calling and emailing, and marketing is sending content to get the prospect on a discovery call and demo with a sales account executive. Marketing supplies high-level content (such as blog posts, ebooks, whitepapers, and infographics) to increase awareness and appointments for sales.

>> **Prospect to opportunity:** The sales account executive has a successful demo and engages with the opportunity. The sales AE is working with the contacts in the account to answer any questions about pricing or handle objections, while marketing supplies educational content (such as case studies, customer video testimonials and webinars to increase engagement and create velocity to close more deals, faster).

>> **Opportunity to customer:** The sales account executive is engaging the account in negotiations to close the deal. Here, marketing supplies "how to" content, demonstrating a return on investment (ROI) and competitive analysis. The value is in increasing engagement with contacts in the opportunity accounts to turn them into customers.

Advocate

The goal is to get the accounts you closed to become advocates for your company. Accounts become advocates through the successful adoption of your product or service. When they can use your product to fulfill a business need, they continue paying your company. Seeing customers successfully adopt and use your product increases retention and reduces customer churn. Marketing supports customer success in the creation of advocates by supplying content, such as implementation guides, video tutorials, "how to" resources, free training webinars, and hosting customer events.

REMEMBER

This may or may not fall under the responsibility of a marketing team. Larger organizations may have entire departments dedicated to creating training and onboarding resources, especially if the product or service is more technical.

Serving and selling

With "smarketing," marketing and sales work together to serve accounts with solutions that answer a business need. The idea of serving instead of selling comes down to the fact that you should service an account instead of always asking them for more: more of their time or more of their money. Selling comes down to brass tacks: The salesperson asks an account for money. Account-based marketing is about building relationships with accounts to make it easier for sales. This is where a combined "smarketing" team can leverage its strengths. Marketing activities help engage accounts to determine whether there are additional needs to fulfill for an account. A "smarketing" team can serve an account by

>> Hosting free webinars

>> Inviting them to relevant events

>> Sending case studies

>> Including them in industry research

>> Interviewing for video testimonials

Greasing the wheel to revenue

All of the "smarketing" team's efforts are to drive revenue. It's an organic effort that starts by identifying the best-fit accounts you need to work with, then determining how to reach all the contacts in the account to engage them through activities and programs. By serving up relevant content, inviting them to events, and thinking of them as future partners and advocates, you're on track to building long-term relationships and a sustainable revenue model.

MARKETING IS WHAT "GREASES THE WHEEL TO REVENUE"

My colleague Jim Williams, VP of Marketing at Influitive, once told me marketing is what greases the wheel to revenue. This saying stuck with me. Sales has a tough job. There are an increasing number of decision-makers in a B2B purchase decision, and sales must sell each contact on the benefits of your product or service. Marketing helps support sales in this endeavor by creating content, designing activities, and engaging accounts to make it easier for sales to win trust, and ultimately win more deals.

4

Engaging Accounts on Their Terms

IN THIS PART . . .

Accelerating sales opportunities in your pipeline

Surrounding your accounts with digital advertising on the right channels

Customizing content to personalize the journey for all contacts in the account

Running a strategic combination of advertising campaigns and "smarketing" activities

Chapter 11

Generating Velocity for Sales

The third stage of the account-based marketing funnel is Engage. With account-based marketing, it's about engaging contacts in your target accounts on the channels where they're most active.

You need a detailed program of content and activities to generate engagement among your contacts. This engagement helps drive revenue opportunities within the account. It's why marketing and sales are tightly aligned as one "smarketing" team dedicated to winning more accounts. So how can your "smarketing" team accelerate accounts from the moment they first connect with your business to becoming customers?

In physics, the formula for velocity `= distance/time`.

In this chapter, I show you how to create velocity to advance accounts through each stage of the account's journey faster and bring on new sales. I explain how marketing activities align with each stage of the account's journey, linking an ABM strategy to growing revenue.

Accelerating Your Pipeline from Click to Close

The term "click-to-close" means from the time the prospect first interacted with your company until becoming a customer. The first "click" interactions include coming to your website, filling out a form, opening and email, or an in-person activity (such as meeting at an event, or being referred by another customer or industry thought leader). For "smarketing" teams, you measure how an account progresses from the first "click" to becoming an opportunity, then closing the deal as a customer. The progression of accounts is measured with a *sales pipeline.* A sales pipeline shows you all the revenue opportunities for the coming months and quarters. It notes how much the deal is worth in revenue, and the anticipated close date.

The sales pipeline is what C-level executives and stakeholders examine to forecast the revenue for their company. When a revenue opportunity is entered by a salesperson in the CRM system, the opportunity is added to your pipeline. Pipeline velocity is the rate that revenue opportunities move through your pipeline from the time they're first entered until becoming Closed-Won deals. Account-based marketing can accelerate your sales pipeline from first click to final close. With account-based marketing, you are trying to engage with as many contacts in the account, as this connection and activity increases excitement and energy, which generates velocity for accelerating revenue opportunities in your sales pipeline.

Launching a pipeline acceleration campaign

Pipeline acceleration is also known as sales velocity. Using the formula for velocity (`distance/time`), your company wants to generate as much velocity as possible to see a revenue opportunity move through the sales pipeline to becoming a Closed/Won customer. An acceleration campaign is used in collaboration with marketing to help generate velocity and move a deal through the pipeline. Before technology, salespeople had to do a lot of manual work to accelerate deals through the pipeline. This involved taking clients to fancy dinners, sending gifts, and wooing executives to buy from their companies. Marketing supported these activities by sending direct mail or hosting events.

With account-based marketing, there are several ways to launch a pipeline acceleration campaign. Because you have aligned your sales and marketing teams as one cohesive "smarketing" team, you have more resources to create effective campaigns. The goal is to develop a multi-touch strategy to engage with the right contacts in your opportunity accounts. Your goal should have associated success metrics. The success metrics for a pipeline acceleration campaign are *time* and *engagement.* With your pipeline acceleration campaign, did you see the following?

>> **Decrease in sales cycle:** The amount of time it takes from the first touch ("click") to the account becoming a customer ("close"). When your typical sales cycle takes 90 days, your goal for a pipeline acceleration campaign should be to shorten the number of days to close an account.

>> **Increase in engagement:** The amount of activity with contacts in your account. The activities are recorded with your marketing automation system. Using marketing automation, you can see an increase in the score for your contacts. The score increases when contacts are engaged in more activities, such as downloading content or attending webinars.

> The goal for pipeline acceleration campaigns is to decrease the amount of time it takes to close the deal, and increase the amount of engagement with all the contacts in the account. Your "smarketing" team, working together, can make these goals a reality.

Ask your "smarketing" team these questions before launching a pipeline acceleration campaign:

REMEMBER

>> **Who are the influencers, decision-makers, and "champions" in the account?** When you're selling a product to an IT department, this is the IT manager, his supervisor, the department head, and any additional contacts you have connected. Your "champion" is your primary point of contact who will be a "power-user" of your product or service.

> This is why it's important to capture an organizational hierarchy, noting which of your contacts in an account can influence the purchase decision.

>> **When do you want the deal to close?** In your CRM, the sales account executive should have assigned an anticipated date for the deal to be closed. Based on this date, how many days, weeks, or months do you have? This is the timeline for your acceleration campaign, and also helps you track your goal of decreasing the time to make a sale.

>> **What needs to happen?** Working with the sales account executive, determine what questions need to be answered. Are contacts in the account concerned about training, or implementation? Are there objections that need to be overcome, such as pricing or contract terms?

>> **How can we engage the contacts in the account?** Which channels are appropriate to connect with contacts? In your marketing automation system, you can see a record of activity. Strategize how you will connect with each contact who has a stake in the purchase decision. Consider the following items for the context of your relationship with the account:

- *What's worked so far to engage contacts.* Have they attended webinars or downloaded content? Did you send direct mail? How was it received?

- *The job titles of the contacts.* When you know your "champion" is a marketing manager who read all of your content, what else can you send him or her?

- *What's been done to engage the decision-maker.* When the marketing manager's director or CMO hasn't been engaged (from your marketing automation system, you know they haven't read much content), how do you engage your champion's boss?

Executing with your sales team

Sales and marketing are in alignment for one "smarketing" team. Your steps need to be in sync, too. After establishing the goals for your pipeline acceleration campaign, you work together to execute the campaign. Here are the individual responsibilities of the "smarketing" team members when executing a pipeline acceleration campaign:

>> **Communication:** A 1-to-1 effort with the account executive who is communicating directly with the contacts in the account. The AE has established the relationship and should own email communication and directly calling the contacts.

WARNING

Marketing shouldn't have direct communication with contacts during a pipeline acceleration campaign. This can confuse the contacts about who from your company is their point of contact. The primary point of contact at your organization is the salesperson who is trying to close the deal.

>> **Content:** What is the message that needs to be conveyed to help move the opportunity through the pipeline? This is where marketing supplies content that answers these questions, such as

- What type of training is offered?

- How have your customers have been successful?

- What do industry leaders think of your offering?

- How can I demonstrate an ROI to executive leadership, proving your product or service is worth the investment?

>> **Channel:** How you will engage the contacts in the account. This can be on several channels, including

- *Email:* Sales account executive sends a recent blog post, whitepaper, ebook, case study, implementation guide, or whatever content will answer questions the contacts have.

- *Event:* Hosting a breakfast or dinner in their city, and bringing customers or a thought leader.

- *Advertising*: Launching a targeted advertising campaign with your ABM platform to surround the contacts with your message.

- *Direct mail:* Sending swag, cookies, personal notes from your CEO or executive leadership, and other items to your contacts.

For your pipeline acceleration campaigns, think about how much velocity is currently in the account. To accelerate accounts through the sales pipeline, you need a combination of personalization and activities to drive engagement. Think of it as *touch* and *tech*. The combination of touch and tech creates velocity. Here is how to measure your touch and tech:

» **High Touch:** The longer it takes to make a connection. The more time an account executive must invest in this personalized touch.

» **Low Touch:** Less time is required by your "smarketing" team. The outreach isn't as personal, but still effective for creating velocity.

» **High Tech:** More technology is needed, such as employing your marketing automation system to send content, or using a targeted advertising platform.

» **Low Tech:** Less technology; however, a low-tech campaign can also be high touch or low touch, as it depends on the context of the campaign and how close the opportunity is to closing.

Focusing on the right deals

Not every sales opportunity is worthy of a high-touch/high-tech pipeline acceleration campaign. It's important that you're focusing on the accounts that have an opportunity with a high likelihood of closing. The opportunities that are more likely to close should have more velocity. Here's how you should focus on the right deals for creating velocity.

» **High velocity (close in 30 days or less):** The pipeline acceleration campaign should be high touch and high tech.

» **Mid velocity (30-60 days to close):** A combination of personalization and marketing technology, high tech/low touch or low tech/high touch.

» **Low velocity (more than 60 days to close):** When your sales team isn't likely to close this deal within the business quarter, don't invest too much time, energy and resources. That's time for high tech/low touch.

TYPES OF PIPELINE ACCELERATION

The renowned research analyst firm SiriusDecisions helps its clients plan pipeline acceleration programs to increase sales velocity. According to SiriusDecisions, there are three types of pipeline acceleration programs:

- **Rapid entry:** In this zone, pipeline acceleration involves tactics designed to fill the pipeline with pre-qualified accounts that are more likely to move quickly through qualification stages.

- **Intra-pipeline:** In this zone, acceleration includes the creation of targeted offers and sales enablement assets that facilitate movement of opportunities through early and middle pipeline stages toward closed status.

- **Last mile:** Pipeline acceleration tactics in this zone are designed to drive positive interactions that can help push late-stage deals across the finish line.

REMEMBER

This is why it's important to have a target list of accounts, tiered by Tier A, B, or C for the best fit for your product or service, according to ICP and persona criteria. It's also important these accounts have met BANT or other criteria demonstrating they're ready to buy.

WARNING

Launch pipeline acceleration campaigns only when there's a revenue opportunity associated with the account. When the account isn't in pipeline, such as accounts that are in the new or prospect stage and haven't been qualified, should remain in nurturing programs such as email drips.

The best way to think about your pipeline acceleration campaigns is in the context of high tech/high touch and low tech/low touch. The purpose of generating velocity within an account is to convert it from an opportunity to Closed/Won revenue. The closer you are to the revenue in terms of the time it takes to close (high-velocity opportunities), the higher the touch needs to be. A classic example of this is a direct-mail campaign to a list of target accounts who are likely to close in the next 30 days. You know these are high-value accounts that are worth the investment in customizing a direct mail piece.

On the flip side, the accounts that you are targeting that aren't necessarily ready to buy (the mid- to low-velocity accounts), you could continue to have a high-tech but low-touch campaign. Here are examples of each type of pipeline acceleration campaign for high, mid, and low velocity.

>> **High velocity with high touch/high tech:** Personalized videos. When you have an account you're trying to close in the next 30 days, send them a video you created just for them.

>> **Mid velocity with high tech/low touch:** Display advertising. When you're using an advertising technology platform, this is high tech but low touch. Even when the contacts you're targeting don't click on your ad, they're still seeing your brand and message.

>> **Low velocity with low touch/low tech:** Sponsoring large events. You're investing money in a sponsorship opportunity for a large event, such as an industry tradeshow or conference, because you know your sales opportunities in the industry will attend the event.

Figure 11-1 demonstrates how a combination of "touch" and "technology" generates velocity for a sales opportunity to drive engagement.

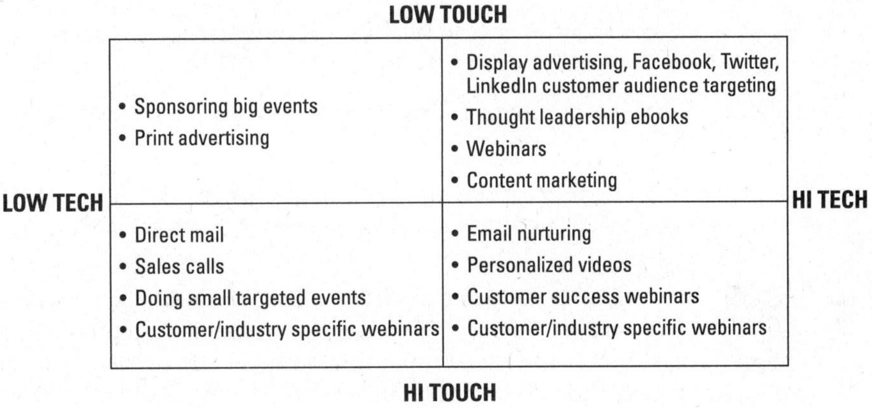

LOW TOUCH

LOW TECH		HI TECH
• Sponsoring big events • Print advertising	• Display advertising, Facebook, Twitter, LinkedIn customer audience targeting • Thought leadership ebooks • Webinars • Content marketing	
• Direct mail • Sales calls • Doing small targeted events • Customer/industry specific webinars	• Email nurturing • Personalized videos • Customer success webinars • Customer/industry specific webinars	

HI TOUCH

FIGURE 11-1: Accelerating a sales opportunity with engagement.

Advancing Opportunities to Closed-Won Deals

Sales velocity moves opportunities through the pipeline faster to Closed/Won revenue. To advance an opportunity to a Closed/Won deal, your "smarketing" team must work together on activities to drive engagement while also answering any questions or objections that arise from the contacts in the account. For opportunity to advance to becoming a customer, you must supply the account with relevant activities and on the right channels.

Nurturing throughout the buying process

Before ABM, marketing would generate a lead and give it to sales, hoping they could close it. Now, marketing partners with sales to collaborate in getting the account through the entire buying process. This way, marketing can show how it contributed directly to pipeline (also called a *marketing-sourced pipeline*). Sales manages the relationship and the 1-to-1 communication with contacts in the account. Marketing supports sales by providing content for nurturing the account to create velocity.

WARNING

Generic email drips won't progress an opportunity to a Closed/Won deal. The content provided to contacts in opportunity accounts needs to be personalized for this stage of buyer's journey.

To successfully nurture an account throughout the buying process, your activities need to be varied. Nurturing activities include

» Advertising on such channels as mobile, social, display, and video

» Content marketing, such as emailing whitepapers, case studies, infographics, ebooks, and recent blog posts

» Events, such as in-person events (industry tradeshows) and digital events (webinars)

» Social media, such as having the salesperson connect on LinkedIn, or having marketing serve up LinkedIn posts targeted to the contacts

REMEMBER

The types of nurturing activities should be specific to where your contacts are in the purchase decision. Your salesperson shouldn't connect with a new account on LinkedIn as soon as a form is completed (the first "click"). It's about engaging the contacts in the account on their terms.

TIP

Install a "live chat" application on your company's website. The chat box will pop up anytime a contact visits the site with an automated prompt: "Can I help you today?" or something along these lines. This chat functionality helps to close business faster. Tools, such as Olark or Intercom Acquire, can be managed by an SDR or sales account executive to manage your chats.

Selling value, not product features

You're working with your "smarketing" team to advance accounts to becoming Closed/Won deals. The reason marketing exists is to create awareness. Product marketing is about extolling the virtues of your product or service; content marketing exists to help demonstrate the value of your product. Instead of saying "here is why you should buy my product," it's marketing in the context of "the value of having a solution like this for your company."

START WITH "WHY?"

Simon Sinek presented an amazing TEDTalk, "Start With Why: How Great Leaders Inspire Action." The highlight of Simon's presentation is his discovery of The Golden Circle. There are three parts of The Golden Circle: *Why, How,* and *What.* Here's my interpretation of this model as it applies to B2B marketing and sales professionals:

- **Why?** Simon suggests that "very few organizations know why they do what they do. And by why I don't mean to make a profit: that's a result . . . I mean what's your purpose?" Very few B2B "smarketing" professionals answer this question. Why does your organization exist? And this is a question that applies directly to the B2B buyer's journey, and extends into the customer journey.

- **How?** Some B2B "smarketing" teams know how they have achieved success for their customers. Some may have written a value proposition, looked at sales data, and have a few keen insights into how they can deliver their offering to the best-fit customers.

- **What?** Every B2B sales and marketing ("smarketing") organization knows what they do. They know their mission, the product or service they're offering, and what they charge their customers to do business.

By aligning your "smarketing" team with account-based marketing, you're serving up new content, depending on the stage of the buyer's journey, and not just talking about why your product is great. You're educating the contacts in the account about specific value and why it matters to them based on their role.

Your targeted contacts may not remember all the features of your product or service, but they remember why initially they were interested in learning more about your company. Demonstrating value is more important, especially when you can connect that value to an emotional pain point or need.

Converting opportunities

You won't win every deal. Your sales team creates opportunities when there is a potential to generate revenue within an account. These opportunities can fall out of the sales pipeline for a number of reasons, or you're successful and win the deal. In your CRM, you either mark an account as

>> **Closed/Lost:** The opportunity failed to generate revenue, and is therefore a lost deal. The account is now marked in your CRM as Closed/Lost.

>> **Closed/Won:** The account decided to purchase from your company, and the deal was won. The account is now marked in your CRM as Closed/Won, and will become a customer account.

TIP

With Closed/Lost accounts, you need to document in the notes section of your CRM (or create a field for capturing this data point) for why this account failed to generate revenue, such as wrong timing, selected one of your competitors, or couldn't get the budget approved.

WARNING

Never delete accounts from your CRM. You need to preserve the history of the account to remember why you lost the deal should a new revenue opportunity present itself in the future.

With Closed/Won accounts, in the notes section you need to include as much information as possible for your Customer Success team. This information should include their primary point of contact in the account, (the champion) and any special requests they have.

After converting the opportunity to Closed/Won, you need to send an introductory email that connects your new customer account to your colleague or coworker who will be the new point of contact in your organization. This contact can be a number of people, including

>> **Project manager:** When your product or service requires an implementation, then a trained, capable project manager is needed next.

>> **Training manager:** When your product/service is somewhat easy to adopt, the next contact will train your new customer and help them to go live.

>> **Customer Success Manager (CSM):** The CSM may also be responsible for training and onboarding the new customer account then continue to provide support.

Growing Revenue Using ABM

You decided to read this book on account-based marketing because you're looking for ways to grow more revenue for your company. ABM is about connecting with the right accounts. This is the B2B industry, and it's called that because your business sells to other businesses, not to leads. It's about the quality, not the quantity, of our customers. I'd rather have a dozen best-fit customers willing to do business with my company for years than 100 bad-fit customers that churn within the first six months.

Creating clear metrics

The metrics to define success in account-based marketing are different from traditional B2B lead-based marketing. Marketers have to commit to changing to these metrics, as it will help you as a marketer to be more successful. With ABM, marketing teams show how they're driving engagement in the right accounts for more impact. Marketing is ensuring that content and messages are reaching all the decision-makers in the account to help move accounts faster through the sales pipeline.

In ABM, the number one metric is revenue. But revenue doesn't happen overnight. Creating velocity helps to grow revenue, and this takes time. Your "smarketing" team creates the list of accounts to target, strategizes campaigns for the accounts based on their stage in the purchase decision, then modifies those activities accordingly based on the success rate.

REMEMBER

With account-based marketing, it takes time to show that your ABM campaigns are working, especially when you're switching from a traditional lead-gen strategy to demand generation in your best-fit accounts.

Your one "smarketing" team marketing shares ownership with sales on your target accounts. Because your target accounts won't immediately start generating revenue, what you can do is pay attention to additional key performance indicators (KPIs). These KPIs are documented in your CRM and will correlate with revenue growth. These KPIs include

>> Number of qualified accounts generated by marketing

>> Number of opportunities added to pipeline, or marketing-sourced pipeline

>> Time for stage-progression from prospect to opportunity to close

>> Engagement in accounts, showing an uptick in the account's score in your marketing automation system

Linking your ABM strategy to revenue

One inherent problem with traditional B2B marketing is that marketers were always trying to assign a lead to one source. The lead came in through a webinar, a form completion, a referral, and then the lead was attributed to a source in your CRM. Marketers used to think that worked. But with account-based marketing, you accept that you can't attribute a lead to a single source.

Think about it this way: David is a marketing manager who comes to your website and downloads an ebook. Tim is a marketing director who attends one of your webinars. Michael is a CMO who comes to an event you sponsor. David, Michael, and Tim work for the same venture capital firm, DTM & Co. You've identified venture capital firms as the best fit for your product or service. DTM & Co. is an account on your target list to close this quarter. Your "smarketing" team will engage David, Michael, and Tim in many activities to create velocity and close the account. The ABM strategy you employ for the contacts at DTM looks like this:

>> David is emailed a case study that shows how VC marketing managers are successful with your product. This is followed by a video testimonial from another marketing manager in his industry detailing his success with your product.

>> Tim receives an email with a recording of the webinar he attended, and a copy of the slides. The next week, he gets a case study, featuring a marketing director who details the problem, the solution, and why he chose to do business with your company.

>> Michael is sent a handwritten note in direct mail from your team member he met at the tradeshow. He's also emailed a copy of a whitepaper that was developed for C-level executives; it details the value of your solution for his industry.

Which of these activities contributed to revenue? It's a waste of time to track it by a single activity. Think of it as a strategy, as multiple activities will create velocity and engagement within an account. Contacting multiple touch points in an account helps you to build a relationship in the account toward the ultimate goal of closing a deal.

Turning opportunities into deals: a case study

One of the best case studies I've seen for proving that account-based marketing works to advance opportunities to Closed/Won deals is at my own company. In 2015, I joined Terminus as co-founder and CMO, because I truly believed that account-based marketing represented the future for B2B marketing and sales. At the time, Terminus didn't have a product. The account-based marketing platform launched in March 2015. In just nine months, our annual recurring revenue (ARR) went from $0 to $1 million. How did we do it? This comes down to our ABM efforts.

The sales and marketing team are aligned as one "smarketing" team to generate velocity and close more accounts. Our "smarketing" team includes

» **Sales Development Representatives (SDRs):** The SDRs are divided to focus new accounts obtained on either inbound or outbound. The inbound SDRs are answering form completions then qualifying those contacts to determine whether they meet our ICP. The outbound SDRs are prospecting into accounts by using a cadence of calls and emails using SalesLoft's cadence to monitor lots of touch points there and sending relevant content created by marketing. The goal for the SDRs is to set demos for sales with qualified accounts.

» **Sales Account Executives (AEs):** After a demo is scheduled, an account is transferred from an SDR to an AE. The AE engages the contacts in the account in a demo of our product. When the account demonstrates intent and asks for pricing, a revenue opportunity is created in our CRM. During this stage, a complete profile of the account is created with other contacts in the account.

» **Director of Sales:** Continuously maintains and updates an ongoing list of target accounts the sales team wants to close this month and this quarter. She's looking at the revenue opportunities for each AE. Her job also includes defining the ideal customer profile (ICP) and the personas to target within accounts. Ultimately, her biggest goal is to meet or exceed our monthly and quarterly sales goal. Going from $0 to $1 million in ARR in nine months, she and her team are crushing it.

» **Marketing Manager:** Our marketing manager does a ton. She's in charge of managing our marketing technology (MarTech) stack with all the software and applications we use, including our CRM, marketing automation system, website, blog, social media, communications channels, and project management tools. Also, she plans all of our events.

» **Storyteller:** We call her our "Storyteller", as she's in charge of all the content and communications that define the narrative of our brand. She's tasked with creating new content for sales enablement, posting it to our blog and social media, and working with the sales team to supply any content that answers questions from contacts in accounts.

» **CMO:** Hey, that's me! When I'm not writing a book about account-based marketing, I'm helping my team however I can. I frequently join our AEs on calls to help them close accounts and guide my marketing team to "Dream Big." I joke that I should rebrand myself to be the chief "smarketing" officer.

Our "smarketing" team used several strategies to increase engagement and generate velocity in our target accounts. In addition to our content and social media, the biggest way we've reached our targeted accounts is through event marketing. We host an event series called #FlipMyFunnel. Our SDRs are inviting people to the next #FlipMyFunnel event. During the event, sales AEs are talking to those people from our target accounts. Before and after the event, we run targeted advertising campaigns to contacts in those accounts.

REMEMBER

This is just what's worked for me. Each B2B "smarketing" organization will have success from different activities. You will have to test different content, strategies, and campaigns to determine what works best for you.

Chapter 12

Personalizing the Buyer's Channel

According to LeapJob, only 2 percent of cold calls result in an appointment. While traditional lead outreach tactics (such as cold calling and mass emailing) have their merits, they also have significant limitations. Your buyers are busy, which means they'll only respond to marketing messages that really resonate with them; generally, cold calls and mass emails don't fall into this category.

What buyers are looking for is personalized, targeted marketing that really caters to their needs and pain points. In other words, they're looking for a relationship. But how can companies build these relationships when their buyers won't pick up the phone or respond to emails? The answer is account-based marketing. Having an ABM strategy with activities on multiple channels helps your sales and marketing ("smarketing") team to connect with your best-fit accounts on their own terms.

In this chapter, I show you how to run advertising campaigns personalized to your contacts in accounts. I explain how connecting with contacts across various channels (such as mobile, social, and video) helps to make your message resonate, thereby generating sales velocity and driving accounts to make a purchase decision.

Mobilizing Your Message

In the modern age of marketing, your message must translate across multiple platforms. The number of people accessing the internet on mobile devices now exceeds the number of people surfing the internet on a desktop computer. The average adult spends more than two hours every day on a mobile device! The proliferation of mobile devices, such as smartphones, tablets, and laptop computers, means that there are more ways than ever before to connect with your buyers. As your buyers are going mobile, so must your marketing tactics and efforts.

Advertising the way B2B marketers did before just doesn't work today. As a marketer, you don't own time in the day from people as we owned it in the past. Traditional advertising channels included TV, print, radio, and billboards. When you bought a TV ad, the viewer couldn't skip commercials. Your buyers, especially the millennial generation, don't read newspapers; they go online or social media to scan the headlines you want to read.

The point is that buyers control what they want to watch, and the content they want to engage with, so your message needs to be on their terms. Their terms include the web, social media, and the videos they watch, which are all accessible on mobile devices. Making sure that your message is mobile will help you to reach your targeted prospects and ensures that your message resonates.

Working outside of business hours

The 9-to-5 schedule just doesn't exist. I often get asked a question, "What's your work/life balance like?" There's no such thing anymore! When you like what you do for work, you're engaged all the time. People always check their phones for updates. When your commute is an hour, you're picking up your phone while you're sitting in traffic. On Saturday mornings, the executive who is standing on the sideline watching his kid play soccer is on his phone getting caught up on emails, scrolling through newsfeeds, and checking social media. Your contacts in your accounts are doing many things outside of 9-to-5 business hours. A modern B2B marketer understands the importance of engaging people on their terms and at the right time.

Marketers are notorious for doing interruption marketing. You're interrupting your prospects by attempting to get your message in front of them. Sending an email interrupts whatever they were working on when they have an alert set on the computer. Calling your prospects at the office, or on their mobile phones, is an interruption because they're checking to see who is calling and deciding whether they want to pick up the phone. With technology, marketing and salespeople don't have to interrupt the people we're trying to connect with. This is where advertising comes into play.

WHY B2B MARKETERS MUST INVEST IN MOBILE

Capterra recently surveyed more than 100 B2B software marketers about their mobile plans for 2015. Alarmingly, 41 percent said they had no mobile plans in the works for the coming years. As a B2B marketer, you must acknowledge that each and every one of your prospects and customers has a mobile device they're engaging with more than a computer.

The amount of money advertisers spend on mobile research is steadily increasing. According to research from eMarketer, mobile ad spending in the US for 2015 will increase 50 percent, reaching $28.72 billion and accounting for 49 percent of all digital ad spending. By 2019, mobile ad spending will rise to $65.87 billion, or 72 percent of total digital ad spend. Does your marketing and sales ("smarketing") team have a plan in place to connect with your buyers on mobile?

Here's the good news: Because your prospects have gone mobile, they're more likely to engage with something that interests them after business hours. Outside of the office, there are fewer distractions at home, especially from the hours of 8 to 11 p.m. Dinner is done, the kids are in bed, and there's finally some down time to catch up on emails and social media. Working outside of business hours doesn't mean you have to do a sales pitch. It's about giving your contacts the right content to help them start thinking about why they should do business with your company.

That's the beauty of account-based marketing. It's about not interrupting your best-fit contacts, but about being on their terms to engage with the contacts in accounts you're targeting. When it's after hours, you can engage them in something they care about. Being where your buyer is means going mobile and social. Today's buyer has more power than ever before because of easy access to information. You can connect to them in several ways:

>> **Advertising on multiple channels:** Targeted advertising helps to get your message in front of your contacts as they surf the web. Even when they don't click on your advertisement, they see your logo and message.

>> **Connecting with contacts on LinkedIn:** When you invite a contact to connect on LinkedIn, the contact receives an email alert to accept the invitation to connect, which they can do at their own convenience.

>> **Sponsoring posts on social media:** Posting content to Facebook, LinkedIn, Twitter, Instagram, and other social media platforms is free. To help your posts reach a wider audience, you can pay to "sponsor" or have your post reach targeted contacts.

> » **Emails with links to content:** During 9-to-5 office hours, your contacts don't read a 700-word blog post or attend an hour-long webinar. When you send emails with links to relevant content (which you can time to send in your marketing automation system), they can read or watch your content on their own time.

TIP

Consider posting your blog content outside of business hours. When I write a new blog post for LinkedIn, I always post on Sunday afternoon. That's when people are catching up, reading a few articles, and preparing for the week ahead.

Networking in-person and online

Networking in the 21st century is a beautiful thing, because you can connect with people in person and online. It's through these connections you establish relationships. Building relationships with contacts in your target accounts makes it easier to ask for a sale at the time of a purchase decision. The primary way to build a relationship with someone you don't know is to start by connecting with them online. Social media makes it easy to network online with people you might never meet face to face.

Building a professional network is essential for modern marketers. With account-based marketing, you're building relationships with contacts who work in all types of industries. I like to think of networking as building my personal board of advisors. Using social media allows you to connect with your potential customers in your target accounts. Account-based marketing is about engaging our prospects on their terms. Here are the platforms to use for networking online:

> » **Twitter:** Search for your contacts in the search bar, and follow them.
>
> » **Facebook:** Search for your target account company pages, and "Like" them.
>
> » **LinkedIn:** Connect individually with your target accounts.
>
> » **YouTube:** Create and upload personalized messages for your contacts.

When I was putting together the first #FlipMyFunnel conference for account-based marketing, I compiled a list of all the people I knew I wanted at the event. This included industry thought leaders, analysts, and C-level executives I had a ton of respect for. I made this my A-list and created videos for each contact on the list, because I knew how important it would be to have them at the event. I started each video with "Hi (first name). Sangram here." and uploaded these to a landing page with a link for each contact to see his or her personalized video. Figure 12-1 is a screenshot from a "Sangram here" video for #FlipMyFunnel.

#FlipMyFunnel
BE INSPIRED. GET EMPOWERED.

Sangram Vajre
#FlipMyFunnel Host

FIGURE 12-1: An example of a personalized video to connect online.

TIP

Insert yourself into a conversation that's already happening. Look for existing hashtags (such as #ABMChat and #FlipMyFunnel for Twitter conversations about account-based marketing).

TIP

If you're an introvert, networking online helps to start the conversation before having to pick up the phone or meet someone in person.

For in-person networking with contacts in your target accounts, it's about meeting them on their own turf. If you're trying to schedule a meeting with a contact, start by connecting with him/her online. Through email, suggest options for meeting in person. Here are ways to network with your contacts in-person:

» **Find a professional organization or trade association hosting events.** Ask your contact if they're going; if so, meet there.

» **Host your own events for your target accounts.** The first #FlipMyFunnel roadshow is one example of how I connected with my target contacts to talk about account-based marketing.

» **Travel to their city and invite them to coffee or a meal.** It's amazing what happens, and what you can learn about your contacts, when you connect with someone over food.

When inviting contacts to connect in person, I like to schedule multiple meetings over the course of a few days. If I'm heading to a big city like New York, San Francisco, or Boston, I'll look up my network of contacts I want to connect with and send a personal email to find their availability. The age of social media gives us infinite abilities to connect online and then meet up.

INFLUITIVE'S "MOST WANTED" LIST

Salesforce's Dreamforce event is the largest tradeshow for B2B marketing and sales professionals. To stand out at Dreamforce 2015, Influitive (a customer advocacy company) put together a list of their "Most Wanted" contacts. Because Dreamforce is such a huge event, with more than 100,000 attendees, the Influitive team knew they had to be strategic to reach all the contacts they wanted. These contacts included C-level executives, VPs, Directors, and Managers of Marketing, Sales, Demand Generation, or Customer Success. All were contacts in accounts they were targeting.

The "Most Wanted" list was posted to Influitive's website and cross-promoted on social media with the message "Bring these savvy marketers to our booth so that we can help them round up their advocates with a formal advocate marketing program. Come to Influitive's booth #N2104 with one these marketers and collect your cash bounty. We are giving away a Benjamin for each bounty ($50 to the bounty hunter and $50 to the captured marketer)." Throughout the conference, attendees would bring the "Most Wanted" to Influitive's booth. Influitive posted to social media throughout Dreamforce with the "Most Wanted" and saw awesome results.

Ensuring your message resonates

Personalized messaging is more effective than generic email blasts. Because you're strategically reaching out to contacts in accounts, an increased level of personalization is needed. More importantly, your message and content must resonate. Making your message resonate means it hits the right nerve with your contact, connecting your message to a pain point or business need. This is a big problem because everyone has something to say. Everyone is talking. There are billions of voices shouting their message into the abyss of the internet, so you have to make your message is specific. Here are ways to test your messaging before putting it out there:

>> **Proofread for grammar and accuracy:** Typos kill an email you worked hard to create. They might reply to your email to correct your typo, but you've made a poor first impression. Be sure your text is clean!

>> **Read your message aloud:** Even though you've typed it up, read it aloud to hear how your words sound. Make sure they resonate!

>> **Check the contact information:** Is the name of your contact and his or her company spelled correctly? If not, they probably won't reply to your email!

>> **Share it with your teammates in marketing and sales:** Ask whether the message aligns with the needs you've identified of the personas in your ideal customer profile (ICP)!

TIP

Before sending an email, draft your message in a platform like Google Docs and invite your teammates to read it and make comments before you send it to your contacts and accounts.

REMEMBER

Because account-based marketing is business-to-business marketing, you are targeting a specific industry vertical or market segment, and you're targeting a specific persona from within that vertical.

Your message should be customized for the individual job roles at the companies on your target account list. If you're targeting the manufacturing industry, and trying to engage IT people in that industry, create specific messages that address the challenges/pain they're experiencing.

Advertising on the Right Platforms

Account-based marketing is a strategic approach to focused B2B marketing. A big part of this strategy is advertising. As B2B buyers spend a huge amount of time researching products and services on the web before making a purchase decision, you need to surround your potential customers with your message wherever they go on the web. This means launching advertising campaigns targeted at your contacts, prospects, and opportunities, in your best-fit accounts.

The right platform depends on the industry verticals you're targeting. If you're focused on the healthcare industry, you're attempting to get your message in front of doctors and nurses. Those contacts in your target accounts are super busy and not on their phones throughout the day. But they're people who will check their phones and email, just like everyone else, so running an advertising campaign after 9-to-5 business hours will help you to engage on their own terms. Account-based marketing platforms allow you to do this type of targeted digital advertising. Advertising campaigns will vary with on the ABM platform you select. The types of advertising you can do across multiple digital channels include

>> **Mobile:** Advertisements are automatically adjusted in size to appear on any device.

>> **Social:** Advertisements are shown on social media platforms, such as Twitter, LinkedIn, Facebook, and Instagram.

>> **Display:** Advertisements appear in web browsers that show your ads while your contacts are reading articles or surfing the web.

>> **Video:** Advertisements play before the video starts, or they appear in the sidebar of a website (such as YouTube).

Building your advertising campaigns

The first step of building your targeted advertising campaign is knowing who to target. These are the companies, or accounts, that you should have data, records, and profiles for in your CRM. The data you will use from your CRM includes the contact information for the people in your target accounts. Choose your targeted contacts according to the personas in your ICP. This will help you reach all the relevant decision makers and influencers at the accounts you want to do business with. This list of contacts is your audience.

After you decide which contacts are in your target audience, you will pull the list of contacts from your CRM into the advertising platform. The fields from your CRM you need to pull include

>> Company

>> Job Role or Department

>> Job Title or Seniority

TIP

You can also target regions or demographics with your targeted advertising campaigns. Any fields in your CRM can be used.

When you know the contacts and accounts you need to target, you create rules for your advertising campaigns. The rules are defined by the goals for the individual campaign. Examples of campaign goals are

>> **Demand generation:** Increasing awareness within your target accounts that are new from a recently acquired list or in the prospect stage. The goal of this campaign is to warm up the contacts in the account so you can set an appointment or a demo for the sales team.

>> **Stage progression:** Advancing your account to the next stage in the buyer's journey, from prospect to opportunity, or opportunity to Closed/Won customer. This is also known as a pipeline acceleration campaign, as it moves the account faster through the sales pipeline.

>> **Expansion of reach within an account:** You may only have one contact in your target account; the goal of this campaign is to reach all the relevant decision makers in an account.

Figure 12-2 shows how you begin to set up your advertising campaign in an account-based marketing platform.

FIGURE 12-2:
Setting up your advertising campaign in an ABM platform.

Your account-based marketing platform can append data to your campaign by supplying additional contacts that match the company data pulled from your CRM. Your ABM platform pairs this data with cookie- and/or IP-based targeting. Starting with the account first has a much higher match rate for ensuring your advertising reaches new contacts in your target accounts.

The ABM platform is proactively engaging your target audience across all digital channels including mobile, social, display, and video. ABM platforms are connected with dozens of ad exchanges and enable you to engage decision-makers on their terms. Within your ABM platform is where you load the graphics for your advertisements, also known as your "creative." Advertising "creative" elements include

>> **Message:** The words or "copy" included in the ad.

>> **Graphics:** The design elements or pictures in the ad.

>> **Call-to-action (CTA):** What you want the contacts to do, such as "Read More", "Register Now" or "Request Demo."

>> **Landing page:** Where you want your contacts to "land" after they click on your ad. Examples of landing pages include

- Form to request a demo (also known as a *gated* page) to capture information from your contacts in the form.

- *Un-gated* content without a form, such as an infographic, case study, or blog post.

REMEMBER

You need to create the landing page in your marketing automation system. In your marketing automation system is where you will record the activity for all the contacts in the accounts. The marketing automation system will record whether your contacts click on the advertisement and capture which landing page they came to. This data is important for measuring the success of your advertising campaign.

Figure 12-3 shows examples of advertisements to be used for campaigns.

The advertising "creative" should fit within the defined parameters of your account-based marketing platform. For each campaign, you need to create advertisements in different sizes. Having the correct sizes ensures they will be responsive on any mobile devices. The types of advertisements you're designing include

>> **Banner advertisement:** These appear at the top of a web page.

>> **Mobile advertisement:** Responsive ads for mobile devices, including smartphones and tablets.

FIGURE 12-3: Advertising examples for an ABM campaign.

>> **Social advertisement:** Included in social media, such as LinkedIn, Twitter, Facebook, and Instagram.

WARNING

If you don't use the correct sizes when designing your ads, they don't display correctly across all platforms.

Your account-based marketing platform will store all the creative content you load for your advertising campaigns. The ad creative content is kept in a library so you can use the same ads for future campaigns at new, target audiences. Figure 12-4 shows how you would load your creative for your advertising campaign in an account-based marketing platform.

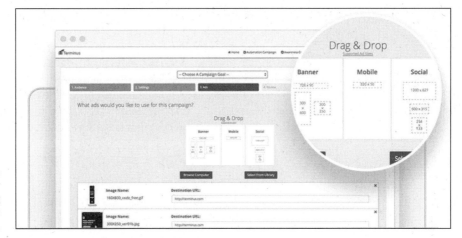

FIGURE 12-4:
Loading your
advertising
creative in an
ABM platform.

Pushing the envelope

There's a flood of ads on the web. It's important that your message stands out above the crowd. Think about how you're differentiating your brand from other brands when trying to connect with your target audience. The good news is that you can push the envelope to make your message stand out. Here are considerations for pushing the envelope:

>> **Message:** "Schedule a demo now to learn more" is as dry as a piece of toast.

One of the best lines of copy I ever read was "Who is Willie Sutton?" Willie Sutton was a famous American bank robber. While this had nothing to do with the industry, the content garnered tons of clicks because it piqued curiosity.

>> **Creative:** Eye-catching graphics grab your targeted contact's attention. Stock photography and clipart won't get you very far above the noise. "Memes" go a long way. A meme is a funny picture with only one or two sentences.

CRM RETARGETING TO EXPAND YOUR REACH

Targeted advertising is part of your account-based marketing strategy. You're pulling data from your CRM to target contacts in accounts. It's a laser-focused B2B marketing technique. Another way to connect with your accounts is through CRM *retargeting*. The retargeting component includes taking the data in your CRM and syncing it with third-party sources for cookie- or IP-based targeting. If you know the name of an account you want to target, and this account is in your CRM, then additional platforms (such as AdRoll and LiveRamp) match your data for CRM retargeting.

Account-based marketing platforms add another layer onto CRM retargeting with *account-based retargeting*. Account-based retargeting proactively targets the entire set of people in the account. CRM retargeting uses the first email or contact who came to your website. Because Bob from ACME came to the website, he is the first contact associated with the account in your CRM. You know Bob isn't the only decision-maker in the account. If Bob is a Marketing Manager, you need to find Bob's Director of Marketing or CMO. Your ABM platform will use Bob's company name, ACME, and find more contact data for the marketing team members at ACME. This way, the entire marketing department at ACME will see your advertisement. This helps to expand your reach in your target account.

Another great way to push the envelope is direct mail. Companies like PFL (www. pfl.com) take the contact information from your CRM and use it for direct mail campaigns. You can print collateral with personalized messages, and ship this direct mail to hundreds or thousands of people. From within your marketing automation platform, you can use automation rules to update a predetermined CRM field that then triggers the direct mail piece to send. After that collateral is sent, PFL will show the delivery status in the lead or contact section of your CRM. You can then set up task assignments to have your sales reps follow up.

One of my favorite ways to really push the envelope and have a 1-to-1 connection with contacts is to use personalized videos. B2B marketers are notorious for producing video content that's "evergreen." These evergreen videos were designed to target the message and generate leads to fill the top of the funnel. Thanks to video marketing platforms like Vidyard (www.vidyard.com), you can personalize videos for each individual in your target accounts. Figure 12-5 is a screenshot from a personalized video created for a contact in a target account.

FIGURE 12-5:
Screenshot from a personalized video.

Changing your message at every stage

Depending on the stage of your account's journey, you need specific advertising creative. The creative and message should change at every stage of the account's journey. Your message needs to develop so the contacts in your account continue to stay engaged. Here is how to align your advertising creative with a stage-based progression:

» **New/Prospect:** The advertising message should focus on awareness; why the contacts in your target account should consider your solution. At this stage, you want them to have an opportunity to learn more about your company before unveiling your product or service demo.

» **Marketing Qualified Account (MQA):** The advertising message should focus on education; what your solution can do for this account to alleviate any pain or fulfill a business need. At this stage, you want them to get as much information as possible about your company's value proposition.

» **Sales Qualified Account (SQA):** The advertising message at this stage of qualification demonstrates your success with other customers like your account. Advertising here should link to landing pages with client case studies and video testimonials so your contacts can hear from your customers in their own words.

WHAT *MAD MEN* TEACHES ABOUT ABM

In the hit television series *Mad Men*, the agency of Sterling, Cooper, Draper & Price is a team of creative people and account men. The enigmatic Don Draper is the creative director. Don works closely with Roger Sterling, who oversees all the activity of signing up new accounts and then keeping them happy. In many scenes, the team gathers in a board room to review the list of accounts, discussing where there are opportunities and which clients are in danger of leaving. Although the *Mad Men* story began in the 1950s, long before anyone had ever heard of a sales and marketing funnel, the agency actually was doing B2B account-based marketing:

- **Identify target accounts**. They targeted companies in such industries as automotive, cosmetics, fashion, travel, and commercial goods, because they had success with those types of companies before. The account executives found the ultimate decision makers.

- **Expand the account with contacts**. They determined who else from the account needed to come in for a pitch about creative. For example, when the agency was pitching a big tobacco company, they would need to know all of the executive stakeholders.

- **Engage accounts on their terms.** Invite them to the office for a swanky board-room meeting or to dinner to sip martinis. Find out their hopes and dreams for their product or service, then design creative to help tell the story. The big pitch with storyboards showing messaging that spoke to them and tugged at their heart strings would help win the deal.

- **Create customer advocates**. They accounts then tell all their friends about the amazing work the agency did to help increase sales at their business. This word of mouth marketing gave the agency its excellent reputation.

Because *Mad Men* covered the Fifties to the Seventies, the agency didn't have access to the technology we have today. Contacts were kept in a Rolodex on a pretty mahogany desk. When an account man left an agency, all he had was his Rolodex and his reputation. Today, your reputation follows you on social media, but the way you manage accounts is much more sophisticated. Imagine what Don Draper would think about all these B2B marketing automation software and sales prospecting tools.

The advertising creative at these early stages should be geared toward getting the prospect to open the door and start a conversation. The call-to-action (CTA) options to consider for these ads include

>> "Schedule a Demo" and link to a form to schedule an appointment with a sales development representative (SDR) or account executive (AE).

>> "Learn More" and link to a whitepaper, infographic, or blog post that explains more about how your solution has helped people like your prospect in the same industry.

TIP

Your message should be focused on that goal; the logical next step is to a demo. The CTA for your advertising should be after the demo is completed.

Automating stage-based advertising for every opportunity

If you're doing advertising campaigns for accounts in the early stages of the buyer's journey, then you will need to be sure you have new advertising creative for accounts in the middle stage of the buyer's journey. This is called the opportunity stage. A revenue opportunity has been tied to the account in your CRM. The advertising campaigns you create for your contacts in accounts with revenue opportunities need to be highly personalized campaigns. When thinking about the narrative of advertising campaigns, think about how your message will evolve throughout the account's journey.

Your advertising *must* change every time the account moves from one stage to another in your CRM. Because your account has progressed in the buyer's journey from a prospect to an opportunity, you want them to receive a new message that will help get them further down the sales pipeline to becoming a customer. You don't want them to download another ebook or read another whitepaper. You want them to learn how your company has helped other people who are similar to your contact do the same thing but better.

REMEMBER

After the first demo has been completed with the account, you need to change your advertising creative. This additional level of personalization will help to create sales velocity. Sales velocity is created by activities from marketing which drive engagement with all the contacts in an account.

In the opportunity stage, it's important to show how you support your customers and how happy they are doing business with your company. The messages in your advertising should be related to customer sentiments. In the advertisement, the CTA should link to customer case studies or video testimonials. This contact should include quotes or have your clients talking about the great experience they've had with your company.

Automating stage-based advertising wasn't possible before marketing automation. It is through the evolution of marketing technology (MarTech) that it's now possible to engage the entire account across the different stages at scale. Technology makes it possible to do targeted advertising based on the stage in the account's journey.

As the account progresses through its journey, your salesperson is going through the process of updating the account in your CRM, such as when the account crosses from prospect to opportunity stage. Because your CRM is synced with your account-based marketing platform, and you have loaded your library of advertising creative for each stage, as the account moves into different stages, there will be different messages to engage on their terms.

Launching form-free

If you know who you're targeting, and which companies you're focusing on, the guesswork is gone. The whole idea of traditional lead generation was finding people who were interested in you. Because you're starting with the people you know you want to engage with, you don't need a form to capture information from your contacts.

Form-free means un-gated content on a landing page. In your marketing automation system, you create landing pages to host your content. This content includes whitepapers, infographics, videos, case studies, or anything else you want your contacts to read or download. This same content is hosted on your company's Resources page of the website. In the Resources section, content is "gated" by a form. Your contacts must complete a form in order to download the content. This ensures the contact information is captured in marketing automation and added to your CRM.

Because your account-based marketing platform is doing targeted advertising using the data in your CRM, you don't need to gate content with a form. The contacts you're targeting with advertising are already stored in your CRM. You're doing advertising to surround the contacts with your message about why they should do business with your company. There's no reason why they should fill out another form with all the MarTech solutions available.

Form-free campaigns are possible thanks to marketing automation. It is through marketing automation you're able to identify which contacts are coming to your website and landing pages. Through IP-based targeting, the marketing automation system does a reverse IP lookup, so you actually know who is coming to your website without asking for information.

Marketing automation syncs with your CRM. The CRM information is used to proactively target who is getting your message, so you're eliminating the need for a form. Forms are erroneous at this point.

Engaging on Social Media

Connecting socially through the internet first became popular in the early 1990s with the rise of chatrooms through AOL and AOL Instant Messenger. By the early 2000s, connecting online evolved into networking platforms. Facebook and MySpace were the first to enter the digital arena. Analysts called these sites "new media." Then came LinkedIn, where people could connect on a professional level instead of connecting with friends. Twitter soon followed, giving users the ability to publish their own stories (in 140 characters or less) to the entire world and gain Followers while Following other users.

Today, social media is the primary media used by the millennial generation. Millennial young adults rarely read printed newspapers. They gain their news and information online and using social media. It is through social media they connect to their peers. In order to evolve your marketing strategy for an account-based approach, you have to consider how you will engage with contacts of any age. This is why social media is essential for a comprehensive ABM strategy.

Connecting with your contacts

The number of social media channels is endless. Each social media channel serves a different purpose designed for a certain audience. Depending on your audience and purpose, you will find yourself with using some social media channels more than others. It depends on the types of accounts you're trying to connect, and with what message. As of 2016, the biggest social media channels in the world are

>> Facebook

>> Twitter

>> LinkedIn

>> YouTube

>> Reddit

>> Instagram

>> Pinterest

REMEMBER

It's important to recognize the most popular social media platforms, as they all offer ways for your company to do advertising or promote sponsor content. These media help you reach your contacts in your target accounts.

WARNING

TIP

It isn't possible to be on every channel and be effective. Identifying the right channels is important for connecting with your contacts.

LinkedIn is the best place to connect with your contacts on a 1-to-1 basis utilizing social media.

As the largest professional networking site in the world, every B2B marketing and sales professional should understand the importance of being on LinkedIn. LinkedIn has several ways for you to connect with your contacts, including

» Liking or commenting on status updates

» Reading your contacts blog posts and sharing them with your network

» Joining groups

» Inviting them to connect

Here is when you should invite a prospect to connect on LinkedIn:

» **Business/Sales development representative (BDR/SDR):** If you're engaging in conversation with a prospect, after completing an initial discovery call or scheduling an appointment for sales.

» **Sales account executive (AE):** If a demo was successful and the account is progressing to a revenue opportunity. You need to connect with all the relevant decision makers in the account.

» **Project manager:** If the account has become a Closed/Won deal, and the implementation of your product or service requires a project manager or professional services consultant, this individual should connect with your customer accounts on LinkedIn.

» **Customer success manager (CSM):** After the account has been handed off to a CSM via email, the CSM should connect with their customers, (especially the "champion," or biggest user of your product or service). This champion can become your customer advocate, and LinkedIn can help to further engagement.

» **Marketing team member:** A member from your marketing team needs to collaborate with your customers to create content. This customer content includes case studies, video testimonials, webinars, and planning for events. When marketing team members are collaborating with customers, they should connect on LinkedIn to build a relationship.

WARNING

Don't ask your contacts to become your Facebook friend. If you get to the point where one of your contacts offers to connect with you on Facebook, consider what message you'll send by accepting his or her friend accounts.

Following accounts

There are options for following accounts instead of using social media to connect with contacts in accounts at a personal 1-to-1 level. You can follow accounts at the company level. The value in following your accounts at a company level on social media includes

>> **Staying informed:** You're updated with the latest company news, such as hiring a senior executive, acquiring another company, or being acquired by a larger company.

>> **Knowing the decision makers:** When you follow a company on LinkedIn, you can see the employees on the Company page. Using your personas, you can identify who you will need to work with to get the deal done.

REMEMBER

You need to create a plan for your target accounts, recognizing the organizational hierarchy to determine your influencers and decision-makers in the account. LinkedIn can provide you with this account information if it's missing from your CRM.

TIP

If you're a salesperson (either an SDR, AE, or senior sales leader), you need to follow the accounts on your target or Tier A account list.

Being armed with the latest information will help you create sales velocity to accelerate the purchase decision. The purchase decision is based on what's going on within the account. If you see the account is in the process of merging with another company, you can anticipate that the sales process will be delayed because of internal reorganization.

Here are ways to follow company accounts:

>> **LinkedIn:** Search the company name to pull up the Company's page. "Like" the company to be updated with the latest news and find your key contacts in the account in the employee list.

>> **Twitter**: Follow the main company account, usually like *@CompanyName.* You can find company accounts by using the search bar on Twitter. Also check whether the company is using a certain hashtag to follow the conversation on Twitter.

>> **Facebook:** "Like" the company Facebook page to stay updated about the company. Here is where the company will share content, so you can gauge their interest in specific topics or events.

>> **YouTube:** Your account may have a company YouTube channel. Search in Google for videos from your account. You can follow your account's YouTube channel by clicking the "Subscribe" icon below the video.

REMEMBER

Depending on your industry, your accounts may have accounts on Instagram or Pinterest. You can follow these accounts as well, although it's difficult to engage on a professional level.

Sponsoring posts

In addition to following accounts on social media and connecting with contacts in accounts on a 1-to-1 level on LinkedIn, another way to engage your accounts is to sponsor posts. Every time you update your company's social media channel, it's a post. LinkedIn, Facebook, and Twitter will all prompt you to sponsor a post if you're posting from your company's account. Sponsoring posts is a form of advertising.

Sponsored posts are targeted to anyone who is following you on the social media channel. This isn't as easy to target to give account-level attribution. What you can do is run advertisements on social media from within your ABM platform. This way, if one of your contacts in your CRM clicks on an advertisement which is launched from your ABM platform, you're capturing this engagement and connecting directly with one of your targeted contacts.

Chapter 13

Developing Content for Campaigns

The content marketing revolution transformed the B2B marketing world. The birth of marketing automation platforms launched in the mid-2000s also launched the digital content marketing industry. Content marketing is all about telling the story of your company's product or service in an unbiased way and demonstrating thought leadership. Establishing a thought leadership position is accomplished through creating meaningful content that leaves an impression on your targeted accounts.

Marketing automation systems need content to fuel demand generation. Without content, there's nothing to link to from your CTAs on landing pages. Demonstrating thought leadership would be impossible. Your company needs content to demonstrate its knowledge of industry subject matter. Content has become the lifeblood of a successful marketing program.

You've got to get the content engine revved up and keep it full throughout your account-based marketing campaigns. A comprehensive ABM strategy is paired with content for each stage of the account's journey. Content should be engaging, entertaining, and based on the stage of the relationship. All throughout the account's journey, you'll use marketing technology to help deliver content at the right stage, at the right time, and to the right contacts in your account.

In this chapter, I show how to produce content the key contacts in your accounts. I discuss how to drive a response from your various types of content, giving you a framework to start your own content marketing program. I also outline the best practices for measuring the success of your content marketing programs by using your marketing automation system to see the results.

Creating a Content Library

According to the Content Marketing Institute, 80 percent of business decision makers want their company information in a series of articles, not in advertisements. The account's journey is a comprehensive lifecycle, from the time a contact in an account first connects with your company. Your contacts in accounts want to read and digest information at their own pace instead of being spoon-fed by a salesperson. By having a library full of content, your prospects can select the content they want to read or the videos they want to watch. This content informs them about the *value* of your company's product or service without a sales pitch.

REMEMBER

Your company's content library will be hosted on your website, labeled as "Resources," "Resource Library," or "Knowledge Center."

A content library will have gated content protected by a form. This way, you capture a contact's information before they download content. Content is used to draw inbound activity to your website to discover new contacts and nurture existing contacts. Lots of different content is needed, as it will serve a different purpose to all of your accounts in the buyer's journey.

TIP

When brainstorming ideas for content, think of people outside of your company you need to interview. To remove any bias from your content, I recommend interviewing at least three thought leaders outside your industry, then sending them quotes to review before including them in your content.

Your content library should showcase your company's expertise and thought leadership position in the industry. All the different pieces of content should inform your prospect, educate them on best practices, and guide them through the buyer's journey. I've seen these tools work in all stages of account-based marketing:

>> **Whitepapers:** This long-form content is created in .pdf and should be served up early in the buyer's journey. A whitepaper is a great way to demonstrate thought leadership in your area of subject matter expertise. Across all industries, producing and distributing whitepapers to your prospects is considered a

best practice for moving prospects through the sales process. Whitepapers can be as short as six pages to make the information easy to read.

>> **Ebooks:** An ebook is an even longer version of a whitepaper. Ebooks are used to incorporate even more quotes and content from other thought leaders and industry insights. These should also be served up early in the buyer's journey.

REMEMBER

The difference between a whitepaper and an ebook is both the length and design. An ebook is a longer work, averaging at least 20 pages or more. Whitepapers usually are around ten pages, and they got their name because of all the whitespace included in the design to make the text easier to digest. An ebook should incorporate more color and graphic design elements. Figure 13-1 shows a sample of an ebook.

IDENTIFY: WHY IT'S "CUSTOMERS FIRST," NOT "CHANNELS"

The #FlipMyFunnel movement starts with identifying your best-fit customers. While a lead generation model based on the traditional funnel might begin by selecting a set of channels, a more logical first step is to identify a set of potential customers first. In a marketing landscape that is increasingly focused on the customer's needs, not the marketer's, why start anywhere else?

FINDING THE BEST FIT

Let's use a simple analogy. Say you're going fishing and you're hoping to catch a few trout. You can throw a giant net into the water and catch a number of fish at once — that may or may not be trout — or you can specifically identify the trout you're after and reel it in from there. Now, in the world of fishing, those extraneous fish caught in your net might not be such a bad thing, but step into the shoes of a B2B marketer, and those fish just become clutter in your database — and quite frankly, a waste of your time and money.

Let's go back to our funnel. With your best-fit customers identified up front, it's much easier to allocate resources and budget where they're going to be most effective. Armed with the knowledge of your customers' pain points, motivations, and interests, you can target them on the channels they're using with messaging that's been developed specifically for them (we'll learn more about this in chapter two).

FISHING FOR THE RIGHT CUSTOMERS

MOTIVATIONS **CUSTOMER PROFILE**

INTERESTS

PAIN POINTS

FIGURE 13-1:
Example of an ebook.

TIP

Include a table of contents in your ebooks and whitepapers over ten pages. This helps the reader to find the content they want to read.

Figure 13-2 shows a sample table of contents from an ebook.

>> **Infographics:** When you only have eight seconds to capture the attention of your prospect, an infographic helps keep you top of mind. These graphics should also be served up early in the account's journey to help increase the awareness of your product or service. Figure 13-3 shows a sample infographic.

Contents

FIGURE 13-2:
Example of a table of contents.

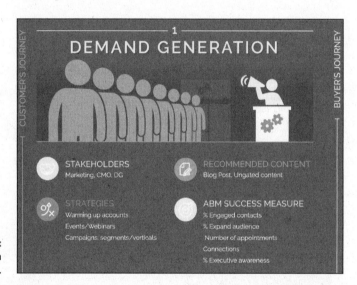

FIGURE 13-3:
Example of an infographic.

WARNING

With ebooks, infographics, and whitepapers, the goal is education of the problem your company solves, not about your company. Don't include detailed information about your product or service in this early-stage content. Save it for later in the account's journey.

>> **Case Studies:** Letting your customers share their success stories in case studies is good for you (prospects will hear about authentic results from real clients) and good for your clients (their stories promote awareness of their businesses, too). This content should be presented by the sales team after the qualification process, when you're trying to progress the account into an opportunity or Closed/Won deal. Two ways to develop case studies into content include

- *Document:* Designed in a .pdf covering the problem your customer was experiencing and how your company provided a solution.

- *Video:* Short recorded interviews with your customers, where prospects can hear from customers in their own words about why they do business with your company.

>> **Webinars:** In the early stage of the account's journey, webinars are a great tool to drive awareness and engagement in your target, qualified accounts. The goal of producing webinars is to create more interest with the contacts in your account and move them further through the sales process. With your prospect webinars, you need a panel of presenters. When you'll have three presenters, I recommend these roles:

- One thought leader or industry influencer from outside your team

- A customer "champion" who can be an advocate for your product or service and can speak eloquently to your audience

- One of your executive team members or a leader in your company

TIP

Edit your recorded webinars into shorter segments, such as a 15-minute video. Short video recordings are easy to digest, and can be replayed at your contact's convenience. Figure 13-4 shows a sample webinar.

Flipping Funnels with Account Based Marketing

featuring Dave Rigotti and Sangram Vajre

FIGURE 13-4: Example of a webinar replay.

TIP

Have a quarterly plan for your webinars. Hosting at least one webinar per month is great way to create velocity for the sales team. Your "smarketing" team should create a promotion plan to share this new content.

Because you're going through the effort to create a content library, you need to have a plan to share this content with your target audience. When you spend this time, money, and effort to create content, it needs to be shared with the contacts in your accounts.

REMEMBER

You need to create content that doesn't live in your "Resources" section, as other content and communications are needed to serve other purposes to drive awareness.

This content can be strategically used in campaigns to target accounts that are in the early stage of the buyer's journey. Here are other types of content you'll need to develop:

>> **Blog posts:** Your company's blog is a key component of your marketing website. Your prospects and influencers will check out your blog for the latest topics your company is writing about.

REMEMBER

New content should be published to your blog at least once a week. Make it current and topical.

>> **Press releases:** This is how your company will distribute major news. These news announcements can include a strategic round of funding, a new customer acquisition, merger, partnership, or hosting an event.

The benefit of distributing a press release on a web-based platform, such as PR Newswire (www.prnewswire.com), MarketWired (www.marketwired.com) or PRWeb (http://service.prweb.com/home), is that it's an official press release, which you can then link to from other sources.

>> **Social media:** The content you publish to social media platforms, (such as Twitter, LinkedIn, and Facebook) should be fresh and timely. Social media content should be created specifically for the channel you're publishing it on. A Twitter post can only be 140 characters (including the link to your content), so what you write for Twitter can be expanded for a Facebook or LinkedIn post.

TIP

Every time you post a link to Twitter, use a platform like Bit.ly to track how many times the link is clicked. When you're sharing the same piece of content on multiple social media channels, such as sharing the same case study on both Twitter and LinkedIn, create different tracking links on Bit.ly (https://bitly.com) and Ow.ly (http://ow.ly/url/shorten-url) to attribute it to different channels. Many marketing automation systems can also generate tracked links or integrate with tools that track social media engagement.

>> **Direct mail:** Content for direct mailing includes physical objects. You'll need to have stationary printed with your company's logo for your team members to write notes to accounts thanking them for their time. Consider printing postcards to include with "swag" or other items you will physically mail to contacts in accounts.

TIP

Create an editorial calendar for the new content you'll publish to your library, blog, press releases, sending direct mail, and other content. This calendar will help your marketing team manage when and what you're publishing across various channels.

TIP

Having an editorial calendar also provides transparency across your "smarketing" team so everyone knows about new content and upcoming campaigns. Send an email or communicate during your weekly "smarketing" meeting to your sales leaders about when new content will be available and how they can use it.

Storytelling and its importance

The whole point of developing and sharing content is to tell a story. The importance of storytelling for modern B2B marketers can't be overstated. Your prospects don't want to watch a commercial or hear a product pitch. Buyers today want to be informed and educated, so they can arrive at a decision independently. The content your company produces should help tell a story to your buyers, so they can be guided down a path that leads to becoming customers.

The content in your library should be used in campaigns throughout the account's journey. Throughout the sales process, there's an underlying story. This is called the narrative. The narrative tells a story problem you're trying to solve and builds to a conclusion at the end, which is how your company answers the solution. When I think about storytelling, the story should be consistent. No matter who you tell the story, it shouldn't change. However, you might tell the story from a different point of view, depending on the type of contact you want to reach. For example, the angle from which a story is told to an IT manager is very different from a CMO.

Adapting the narrative to fit the buyer's journey means everyone will discover a slightly different version of the same story. A story always has three components: a beginning, a middle, and an end. The same is true for the account's journey. You need to tell a story to the contacts in the account using your content. Here's how to think of your content as a story:

>> **Beginning:** The start of the account's journey with your company. It's about awareness for the early-stage prospects. At this stage, the prospect is becoming educated about the problem and potential solutions. The relevant content at the early stage includes blog posts, ebooks, infographics, and whitepapers.

>> **Middle:** The account has been qualified and the sales team is trying to create an opportunity. At this stage, the contacts in your account are becoming educated about why they should buy from your company. The relevant

content at the middle stage includes case studies, video testimonials, webinars, and engaging on social media (sales account executive should personally connect with accounts on LinkedIn).

» **End:** The sales team is trying to close the opportunity and win a new customer. At this stage, the contacts in your account need to see how your company will continue to support them after the deal is done. The relevant content in the final stages of the buyer's journey includes "how to" content (such as checklists and implementation guides) showing them how they can easily adopt your company's product or service. If there's competition here, a competitive analysis or brief document outlining the return on investment (ROI) can be provided.

WARNING

When you have a lousy product, no good story can sell it. You must have a good product or service, or no amount of marketing will help your company in the long term.

GARY VAYNERCHUK AND JAB, JAB, JAB, RIGHT HOOK

Gary Vaynerchuk (@garyvee) is one of my favorite authors and thought leaders. This dude is amazing. Gary epitomizes what it means to hustle for business. He's a *New York Times* best-selling author. One of his books that's my all-time favorite is *Jab, Jab, Jab, Right Hook: How to Tell Your Story in a Noisy Social World.* In this work, Gary basically provides a blueprint for marketers to communicate across multiple social media channels and mobile devices. Essentially, Gary's blueprint is a combination of "jabs" with different activities. This involves treating people like people, not as numbers, which is also the underlying theme of account-based marketing.

Instead of thinking of our prospects as leads, we're tailoring our marketing efforts to make everything personalized. You must consider who you're talking to, where they are in the buyer's journey, and what information they are looking for to deliver the right "jab." The storytelling process includes a number of "jabs" and content before landing that "right hook" to close the next sale. Gary is a master storyteller. This book is both entertaining and highly informative for any B2B marketer wanting to take their content to the next level. I highly recommend reading this work as you think about how you'll develop content for campaigns.

To win the deal, you need a solid product offering, but it's so much more than that. The account will choose to do business with your company because of the relationship built with the sales representative and the content that was produced and shared throughout the buyer's journey. The storytelling process helps your "smarketing" team to tell the right story and sell the dream to close the deal. It's part of the psychology of sales.

Now, the content that supports the overall narrative can be different depending on the particular problem they're trying to solve. How others are looking at results, make you a hero in your own organization. The story needs to tailor to that angle and may require a change in focus on which portion of the story based on the stage in the buyer's journey.

TIP

Every quarter, your "smarketing" team should get together to determine what type of content marketing needs to produce for sales enablement. "Smarketing" should also meet with customer success to discover which content will be needed for customer accounts to support adoption and provide training.

Taking an ABM lens to your content

Imagine you walk into a store. The shopkeeper knows your size, the colors you like, your fashion sense, and your price range — all of the information about the types of clothes you like. They select items to present clothing options that they know you'll be likely to purchase. B2B marketers need to think more like the storekeeper who treats all clients like they're VIPs with tailor-made clothing. With account-based marketing (ABM), you're tailoring your message to contacts in an account. These contacts should match your personas (the type of people who are the best fit for your product or service). Keeping the accounts and contacts in mind when developing your content will make sure it resonates.

To think about your content from an account-based marketing perspective:

>> **Know your audience:** Remember that your audience is extremely important as you're taking a targeted account approach.

>> **Deliver content meaningfully:** Don't just blast an email to thousands of people every time you publish a new infographic or whitepaper. Your content was designed with your audience in mind.

FIVE OUTSTANDING CONTENT TIPS FROM JOE CHERNOV

I'm a huge fan of Joe Chernov (@jchernov). He's one of the content marketing gurus in the B2B world, having run marketing teams at HubSpot, Kinvey, and Eloqua, and now InsightSquared (www.insightsquared.com). He was kind enough to share these tips for developing content:

- Think about all the content your company has published and could publish as a "Total Address Content Market." Everything you published includes internal content (such as presentations and reports) and external content (such as blog posts, resources on your website, and advertising). Next, think about everything you could publish, such as stories and anecdotes, plugging your readers into the thoughts and minds of your company's leadership.

- The value of having a content library begins with identifying what you have and what you need. Catalog all of your existing content, everything you have published internally and externally, and then identify areas needing collateral.

- Marketing needs to interview sales leaders for questions they're frequently asked. Salespeople are on the frontline between your business and future customers. Which topics or subjects regularly come up on sales calls? Match these questions to existing content, or brainstorm new content that needs to be developed to answer these questions.

- After talking to sales, marketing needs to talk to the customer success team. These are the folks on the front line of customer service for implementation, adoption, and usage. Use them to generate ideas for content to support customers with training and successfully using your company's product or service. They have the pulse on customer needs.

- Resist the temptation to create content that speaks to you and your boss. Reduce your own role, and replace it with your prospect or customer.

  This sounds obvious, but not everyone loves the product like you do. . .at least, not yet.

Producing content by industry vertical

Your content should be specific to the industries and segments of the market in your ideal customer profile (ICP). When you start planning your first account-based marketing strategy, you'll work with your sales team to identify an ICP that includes both company size (based on the number of employees and the amount of revenue) and the type of industry.

WARNING

You *must* create an ICP for the types of accounts you want to target before producing content.

Writing content without basing it on an industry is like speaking a foreign language to someone who isn't fluent.

TIP

Publish a case study for each industry vertical you're targeting. When you're targeting that industry, you must provide proof of how your solution works for their peers.

Figure 13-5 shows a sample case study tailored to target accounts in a specified industry.

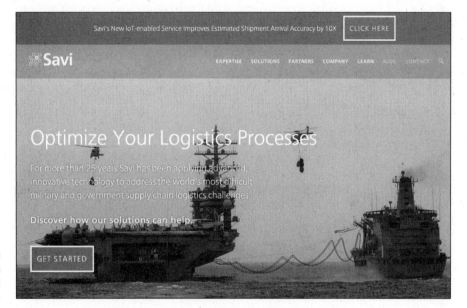

FIGURE 13-5:
Example of a case study for one industry.

Basing content on personas

For your content, consider the stage of the account's journey and who is in the account. Your marketing team needs to both educate one person or contact, and also all the contacts within the account who have a stake in the purchase decision. The content should be as specific as possible for each individual decision maker, ensuring they're engaged in the process.

You must consider who your audience is for each individual piece of content, and how they will obtain this content. Every piece of content should be created and tailored with your personas in mind. The personas are based on job role, responsibility, and seniority in an organization.

REMEMBER

This is why it's essential to have your personas created before you start developing content. You can read more about building your ICP and personas in Chapter 5.

When you're developing persona-based content, write the content targeted toward the persona's role and business needs. Think about how your solution focuses on supporting the needs of the individual role.

REMEMBER

The story you're telling with all of your content must align to a narrative. What is the problem, and how is your company the solution?

Your personas for your contacts in your target accounts will range across all levels of the organization. The way a C-level executive wants to consume content is different from a marketing manager, because they're different people who are focused on specific business needs. Your content should provide answers for all the personas in your ICP. Each person wants to hear why your solution will work for him or her, in addition to the company as a whole. Here are considerations for creating content based on seniority:

>> **Individual contributor:** This person is tasked with finding the right solution for his or her own role. They're the most engaged during the buying process, even when they aren't the ultimate decision makers. For content, this individual contributor needs to see "how to" guides. The questions your content should answer for this persona include

- What can your product do to deliver features, functionality, and ease of use?

- Which integrations does your platform support?

- How easily can you pull reports or show metrics?

Metrics are essential. The individual contributor must show why your product is useful.

>> **Manager or Director:** The department manager needs to know your company actually can do what the individual contributor says you can. In most sales situations, your sales account executive will begin by talking to an individual contributor who will be the end user. Content will need to be created for this person's manager. A manager wants to see these types of content:

- Positive product reviews on the internet

- Case studies, customer use cases and video testimonials

The manager is verifying that your company is solid, and that going with your company is the right thing to do.

>> **Executive:** The sponsor of the project who is a stakeholder for the success. He or she is the ultimate decision maker who is conscious of the budget and investment required to use your company's product or service. The types of content this person wants to see includes

- *Financial proof:* A brief or spreadsheet showing an estimated ROI

- *Competitive analysis:* How your company is better than other vendors in the marketplace

- *References:* Connecting with your customers to confirm you truly have a solution.

- *Reporting examples or screenshots of sample dashboards.*

>> **Influencers within the company:** Outside of your end user and his boss, you need to remember that there are influencers in the account who may not directly use your product or service. These influencers can include people in other departments; for example, when you're selling to marketers, an influencer could be the VP of Sales. While this VP role isn't part of the marketing team, because of the leadership position they influence the whole purchasing process. The influencer wants to look at complementary solutions, talk to their peers who have heard of your company, and show their colleagues on the executive team that they did a background check on your business.

>> **Beneficiaries:** When the VP of another department is an influencer, than the beneficiaries are in his or her department asking "what's in it for me?" For example, marketing is looking at technology solutions for ABM, and salespeople benefit from ABM, but marketing who decides which tools to purchase for ABM. Content should be created for the individuals who will benefit from your solution, even when they don't have a say in the purchase decision. They need to know whether the solution is working, and how they will benefit.

REMEMBER

Across the entire account, the end users want to see more tactical examples of how your solution works, whereas the higher you go up the organization more strategic.

The higher you go up the food chain, the more your personas care about how your solution fits into the account's vision and strategic objectives. The executive team in your target account wants to know how doing business with your company will help them reach larger business goals.

Think about how your content aligns with providing answers to all of your personas. Your personas should align with each of the contacts in the account. The story should guide your contacts in the account by what they want to know about your product or solution.

The goal is to get content to the right persona. You need to make sure everyone in the account, all the contacts who can impact the purchase decision, know what your company offers and the benefit it can provide. Here is one example using the different personas in an IT department:

>> **Chief Information Officer (CIO):** The technology leader for an IT department wants to know how your solution works from an integration standpoint. He or she wants to see how it collaborates with the other tools and software that exist in the organization's technology stack. The question to answer here is "Does this new technology play well with what I already have?"

>> **Chief Financial Officer (CFO):** He or she wants to know the return on investment after making this purchase from your company.

VisualizeROI (`www.visualize-roi.com`) is one tool that helps you create an ROI calculator plugging in different variables to demonstrate how using your company's product or service will save time, money, or both. Gartner's Magic Quadrant is another proof of investment. You can leverage the renowned analyst team at Gartner to show your product isn't just smoke and mirrors, but verified by industry analysts.

>> **IT Director:** The department head who will have firsthand knowledge of how his or her direct reports are using your product or service. When something isn't working for one of the director's team members, your customer success manager will hear about it.

>> **IT Manager or Specialist:** The end user of your technology. He or she is the persona who ultimately can turn into a "power user" or "champion" for advocate marketing. You need to empower this person from Day 1, the time they first connect with your company or download a piece of content.

Humanizing Content

The entire marketing industry is evolving. In the future, it won't be business-to-business (B2B) or business-to-consumer (B2C) marketing, but human-to-human (H2H). Humans want to buy from each other, and establish relationships. It's those relationships and personal connections that build trust. Trust makes humans feel more confident in the purchase decision.

SHOWING MY PASSION FOR CHICKEN TENDERS

I love chicken tenders. They're one of my all-time favorite foods. You can trust me as a subject matter expert on chicken tenders, but if I were selling chicken tenders, I wouldn't tell you to buy my chicken tenders. Instead, I would tell you what to look for in a best-in-class chicken tender. A quality chicken tender is crispy, flavorful, and delicious.

Think about this as you start to demonstrate thought leadership in your content. Whatever topic is your subject matter expertise, *own it.* Assume the position of being a knowledgeable person about this topic because you actually are! Become a hero for supporting this cause, whether it's chicken tenders or making a case for account-based marketing. This needs to be a bigger problem you're trying to solve across industry, and show how people can look to you and your company for guidance.

Demonstrating thought leadership

Thought leadership is one of the strongest influences in B2B marketing. A thought leader is someone in your industry perceived to be a subject matter expert. Thought leadership is presented through your content. Demonstrating thought leadership in your content is very different than traditional marketing or advertising. Instead of saying "Here's why you should buy my product!", it's "Here's a problem; in your position, here is how we helped other people in your industry solve it."

REMEMBER

Being a thought leader means sharing the limelight with other industry leaders, giving them the stage. People look to thought leaders when they're bringing the industry's best.

Here are channels and activities you can use to demonstrate your thought leadership position:

>> **Content:** In your ebooks, whitepapers, case studies, and blog posts. Focus on one topic that aligns with your product. If I were writing content about five ways to use account-based marketing to support sales, I'd highlight methods for working with your account executives. I'd also link to quotes from other thought leaders.

>> **Videos:** In all of your video content, from high-level product overviews to detailed demos and customer testimonials, the language used in these videos reinforces your thought leadership.

>> **Press releases:** In your communications to the media, cite industry sources that support your go-to market claims. If I were writing a press release about account-based marketing, I'd include the SiriusDecisions statistic about how 92 percent of B2B marketers surveyed understand the importance of ABM. Also, ask another thought leader for a quote.

>> **Social media:** Regularly post content about your subject matter on Twitter, Facebook, and LinkedIn. If I were a thought leader about IT solutions, I would post content about the latest technology, then find and follow other thought leaders on social media who talk about the same topic to engage them in a discussion.

>> **Webinars and in-person events:** When you're putting together an event, decide on a central theme and topic. Then find other thought leaders to join your event as a panelist, presenter, or sponsor. Having multiple thought leaders participate in your digital and in-person events reinforces your position as a leading influencer in your industry.

Addressing wants, needs, and pain points

Your content should present a solution but not in a sales-y way. The content and messaging your company creates needs to address the wants, needs, and pain points of your personas. Your personas have different motivations, and your content needs to speak to these driving forces. When a contact first lands on your website or reads and email, they don't have a vested interest in your company. They may not even know they have a problem, which your company can provide a solution for. What your contacts know is their own personal motivations.

TIP

Set up a meeting with your sales team to examine your personas and discuss their wants, needs, and pain points.

Because your sales team is on the front line, interacting with prospects and opportunities, they're the best source to provide insight into what's motivating the contacts in your target accounts. Here are the questions to ask:

>> **What does this persona want?** Think about it from the context of their role. When the contact is an individual contributor, like a marketing coordinator or an IT specialist, they want their manager or director to recognize the work they're doing. When you're targeting a manager or director, they want to streamline processes and operational efficiency to achieve more results without spending more money.

>> **What does this persona need?** This motivation most likely will be tied to a strategic business objective or a company goal. When your persona is

someone in the sales department, he or she needs to hit a revenue goal each month or quarter. Consider how your content speaks to helping with this need.

>> **Which pain or stress does this persona have?** When your persona is a marketing director, you know that the pain they're feeling can stem from needing to contribute to revenue growth. When you're targeting an IT director, their pain can come from too many systems that aren't integrated. When it's a CFO at an early-stage technology company, his or her pain may come from not having enough financial resources to grow the organization.

TIP

Before writing your content, make an outline that asks these questions. List your persona, these three questions, and how your content will address each point to help demonstrate your company's solution.

Personalizing your message

There's so much you can do differently in your content to make it personal. The ultimate goal is to communicate on an individual level with all the contacts who can influence the purchase decision. While this may seem impossible to do on a massive scale, your content depends on personas, so you can address the motivations of the contacts in your target accounts.

Developing a brand identity

The content you create will reinforce an identity for your company. You want your content to demonstrate thought leadership and answer any questions your prospects may have, as this reinforces your position as an expert. This also helps create a brand identity. But building a brand identity is a process. You can't become a thought leader overnight, but you need your prospects and other influencers to recognize your brand.

When you think about a brand, the first things that come to mind are probably design elements: the brand's name, logo, color, and text. While these design elements are essential, when it comes to developing a brand identity with your content, you must think about the words you select. Your brand identity is developed through the content you publish, the events you attend, the advertising campaigns you run that link to content, and every interaction you have with your accounts.

WARNING

Your brand is what other people say about your company. Any negative interaction or detracting comment from a prospect can damage your brand.

TEN CONTENT PERSONALIZATION STATISTICS FROM TRIBLIO

Are you ready to start personalizing your customer's experience along their buyer's journey? The web influences every marketing program. For the first time, marketers can target accounts with web campaigns as easily as they can with email campaigns. Jason Jue (@jasondjue), CMO at Triblio (www.triblio.com) compiled these content personalization tips. Triblio's account-based marketing platform empowers marketers to dynamically personalize messaging and CTAs to specific accounts and personas. With Triblio web campaigns, each visitor can view customized websites, overlay cards, microsites, or content hubs that match their interests. Here are statistics to make the case for content personalization:

- Marketers see an average increase of 20 percent in sales when using personalized web experiences (Monetate).

- Personalized CTAs resulted in a 42 percent higher conversion rate than generic CTAs (HubSpot).

- 76 percent of marketers define real-time marketing as personalizing content in response to customer interactions (Direct Marketing News).

- 84 percent of marketing executives plan on developing a process to map content assets to buyer journey stage (Aberdeen).

- 78 percent of CMOs think custom content is the future of marketing (Demand Metric).

- 81 percent of marketers perceive increases in customer engagement as the main benefit of real-time marketing (DemandGen Report).

- 60 percent say that they struggle to personalize content in real-time, yet 77 percent believe real-time personalization is crucial (Neolane and DMA).

- 82 percent of prospects say content targeted to their industry is more valuable (MarketingSherpa).

- 73 percent of B2B content marketers are producing more content than they did one year ago (Content Marketing Institute).

- 46 percent of marketers cited lack of time as the biggest hurdle to content marketing personalization (The Realtime Report).

There needs to be a plan for your brand's identity. Consider the key adjectives, phrases, and descriptions your prospects would use to describe your company. Ask your customers questions about how they perceive your brand in surveys. This will provide insight into the type of content and activities to build and develop your brand.

Reaching Through Technology

Technology, such as marketing automation platforms and CRM systems, has allowed account-based marketing to be possible. The majority of your content is distributed using digital channels. As you're thinking about the type of content you'll develop for your ABM campaigns, consider how the content will be delivered to the contacts in your target accounts. The pieces of content you're producing, such as webinars and whitepapers, will be hosted in a central hub (your marketing automation platform) for all the "gated" content requiring a form to download.

REMEMBER

Host your original content files on your marketing automation platform. It's synced with your CRM. It's your marketing automation platform that monitors who from your CRM is engaging with the content.

Employing a content strategy

According to the Content Marketing Institute, less than 44 percent of B2B marketers meet daily or weekly (in person or virtually) to discuss the progress of their content marketing program. To succeed with account-based marketing, you need a strategy for distributing your content. Having a strategy will help you effectively use technology to ensure that your content is reaching the right contacts in your account. Think about your strategy with this formula:

```
Strategy = Content + Context + Channel
```

>> **Content:** The marketing piece you're sending. It's a blog post, whitepaper, case study, handwritten note, infographic, video, or whatever medium that you've selected for your message and creative graphics.

>> **Context:** The time and situation when you send content. For account-based marketing, the context depends on the stage of the account's journey. Your content will change according to who you're talking to, where they are in the purchase decision, and the context around the account.

>> **Channel:** All the ways you can distribute content and connect with your accounts. The channels include digital methods (such as email, social media, downloading content from forms, and advertisements) and more traditional channels (such as direct mail and phone calls).

You will use a strategy to surround an account with your content, at different times, and across various channels. Surrounding all the right contacts in an account with your message creates a halo effect. To engage all of the influencers in the purchase decision, you run different campaigns across multiple channels. Here are a few technology platforms which help with employing your content strategy:

>> **Uberflip** (`www.uberflip.com`): Uberflip's software that helps marketers create, manage and optimize content experiences at every stage of the buyer journey. The platform puts your marketing team in control of a content Hub equipped with the tools you need to manage content, generate leads, and optimize the entire experience. You can aggregate all your content and easily organize it into Custom Streams tailored for specific buyer personas, topics, events, even prospects, then using Smart Filters and Scheduled Tasks you can automate curation and publishing to serve up the right content experience to your contacts at the right time.

>> **SnapApp** (`www.snapapp.com`): SnapApp's interactive content marketing platform gives you everything you need to create, publish, manage, and measure compelling audience experiences. SnapApp is a powerful, easy-to-use drag-and-drop interface gives you the flexibility to create distinctive, on-brand custom content experiences. SnapApp features templates, asset libraries, design tools, and global account settings to speed your time-to-market while allowing for complete brand control. You can quickly plan, create, optimize, and publish interactive content without the need for internal or external development resources.

>> **Triblio** (`http://triblio.com`): The web influences every marketing program. For the first time, marketers can target accounts with web campaigns as easily as they can with email campaigns. Triblio's account-based marketing platform empowers marketers to dynamically personalize messaging and CTAs to specific accounts and personas. With Triblio web campaigns, each visitor can view customized websites, overlay cards, microsites, or content hubs that match their interests.

WARNING

If you're asking for budget approval to invest in technology to develop content for account–based marketing, make sure your executive stakeholders recognize that publishing more content will not automatically generate more revenue. It helps with nurturing contacts throughout the account's journey.

What does equal more revenue? How can we scale and do more personalization with the same content?

The call to action (CTA) must be different. Don't serve up a demo advertisement when they're in the negotiation stage. When you're doing personalization, it doesn't have to be based on one technology. Within each of these strategies, you will use different tools to help create velocity and drive awareness, interest, and engagement with the contacts in your target accounts. Throughout the process, your job is to make sure you're distributing content to the right people in the account.

REMEMBER

Content needs to be packaged and delivered to contacts in accounts based on stage. Keep your strategy simple. You can't control how people will find you.

When you think about the status of an account, you're thinking about the context. Many interesting things can happen when you think about context.

Because you have accounts that are all in different parts of the purchase decision, there is a different context for each account. By context, I mean the event(s) that impact the status of the account. You contacts in the account can have different context, especially when it's a larger company.

REMEMBER

For all of your named accounts on your Tier A, B, or C list, there will be different context.

There is always a context around the account. In a perfect world, your contacts in the account would say, "We want to do business with you!" But that's just a dream. A specific event will trigger the progression to the next stage of the account's journey.

REMEMBER

The context is important for communicating with your account. Your marketing communications, content, and activities shouldn't just be general, or "blanket," messaging. It should be highly personalized, based on the context. Here are types of situations to consider for the context.

>> **Qualification:** The content you send to a new account who meets your ICP for the right company size and industry.

>> **Big news:** When one of your targeted accounts publishes a fundraising announcement or other press release with a major announcement.

>> **Events:** In-person (such as conferences and tradeshows) or online events (such as webinars and virtual summits). Depending on the timing, there will be different context, such as an attender who came to the event, pre-event registered, or post-event (they registered, but they didn't attend or you didn't have the opportunity to meet them).

>> **Event sponsor:** They may be sponsoring an event that's in your *ecosystem* (the industry or vertical with accounts you're targeting). You sponsor the event for the chance to get in front of your targeted contacts.

>> **Job change:** Alert from LinkedIn that a contact in your account has been promoted.

>> **Article:** You saw one of your accounts in an interview or profile.

TIP

Setting up a Google Alert (www.google.com/alerts) will alert you of any news or media pertaining to your target account. When the company publishes a press release or is featured in a publication, this will pop up in your Google Alert. Whenever there's news, the salesperson who owns the account should reach out.

Delivering content on the right channel

A combination of content and activities will be needed to create velocity for accounts. By publishing content across various channels, and running multiple campaigns, you can create energy and awareness for your targeted contacts. But it's important to know whether these are the right channels to use for connecting with your contacts.

REMEMBER

Your content is only as good as the people who read it. Find new ways to repurpose your content, or to redistribute it on new channels.

Cross-promoting your content

You'll invest a ton of work in creating valuable content. One way to expand the reach of getting your content in front of the right people is to have a cross-promotion strategy.

TIP

Think about it this way: If you're hosting a fancy party, you'll invite a group of people with a formal invitation, but then you will follow up with them individually. When you see Bob at work, you'll ask him whether he's coming to your party, and he'll reply with "Oh, right, I need to RSVP."

A cross-promotion strategy works the same way. When you're trying to engage a new contact in an account, and you invited them to attend an event and they didn't respond, you follow up with an email. Or, when you just published a blog post, you can't just hope people will read it. Hope isn't a strategy. Your content can reach a wider audience by cross promoting across multiple channels. Here are ways you can cross promote your content.

>> **Social media:** You can use social media to share your latest content, such as a new whitepaper or blog. When you've just published new content, you should post a link to this content on social media channels, such as Facebook, Twitter,

and LinkedIn, for your followers to see and read. Also, the "feeds" from Twitter can be integrated into your company's blog through plugins for WordPress.

>> **Blog posts:** When you publish a new case study, whitepaper, or ebook, write a blog post with an excerpt of this content. Include a CTA on your blog post to download the longer piece of content.

>> **Ask customers to share:** When you've interviewed a customer for a case study or video testimonial, and you've just published this to your website, send the link to your customer you interviewed. Ask him or her to share it on social media, or internally with their company.

>> **Ask thought leaders to share:** When you interview a thought leader or industry analyst for your latest whitepaper, ebook, or blog post, send them a link to the content and ask them to share it on social media. If they have a blog, ask whether you can publish an excerpt on their blog as well then cross-promote that link.

>> **Webinar replays:** After a webinar, turn the recording into a video, and publish the webinar's slides on a landing page to download, or on a public-facing site, such as SlideShare (`www.slideshare.net`). Send an email to your webinar registrants and attendees to download the slides and replay the recording. Also, post links to these assets on social media.

>> **Infographic:** Copy the images from your infographics into Microsoft PowerPoint to create a slide deck. These slides can be used for a webinar, a presentation for a sales account executive, or uploaded to SlideShare for people to download. You can also link to the original infographic. so your contacts can see it in different versions.

>> **Monthly newsletter:** Every month, send an email newsletter, featuring multiple pieces of content. Include a recent blog post, your newest piece of long-form content, or a link to reply a webinar. This is a great way to aggregate all of your latest content and email it to contacts in your targeted accounts.

Measuring your content's effectiveness

The formula for our content strategy is `Context + Content + Channel`. To determine whether your content was effective, you must measure the results. You must measure the success of your content and activities across the different stages of the account's journey. Based on the content, here are questions to ask to determine whether your content was effective:

>> Did the whitepaper, ebook, or case study you sent to a prospect advance the account to the next stage (getting the account on a demo or creating an opportunity)?

>> If you sent a direct mail campaign, did they receive your mailing and acknowledge it (replying to your follow up call or email)?

>> If you launched an advertising campaign, did you reach contacts in your targeted accounts? If so, how many impressions did you get? How many clicks did you receive from your contacts?

REMEMBER

Who you're talking to matters. The whole point of cross-promoting your content is to reach your targeted audience.

Think about how your core content can be delivered in different ways for consumption. You'll discover which platforms are most effective for distributing content, based on the number of downloads (tracked in your CRM) and the number of clicks.

DID YOU END UP ON A BLACKLIST?

Every quarter, check your mail server IP address to determine whether you're on any blacklists. You can check with a tool like MX Lookup (http://mxtoolbox.com/blacklists.aspx) or EmailOnAcid (www.emailonacid.com/spam-testing).

You can prevent being on a blacklist by setting up a *sender policy framework* (SPF) and *domain-keys identified mail* (DKIM). Your SPF and DKIM may be fine, but if a company thinks your emails are unsolicited, phishy, or spammy, they may report you as spam to a company-wide or public email service provider. Ask your IT network administrator to make this change in your DNS record. Also, email opt-in and smart cadences in your marketing automation system are tools to help prevent you from getting blacklisted.

Chapter 14

Executing ABM: A Playbook

S ales velocity is created when you're engaging accounts on their own terms, or the right channels. You develop content and messaging for advertising campaigns to surround the contacts in the account, moving them further through the buyer's journey to becoming your customers.

You need a specific strategy for each account. Depending on the stage of the purchase decision that the account is in, different activities and tactics are needed. The message and activities to generate velocity are different for new accounts and late-stage opportunities. Because account-based marketing is narrowing the scope to focus on only your best-fit accounts, having a personalized plan for the contacts in the account will help your sales team grow more revenue, and at a faster pace.

In this chapter, I break down the steps, activities, and strategies to engage your target list of account. I list strategies to execute ABM at scale, based on the stage of the account's journey. I tell you how to strategize your efforts and assign tasks to each of your sales and marketing ("smarketing") team members. By having a playbook with different plays for your "smarketing" team to run, you can win more new revenue.

Centering a Strategy

I'm a graduate of the University of Alabama. I earned my master's degree there, but that's a story for another time. However, I'd be remiss if I didn't use a football analogy. The best football teams have both great talent and brilliant coaches. Think about it this way: You're watching a football game and the offense takes the field. As the offense is in the huddle, they're confirming what play they should run to try to score a touchdown.

Your "smarketing" team can resemble a football team. Here's the lineup of who should be on your team:

>> **Business/sales development representatives (BDR/SDRs):** These individuals are responsible for identifying the target accounts, which are obtained through a variety of inbound and outbound activities.

>> **Sales database administrator:** The guru who is tasked with updating all the contact and account information in your CRM.

>> **Marketing operations/technology manager:** Someone to manage your marketing automation system, ensure that it's synced correctly with your CRM, and align it with content. This role may also manage your targeted advertising or sponsored social media campaigns.

>> **Content manager:** This person (or your marketing manager) is responsible for collaborating with the team to develop creative content, ideas for campaigns, and personalized messaging to a target audience on the right channels. This role could handle advertising and sponsored social media posts, depending on the size of your company.

>> **Account executive (AE):** The salesperson who owns the account after it's qualified by sales. The account executive ultimately closes the deal and brings on new accounts. In smaller B2B companies, an AE also may be responsible for renewing contracts or service agreements for accounts.

>> **Account manager:** In some large enterprise organizations, the account manager is tasked with landing new sales opportunities and upselling or cross-selling in the account to generate even more revenue.

>> **Sales leader:** The Sales Manager or Director running the sales department. The sales leader owns the targeted list of accounts, tiered by accounts they want to close in the next 30, 60, or 90 days.

>> **Customer success manager (CSM):** Owns customer accounts to help turn contacts in accounts into customer advocates.

>> **Executive stakeholder(s):** The leadership at your organization; depending on your size, either the CMO, VP of Sales, or CEO.

Furthering the football analogy, on a football team there are many players who can play certain positions. Some players are better in one role than another. Your "smarketing" team is very similar. Here are the roles your team should play with account–based marketing:

>> **Head coach:** The executive stakeholder calls the shots. Your CMO, VP of Sales, or Chief "Smarketing" Officer decides plays for "smarketing" to execute, based on the stage in the account's purchase decision.

>> **Quarterback:** A good quarterback listens, communicates, and is in sync with the coach. But the quarterback has control because he's the team's leader on the field. In the same way, while the executive stakeholder calls the shots, the Sales Leader must lead the team and score deals. A good Sales Leader anchors and empowers the team to win.

>> **Backfield:** The same way a wide receiver or running back must get the ball down the field, it's the account executive who must score. The account executive is out there trying to close revenue. Either it's a long way to score (like a new account that was just identified and qualified) or a short sprint (to quickly close an opportunity account that's ready to buy).

>> **Offensive linemen:** The offensive linemen help the team move forward by being the brute force. With selling into accounts, the BDR/SDRs are warming up accounts, getting yardage with outbound marketing, and assisting the account executives in setting appointments.

>> **Assistant coaches:** Marketing is the eye in the sky. The marketing team can see the big picture of everything happening on the field. It's the marketing team that is responsible for content, activities, and communication, which provide coverage for sales to score. Like how a coach and quarterback discuss plays with assistant coaches, marketing works with the sales leadership and team members on plays to run to close deals.

>> **Defense:** Customer success keeps the team in the lead. You don't want to take points off the scoreboard. Your customer success team keeps accounts happy to keep revenue coming in.

Customer success can score, too. In some B2B organizations, the CSM is responsible for renewing contracts, and upsells or sells upgrades of the latest version of the product.

REMEMBER

Analogies aside, it's about knowing who on your "smarketing" team will be responsible for which roles and activities in the account's journey.

Listing your accounts

Your universe of accounts is in the hundreds or thousands, depending on market size. With so much data in your CRM, your sales team needs a list of accounts. Having this list helps your entire salesforce, from your executive stakeholders down to the SDRs. When you have a list of accounts that is consistently updated, it helps your entire sales organization get laser-focused on closing the best-fit customers.

Your accounts will be in one of the following stages of the buyer's journey:

>> **New/prospect:** They're starting either as a new account from either inbound or outbound marketing activities.

>> **Marketing qualified account (MQA):** A marketing qualified account that meets your ICP criteria and is being prospected to by an SDR.

>> **Sales Qualified Account (SQA):** Meets BANT criteria demonstrating intent (see Chapter 7). The SQA has been transferred to an account executive.

>> **Opportunity:** The SQA has seen a product demo, and has expressed interest to purchase from your company. This becomes a revenue opportunity, designated with a monetary value in your CRM.

TIP

The sales team should create a list of accounts targeted to close within the next 30 days, 30 to 60 days, and 60 days or more.

You can't give every account an endless amount of love and attention. It's important to prioritize your accounts based on their likelihood to close and become customers. Here is how you should prioritize your account list.

>> **High priority (targeted close within 30 days):** These are opportunity accounts for sales which high velocity is needed with lots of marketing activity. Your "smarketing" team should be doing everything you can to close these accounts.

>> **Medium priority (targeted close in 30 to 60 days):** These are opportunities or sales qualified accounts, depending on your typical sales cycle. These accounts should be receiving nurturing emails, direct mail, and invitations to events.

>> **Low priority (targeted to close in 60+ days):** Qualified accounts that the sales team hopes to close this quarter. These are early-stage opportunities that may have just received pricing and told the sales account executive they need more time to make a decision.

TIP

Keep these low-priority accounts in nurturing campaigns to continue receiving new content, such as a monthly email newsletter.

REMEMBER

To "scale," or expand the reach of your account-based marketing campaigns, you need to focus on accounts that represent the biggest revenue potential. For the sales team, this means having a list of Tier A, B, and C accounts, based on their best fit in your ICP and likelihood to close.

Progressing accounts to the next stage

The account's journey is based on progression across stages. Within each of these stages, you will use a combination of tactics and activities to help your accounts pass to the next stage of the account's journey. To move an account into the next stage of the buyer's journey, you will need to create velocity for sales.

REMEMBER

The formula for velocity = `distance/time`. The goal with account-based marketing is to get more revenue by focusing on your target accounts, so velocity is needed to move accounts through the purchase decision faster. However, not all of the contacts your sales development team connects with will be ready to move forward in the buyer's journey.

REMEMBER

BANT stands for *budget, authority, need*, and *timeline.* It is specific to a person. It's qualification used by a salesperson when talking to the prospect. If the contact meets BANT, matches one of your personas, and is part of an account that's within your ICP, then it's a best-fit for your business.

During the purchase decision, things don't always go your way. You may have thought there was BANT, only to learn later that there was no budget, even if your contact previously said there was during the sales qualification process. Accounts will fall out of the buyer's journey for a number of different reasons. Here are scenarios to consider:

>> **New account through inbound or outbound marketing:** The account may have downloaded a paper and started the education process for making a purchase decision. The SDR tried reaching out to the account and got a reply that "Sorry, it isn't the right time."

>> **Qualified prospect with no BANT**: The account isn't ready to buy. They're a good fit within your ICP, but they don't see the value in your product. . .yet. Your "smarketing" team can't control the budget or authority, but you can help generate demand in the account.

>> **Closed/lost**: The account became an opportunity, but the deal was lost after the opportunity was created. The sales account executive went through the whole process of trying to close the account, and may have lost the deal for a variety of reasons: not ready to buy, not the right fit, or lost the deal to a competitor.

Document the reason you think you lost the deal in your CRM. It's important to keep detailed notes on your accounts, especially qualified accounts that didn't have BANT.

Even though the account wasn't ready to progress to the next stage, the nurturing process should continue. Send them a personal note, either handwritten or email, thanking your contact for considering your solution.

A "Sorry we couldn't make this happen now" email leaves the door open for a conversation at a later date. Just because an account didn't move forward now doesn't mean marketing should stop. There are a number of ways to continuing nurturing accounts that are stagnant or fell out of your sales pipeline. Here are ways to continue nurturing accounts:

>> **Personalized emails:** When your company has released a new version of your product or service, send a note highlighting these product features. The copy in your email could be, "We just released this new upgrade and would love for you to take another look," or "We hope to win your business one day."

>> **Sharing your buzz:** When your company just announced big news, such as a funding announcements or a press release with a strategic partnership, send an email with a link to this buzz to generate interest.

>> **Monthly newsletter:** Keep these accounts on a list to receive your email newsletter. This newsletter should include your latest content, such as a new customer case study, whitepaper, or recent blog post.

>> **Check-in:** Set a task reminder in your CRM to follow up with these accounts every three to six months. Send an email checking in to see whether now is the right time to reconnect.

Don't send product-related content. At this point, it should be education about the problem your company helps solve.

You need to be knowledgeable of all the accounts in this "limbo" stage. One way to do this is to set up alerts in your CRM and marketing automation system. These will trigger when contacts in your accounts engage in different marketing activities.

When your company targets large, enterprise accounts, the sales team may need to go through a request for proposal (RFP) process. In an RFP, you must talk about a feature matrix. This helps your buyers compare different solutions. You must check boxes in the RFP to explain what your solution does, but that isn't how people close deals.

But here's a secret: 90 percent of the time, the buyer knows that most of the features are the same. They choose a solution because of the experience they had during the sales process. It's about the relationship the sales account executive built, and the content your team used to tell the right story and sell the dream to close the deal.

Planning your tactics and activities

In this section, I discuss the content and activities for each stage to help progress your accounts faster through the buyer's journey. Each of these different stages requires different content, especially the further you get down the account's journey. Using my sports analogy, these are plays for your ABM playbook.

Before I get into the use cases, let's talk about all the different strategies. As a modern "smarketing" professional, there are many strategies and tactics you do every day. There are glorious situations where an account executive hangs up after a demo, and then an hour later receives a call from a prospect stating they're ready to buy. This happens when your sales process is transactional in nature and doesn't require a lengthy contract. When they're ready to buy, it's going to happen.

The flow from prospect to customer can happen so fast that you don't need to employ a comprehensive strategy. But these situations are rare for major B2B purchases, so you need to build a comprehensive ABM playbook. This playbook will include different tactics with different activities and content for the stages of the account's journey. All of your accounts will fit into one of these strategies, depending on where they are in the purchase decision.

When your company sells to marketers, this requires more creative content, because marketing departments are always looking for the next new and innovative tactic. When you sell to IT professionals, the strategy you use to reach accounts will rely mostly on email, because most IT pros don't want to talk in person. They need to engage in free trials or hear from their peers about what works, so emailing case studies and video testimonials from users within that community will be effective.

When you're selling to C-level executives in enterprise accounts, you need to host more in-person events, such as a dinner in a major city. When you're selling to SMBs, you should host an event in a city that's conducive for thousands of attendees to attend. This all depends on the size of your organization and processes. The following playbook is an outline for the activities needed for each of these stages.

The stages I will give you plays for are

>> **Demand Generation:** Prospects into qualified accounts.

>> **Pipeline Velocity:** Qualified accounts into opportunities.

>> **Sales Velocity:** Opportunities into customers.

>> **Advocate Marketing:** Customers into advocates.

Demand generation: Prospects into qualified accounts

This is the start of the account's journey with your company. Somehow, an account found your company and identified themselves as interested in your company, your content, or both.

REMEMBER

A prospect came in via inbound or outbound marketing activities.

Here are scenarios where a new contact came in through inbound:

>> **Website visitor:** A contact came to your website, either through organic search or by clicking on a link from an advertising campaign.

>> **Form completion:** The contact completed a form to download a piece of content from your Resources Library, or registered for one of your upcoming in-person events or webinars.

>> **Met at an event:** A new contact your company connected with at a tradeshow when they walked up to your booth.

>> **Referral:** The contact came from such as a customer, industry partner, or vendor.

>> **Requested a demo:** The contact came to your website and completed a form to request a demo with your sales team. they're demonstrating strong intent by requesting a demo.

REMEMBER

When a new account demonstrates intent, it's worth giving more effort with high-tech/high-touch activities. Your sales development team should make these accounts who requested a demo a top priority; that shows intent to purchase a solution like one your company provides.

TECHNICAL STUFF

Whenever one of these inbound activities takes place, the new contact is added to your CRM and marketing automation system (if these platforms are properly integrated). Your SDR team should automatically receive an alert. The account was automatically added to your CRM. The account is created in your CRM when a new contact comes in by completing demo request form, downloading content from a gated landing page, or visiting your website.

For an outbound prospect: The account already is in your CRM. It's a process of prospecting with your SDR team. This is a "named" account that you're now targeting. The SDR must generate demand in the account, going from a "warm" to "hot" prospect who has demonstrated that he or she is interested in your product or service.

>> **The goal:** You want the best-fit accounts to connect with an SDR and set an appointment for sales. The account then gets on a discovery call, demo, or both (depending on your company's sales process).

>> **The questions:** Does the account meet ICP and persona criteria? Are they ready to move forward in the account's journey?

>> **The strategies:** At this stage, the SDR wants to show that your company understands that there is an industry-wide problem, and that your company can help solve the problem. It's about demonstrating your value proposition to the prospect.

>> **The activities:** The SDR is the key player who qualifies the account to ensure that it's the right fit.

An SDR should look at the account's information that your company uses for defining your ICP and personas, such as

- Industry
- Company size
- Department
- Job title/seniority

When the account meets qualification criteria showing it's a fit, the SDR reaches out to schedule an appointment for sales through a series of actions:

- A cadence of calls/emails sending content to warm up the account
- Adding to drip/nurture campaign for emails and webinar invitations
- Updating the status of the account in your CRM to be added to a targeted advertising campaign

REMEMBER

High-velocity accounts request a demo and are qualified by an SDR as a good fit with your ICP and personas.

When an account has expressed interest in receiving a demo, they've demonstrated intent that they're looking to purchase a solution like what your company offers. At this point, the sales team should be focused on this account to turn it into an opportunity as quickly as possible. When a request demo form comes through, the SDR needs to follow up immediately.

TIP

When you examine your closed accounts by source in your CRM, the accounts who had contacts that initially completed a demo request form should have a higher Closed/Won rate.

WARNING

When an account comes in from a content download or lands on your website, they have shown interest in the subject, but not necessarily in your company. The content your company has shared got the contact interested, but they may not yet have realized they need your company's solution.

However good or beneficial your company's product or service is, if the contact doesn't see the *value* of using your solution, they won't buy. The next steps should be to nurture the account and get them engaged. How does an SDR get them to engage with content to start a conversation?

TIP

Keep these accounts in nurture programs, such as email drips, launching targeted advertising campaigns, sending new content, a monthly email newsletter, or direct mailing the key contacts in the account. They're qualified accounts that just aren't ready to buy now.

For accounts that aren't ready to move forward with a demo, the next step is to get them engaged through more content and activities. The SDR has added them to a drip/nurture email campaign to continue receiving content. Using marketing automation, you can see the activity in the account and track which content your contacts engage with. In your CRM, the SDR can set alerts for these accounts; when new activity or engagement occurs; the sales team will be notified and can reach out to the account.

TIP

Create campaigns based on how long prospects have been in your CRM and haven't moved forward. These campaigns will depend on how long it's been in your CRM and the SDR has been unable to connect. Examples include

>> **Warming up:** A new account added within the last 30 days.

>> **Reviving:** An account that downloaded content, then didn't progress.

>> **Waking the dead:** 90 days or longer without progressing to a demo.

Pipeline velocity: Qualified accounts into opportunities

The account has been handed off by the SDR to a sales account executive. A demo has been scheduled by the SDR. The account has been through a discovery call or a product demo with the sales team. The account executive is working 1-on-1 with the contact who initially came into the account.

TIP

Before the demo, the AE should send over a piece of content via email. This email should be along the lines of "Hi (name), I'm looking forward to our demo (time or tomorrow). Before we get on a call, I wanted to share this recent (content, such as case study, blog post, or whitepaper). It discusses (relevant topic), which you might find useful. Please let me know your thoughts, and whether you have any questions before our call."

WARNING

Your sales account executive must nail a demo. An awkward discovery call, or a bad demo where the tour of your product or service isn't working properly, will leave the deal dead in the water.

REMEMBER

Don't ask dumb questions like "What is your job title?" There's LinkedIn, and a bevy of other sources of information about every prospect available on the internet and through data providers.

You need to maximize this time together. A good AE does his or her homework to research the account on LinkedIn, finding them on Twitter, and making them feel like VIPs who deserve special attention.

Your sales team is trying to do account-based marketing at scale to reach hundreds or thousands of contacts, but in that moment, connecting on a call with a prospect, the sales rep needs to make the contact feel like the one and only account he or she is working with. Nailing a demo means having a good conversation that makes your contact feel like they got something out of their time. The time they gave you is an investment, so you need to make sure they learned something new or saw the value in your company.

TIP

Focus on the goals of the contact you're talking to. At the beginning of the first discovery call or demo, ask the contact such questions as

>> What's your goal for this call?

>> What's your goal for this product?

>> Why is it important for us to connect today?

The 30 minutes you took for this demo are valuable. Let them know you appreciate it and want to learn how you can help.

REMEMBER

They may have no interest in seeing the product, but are more interested in understanding your solution. They want to learn more about options, but aren't ready to buy. Giving them what they want in this stage of the experience is important to start establishing the relationship with the account.

TIP

Send a recording of the demo to your contact to replay at their convenience. If you're using a platform like GoToMeeting or WebEx, there is functionality to record the conversation. A recorded demo also lets your prospects show it to the other contacts in the account.

For a qualified account to move forward to an opportunity, there must be a demonstration of intent to purchase. At this point, there are two scenarios for moving forward:

>> **BANT:** The account meets BANT (or other criteria set by your sales team to identify whether the account is ready for the next stage). The contact has asked for pricing, details about using the platform, or terms of service.

>> **No BANT:** The account is ready to buy. The contact your AE is working with specifically said they aren't ready or may have "gone dark" and not responded after the discovery call or demo.

REMEMBER

Because account-based marketing requires your sales team to be laser-focused on a targeted list of accounts, you don't want your account executives to waste time working on an account that isn't ready to progress into an opportunity. ABM requires you to think both strategically and tactically about how to move more accounts faster through the buyer's journey. Think about it this way:

>> **Goal:** Advance qualified accounts further in the purchase decision.

>> **Questions:** Is the account ready to move forward to an opportunity? Who else needs to get involved within the account?

>> **Strategies:** The account executive wants to show that your company understands the pain your account is experiencing, and how your company solves that problem. It's about reiterating your value proposition by providing proof; this comes from multiple sources.

>> **Activities:** The sales team should identify all the relevant decision makers in the account. All of these decision makers are contacts who will need to be engaged with content and marketing activities.

REMEMBER

You're likely to find the most success in this stage of the pipeline, because of the ability to reach the accounts on the channel most relevant to them. As a result, you can see an increase in both engagement and pipeline velocity to accelerate the account into an opportunity.

When the account meets BANT criteria and has asked for pricing, then the sales account executive should ask the account "Who all do we need to get involved at this point?" This will help provide clarity on who these contacts are, and they should be added to your CRM if they don't already exist as a contact record.

After ensuring all the appropriate contacts are added to the account, the "smarketing" team should have a plan to engage these contacts to create more pipeline velocity. It's the combination of activities that will help the account progress into a significant revenue opportunity. The types of content provided at this stage include

>> Whitepapers

>> Customer case studies

>> Video testimonials

>> Webinars (invitations to new ones)

REMEMBER

The content should align with the personas of each contact. You shouldn't send a whitepaper written for C-level executives to an administrator or coordinator, or share a case study written for an IT manager to a marketing director. The content should speak to each of your contacts.

It's hard to create content for every single persona. Think about it by department (what's in it for your business unit) and the role you're selling to and the content you need for them. Read more about this in Chapter 13.

TIP

Create a one-pager or strategic document about the account's problems, and how they can be solved by working with your company. This can be as simple as outlining in an email what the problems your contact said they have, and the types of solutions your company offers for those individual problems.

This one-page document/email can be sent to the other decision makers in the account. It gives everyone in the account involved in the purchase decision a picture of why your company would be a good partner to work with. It also helps build trust and establish a relationship with the account. These activities are important, because they demonstrate that the salesperson recognizes the individual problems of the account instead of lumping the account into a generic sales process.

Sales velocity: Opportunities into customers

After you've turned the qualified account into a viable revenue opportunity, it's time to begin the "smarketing" process. This is when sales and marketing work together to drive as much engagement with all the contacts in an account. It's this engagement that helps all the decision makers see the value of doing business with your company.

The sales team should gather as much information about how the need to approach the contacts in the account. This type of information includes

>> Which problems will we solve for our potential customer?

>> Which version of our product/service will they use?

>> Who will be the end user(s) in the account?

>> Which features are most useful?

Knowing the answers to these questions will help provide your marketing team with context. It's this context that will dictate which type of content should be sent to each contact.

REMEMBER

The formula for using a content strategy to help create velocity is

```
Strategy = Content + Context + Contact + Channel
```

Your comprehensive account-based marketing strategy means reaching all the decision-makers in the account with your message. It's this personalized strategy of content and activities for each decision maker that will help you generate revenue from new customers.

>> **Goal:** Turn the revenue opportunity into a new customer.

>> **Question:** Which activities are needed to move the opportunity to the next stage of the account's journey?

>> **Strategy:** Your "smarketing" team is aligned to accelerate the account to become a customer as quickly as possible.

>> **Activities:** the "smarketing" team will use a combination of content, events, direct mail, advertising, and whichever channels the contacts in your account is most active to create velocity. It's about using all the weapons in your "smarketing" artillery to win business.

REMEMBER

You must prioritize your opportunities on the targeted close date. high-priority opportunities are targeted to close in 30 days. Medium priority accounts are targeted close in 30 to 60 days. Low-priority opportunities are targeted to close in 60+ days.

Through prioritizing your opportunities, your "smarketing" team can better focus on a game plan of activities and content to help create more velocity. The combination of activities will be low/high technology and low/high touch. This combination of activities adds another level of personalization Examples of these strategies include

>> End user: "How to" content, such as implementation guides and checklists, help educate your contact and get them ramped up.

>> Manager: Case studies showing how your customers were successful in solving different problems, thanks to your company.

>> Director or influencer: Competitive analysis showing why your features/solution is better than hiring another vendor or sticking with the status quo.

>> Executive stakeholder: An ROI proof statement demonstrating the return their company will see by doing business with you.

REMEMBER

The more activities you can engage these qualified accounts in, the more velocity you'll generate. It's this velocity from activities that moves accounts further in the sales process of the account's journey to becoming a customer.

So how can you create more velocity?

TIP

Launch advertising targeted to these contacts, with links to download this content. Even when the contacts don't click on the ad to get the content, they see your brand's logo and message. Impressions are a success metric for account-based marketing.

These are examples that will help create velocity and drive the account toward making a purchase decision with your company. The next steps in the opportunity stage toward to a Closed/Won deal are

>> **Evaluation:** The account is evaluating your company's features, platform, terms of service, contract, and other details to decide whether they should try to do business with you.

>> **Negotiation:** A decision-maker in the account has come back to the sales account executive to negotiate the terms of the contract or service agreement.

>> **Review:** A contract or purchase order has been delivered. The account is in the final stage of determining whether they will buy.

The opportunity stage brings the account to the end of the buyer's journey. Either you won a new customer, marking this account as Closed/Won in your CRM, or the deal didn't come through and the account is marked as Closed/Lost.

Advocate marketing: Customers into advocates

The account's journey is just getting started when they've agreed to become your customer. Remembering that rule that 80 percent of your revenue comes from 20 percent of your customer base, account-based marketing is about retaining your best-fit customers you worked so hard to acquire, and turning those customers into advocates. The value of having customer advocates is to use them for organic, word-of-mouth marketing, so they promote your business in an authentic way. Word of mouth is the most valuable, and most often overlooked, marketing tool.

You can turn your customers into advocates by continuing to engage them, treating your end-users and their higher-ups as if they're still prospects and decision-makers:

>> **Goal:** Turn your customers into advocates for your company.

>> **Questions:** Who is the customer in the account to develop into an advocate for our company? What's the use case for this customer, and how can we ensure they're successful? How can we take the account beyond the buyer's journey, and ensure that their customer experience is the best one they can possibly have?

>> **Strategies:** Adoption of your product or service is critical at this stage. The customer must go through a successful implementation, getting ramped up to learn how to use the product/service they just purchased. By making sure that your customers are experts on your product, you'll see higher usage rates and customer retention.

>> **Activities:** Your marketing team supports customer success by providing training content. This content includes

- In-person workshops and training

- Digital training from webinars and video tutorials

- "How to" resources such as checklists and step-by-step guides

- Events, such as user conferences, to learn from their peers

These are just a few ways to make sure that your customers are always comfortable using your product, which leads to them raving about your product to others. I discuss the importance of customer advocacy, and how to turn your customers into advocates, in Part 5.

Coordinating Your Efforts

Account-based marketing is a coordinated effort between sales and marketing, your "smarketing" team, to close the best-fit accounts for your business. Teamwork makes the dream work, right? This is even a book by John C. Maxwell with the same title. It couldn't be more true. The "smarketing" team members each have an individual role and responsibilities for driving more revenue for your company. Together, as a team, you work together to hit your revenue goals.

There's a difference between "feel good" marketing and "make money" marketing. There are activities that can make someone inside your company "feel good," such as listening to your CEO's idea for your next webinar. It might be a great idea, and you should listen to your CEO because it's the right thing to do, but he or she may be out of the loop on the accounts that are on your Tier A target list to close within the next 30 days. When you execute this webinar idea, will it help you hit your goal?

As you're coordinating your efforts, think about "make money" marketing. Which activities should your "smarketing" team focus on to progress accounts faster through the buyer's journey and generate more sales revenue? Think about this from an account-based perspective for each of your target prospect, qualified, and opportunity accounts across the various stages. You need to coordinate activities, based on personas and stages, to ensure you're executing the right tactics at the right time.

Strategizing your content

Having a strategy is crucial for content marketing. As a marketer, a point of frustration for me is when I ask other marketers about their success rates with content. They say, "We sent an email with a webinar invitation to our whole database, and it had a 2 percent open rate, so we had 200 people attend that webinar." You had 200 people register for your webinar, but who are those contacts? Are they a prospect? Have they been qualified as a good fit for your company? Currently, are any of these opportunities? It sounds great when your CMO tells your CEO, "We had 200 people register for our webinar," but will any of those 200 people ever pay your company a dime?

REMEMBER

If you're fully committing to account-based marketing, your generic email blasts should stop. If you're doing a drip email program that isn't segmented (based on industry, persona, or stage in the sales cycle) then it must stop, too. That's "spray and pray" marketing.

As a marketer, you must put yourself in your persona's shoes and ask "What matters to me?" and "What am I trying to do at my job to be successful?"

Asking these questions helps you think strategically about the content you offer to accelerate accounts faster through the buyer's journey. Think about which content you can present, and when, to create velocity. Having a strategy place helps create a full story with a beginning, middle, and end for your content and activities. At a high-level, here are categories of content to offer based on the stage in the account's journey:

>> **New prospect:** Emails from an SDR with links to blog posts, ebooks, whitepapers, infographics, and invitations to webinars or large in-person events, such as tradeshows and conferences.

>> **Qualified account:** Case studies and video testimonials from your customers. This content should be based on which industry your target accounts are in. Continue inviting contacts to webinars and events. If they've gone through a demo, send this recording to replay.

>> **Opportunity:** The end user should receive "how to" content. The executive stakeholders and/or decision-maker should get the case studies, ROI, or competitive analysis. Direct mail can be used here to send personalized notes or gifts directly to their office.

>> **Customer**: Implementation guides, checklists, video tutorials, in-person training workshops and digital training webinars. Host events in different cities where your customers are based and an annual user conference.

Launching advertising campaigns

Advertising is one channel to use throughout every stage of the account's journey. Using an account-based marketing platform lets you target contacts in your target accounts based on their stage and individual personas. Advertising your message on digital channels, such as mobile, social, display and video, creates a "halo effect" around your target accounts. Running advertising campaigns makes your message even more impactful, and generates velocity for sales.

Each of your campaigns should have a specific message and goal. The campaigns also should link to a landing page with a piece of content or message specific to where they are in the account's journey. These are the goals for each of your advertising campaigns, based on the stage:

>> **New prospect:** Create awareness and set an appointment with sales. Use ads that link to content such as a blog post or infographic.

>> **Qualified account:** Move the account to an opportunity. Use ads that link to content, such as a case study or video testimonial.

>> **Opportunity:** Get the account to make a purchase. Content here includes an ROI or video testimonial from your customer.

>> **Customer**: Surround your clients with your message to reinforce them as brand advocates. Link to your newest video tutorial or invitation to your next customer event.

REMEMBER

You'll measure the success of your advertising campaigns by the number of impressions for contacts in your target accounts, and the number of clicks your ads received.

WARNING

Check your CTAs for all of your content in advertising. You need to be sure you're driving contacts to the correct landing page to download the right piece of content.

Assigning "smarketing" tasks

Coordinating your efforts means designating responsibilities to each of your "smarketing" team members. As you scale your account-based marketing efforts, there will be dozens, hundreds, or even thousands of accounts across various stages of your buyer's journey. Each of your "smarketing" team members will have a lot going on every day, so it's important to know who is responsible for each individual task.

TIP

Using your CRM, you can set tasks and reminders for the sales development and sales account executives.

However, your marketing team members may not have access to your CRM. It's also tough for your C-level executive stakeholders to see everything going on for each campaign using your CRM. A key to success with "smarketing" is transparency. Because generating revenue for your company is the goal, you want everyone to have visibility into your strategies and tactics. This type of visibility also helps to prevent communication silos. (A silo happens when information falls through the cracks or gets stuck.)

TIP

Have a weekly "smarketing" meeting to discuss upcoming campaigns, activities, and events. During this meeting, review the targeted list of accounts and the responsibilities of each "smarketing" team member.

Here are examples of tasks to assign to your "smarketing" team.

>> **Business/sales development representatives (BDR/SDRs):** An ongoing list of 25-100 qualified accounts to call/email to set an appointment for sales.

>> **Sales database administrator:** Refreshing account lists for the sales development team and account executives with qualified accounts. Update lists in the CRM to use for advertising and marketing campaigns, based on stage and persona.

>> **Marketing operations/technology manager:** Review activities and engagement scores in the marketing automation platform. Provide regular reports to the sales team with the most engaged contacts and accounts. Grade contacts and accounts by likelihood to buy.

>> **Content manager:** Keep the content library up to date and provide links to sales with all content available to send to contacts, based on stage and persona. Maintain a list of upcoming events and content to be published, and communicate with sales about how to promote these activities to accounts they're targeting.

>> **Account executive (AE):** Have a plan for each account with an organizational hierarchy for all the contacts in the account. This information will help determine what content and activities should be used to engage each contact to create velocity and expedite the purchase decision.

>> **Account manager:** Communicate regularly with the end-user in the account, provide new training content, and stay in contact with the account to provide ongoing service. This is applicable for large enterprise sales teams where the account manager is tasked with landing and expanding to find opportunities for upselling or cross-selling in the account.

>> **Sales leader:** Regularly update the list of target accounts for SDRs and AEs by accounts they want to close in the next 30, 60, or 90 days. Provide reporting on progress toward monthly or quarterly sales goals.

>> **Customer success manager (CSM):** Check in weekly with the users in customer accounts. Communicate on any upgrades and developments, track tickets in your support system and resolution of these issues to ensure the customers have a "joyful" experience.

>> **Executive stakeholder(s):** The biggest task here is to be a team player. The C-level executive also needs to be willing to pitch in when sales or marketing needs support.

Ranking Your "Smarketing" Success

Not every campaign will be wildly successful. Your sales team won't win every deal. These are realities you must face as a "smarketing" team. And you won't maximize revenue overnight. It takes hard work at every level in your organization.

What's important is to review your individual wins and opportunities for improvement. You'll start slowly with your initial account-based marketing campaigns, before progressing to doing ABM *at scale* for every contact and opportunity in your target accounts. Using marketing automation and your account-based marketing platform, you can identify the most successful campaigns by

>> **Clicks:** How many contacts in your target accounts clicked on your ad?

>> **Impressions:** If the contact didn't click on your ad, how many times did your advertisement appear in front of your target contacts?

>> **Content downloads:** How many times was a piece of content downloaded by contacts from *qualified* accounts?

REMEMBER

Account-based marketing is about *quality*, not quantity. You need to view these metrics through an ABM lens. Working with your "smarketing" team, review lists of your target accounts and look at contact-level activity in the account. I discuss this in Part 6 for account-level attribution.

Winning with new revenue

The ultimate goal of bringing together your "smarketing" team in account-based marketing is to generate more revenue for your company. When you're successful with your account-based marketing campaigns, you'll see an increase in the following metrics:

>> **Marketing-sourced pipeline:** The number of new accounts that came from an inbound or outbound marketing activity, then progressed into a potential revenue opportunity.

>> **Increase in pipeline velocity:** More activities and content from marketing will help sales opportunities progress faster through the buyer's journey. The time it takes to close a deal should be reduced.

>> **More Closed/Won deals:** Because you have a tightly aligned "smarketing" team with the same goal, you will see an increase in the number of new customers coming on board.

TIP

Make time to celebrate your wins together. It shouldn't be all work and no play, or your "smarketing" team will get burnt out. Every quarter, take an afternoon to participate in a team-building activity. Go to lunch together, volunteer at an animal shelter or other charity, and enjoy being together outside of the office.

Learning from mistakes and opportunities

There's always room for improvement. Not every campaign and activity will be wildly successful. Salespeople still must work to close every deal. As you're ramping up your account-based marketing campaigns, there will be a few key performance indicators (KPIs) that you should monitor to look for potential ways to improve:

>> **Sales cycle lags**: Progression from one stage to another slows down. If the SDR has qualified accounts that didn't progress to a discovery call or demo, what happened?

>> **Failure to convert qualified accounts into opportunities**: What happened in the sales process after the initial discovery call or demo?

>> **Losing deals**: It's a terrible situation after your sales account executive has worked all quarter trying to close a deal and then it didn't come to fruition. Did the account choose a competitor? Did they decide not to do anything and stick with the status quo?

REMEMBER

Recap in your CRM what happened with each closed account, either Closed/Lost or Closed/Won.

Reassess what content or activities were being used at each of these stages. What could have been done differently to create velocity? What else should the SDR or AE have done to move the account forward? Ask these questions during your "smarketing" team meetings, or individually. Yes, this means a marketing manager must meet with an account executive 1-on-1, but these interactions should already be happening if your marketing and sales teams are truly aligned for "smarketing." Talk to your sales team about what could have been done differently to convert qualified accounts into opportunities.

Brainstorming new ideas

Your "smarketing" team should take time each week for brainstorming new ideas. Salespeople are just as creative as marketers, and provide stellar insights into campaigns and activities that can create more buzz and excitement. It's important to continuously keep the ABM engine going with fresh ideas. Your sales team can be a great source of these ideas.

5

Turning Customers Into Advocates

Chapter 15

Elevating the Buyer to Customer Journey

*T*he party just gets started when the deal is signed.

With ABM, the last stage, Advocate, is about creating customer advocates. A customer advocate is a client who speaks positively on behalf of your business. Turning your customers into raving fans is a process, and it should be taken seriously at all levels of your company. Your company invested time, money, and resources because you know the account you brought on board as a customer is a great fit for your business. You want the customer, and all the contacts in the account, to have an awesome experience with your company. When they have a meaningful experience, they will be willing to talk about it with their peers, or even collaborate with your business for sales and marketing.

In this chapter, I discuss going beyond the typical B2B buyer's journey to a comprehensive customer journey looking at the lifecycle of an account. I tell you about the importance of customer on-boarding and adoption of your product or service. Providing a great experience will create new sales opportunities within your existing customer accounts.

Prospecting to Contacts

With account-based marketing, you'll continue to discover and meet new contacts in both your opportunities and your customer accounts. The same way your marketing and sales teams engage prospects should be done with new contacts who belong to accounts at any stage in their lifecycle.

TIP

Think about it like this: when you're dating a person, whether you just met or you've been together for a year, your significant other has a whole network of people. You want your significant other's family, friends, and such to like you. You smile when you meet them, say polite things, and put your best foot forward.

The same is true for marketing and sales. Think of all of your contacts like they're people you're dating. These are contacts who are stakeholders or influencers who belong to your accounts. Think about each contact as another important relationship. You need to build a relationship based on trust. Even when you've already closed the account and it's a customer, you are starting a relationship with this new contact. You need a good relationship from the start.

On the flip side, when you meet new contacts who are still in the prospect stage, even when they aren't your customers, they'll talk about your company. They talk about you in emails, partnering for events, and when giving interviews to the media. What they say can help drive revenue to your business. Therefore, you need to supply them with relevant content. Recommended content for the Prospect stage includes

>> Blog posts

>> Ebooks

>> Infographics

>> Whitepapers

>> Social media

>> Emails

The goal is to increase the amount of activity you have with your contacts, creating awareness, which will help lead to potential revenue opportunities.

REMEMBER

There can be multiple opportunities within an account. Because you're marketing to an entire company, depending on the size of the organization there can be different buying centers. This means the contacts within an account are at various stages of the purchase decision.

Furthering opportunities through the pipeline

When engaging our contacts in accounts, we call this *creating velocity*. It's the activities from marketing and sales that generate enough interest with contacts in accounts to create revenue opportunities. The goal with account-based marketing is to move opportunities faster through the pipeline. The progression of an opportunity looks like this:

» **Opportunity to Evaluation:** Comparing your company against competitors or other potential solutions.

» **Evaluation to Negotiation/Review:** Competitive analysis is finished, they've asked for a contract or terms of the business agreement.

» **Negotiation to Closed:** The opportunity has either been lost or won, and agreed to become a customer.

Using content and marketing activities, you can help opportunities progress faster through the pipeline. This type of content marketing includes

» Video testimonials

» Case studies

» "How to" content

» ROI documentation

» Competitive analysis

TIP

Surrounding your contacts and opportunities with digital advertising helps to increase velocity, as you're providing "air cover" for sales. Deals will close at a faster rate when they're seeing your message everywhere.

REMEMBER

The stakeholders here are primarily marketing, sales, and sales development, as the progression from prospect to customer reflects on their work. Your executives also have a stake in how fast opportunities turn into closed deals, as revenue is the lifeblood of your organization.

Closing the deal

As your team is doing all this work to accelerate contacts from the Prospect to Opportunity to Customer stages, you will see an increase in how quickly you can close new business. Because you're engaging more contacts across your list of target accounts, there should also be an increase in deal size. Also, the increased level of engagement with your opportunities will result in connecting your business with other successful companies.

TIP

Include the logos of your best-fit and VIP customers on your company's website. It's important to show your contacts the type of organizations who have found success with your company. Create a separate page on your website called "Our Customers," with such copy as "Our customers love us, and you will too."

Establishing a Customer Journey

Account-based marketing goes beyond the traditional B2B buyer's journey into an account's journey. The lifecycle of an account is a comprehensive customer experience. It's about having a long-term relationship with your customers. The last steps of the account's journey are ensuring their satisfaction and encouraging their customer advocacy. You want your customers to have a fantastic experience so they will become advocates for your company. I discuss the stages of the account's journey as a customer in the following section. The stages of the customer's journey in account-based marketing include

>> **Adoption:** Implementing your product/service with your new customer.

>> **Land/expand:** Growing your revenue from within the account by increasing usage or deal size.

>> **Upsell/cross-sell:** Selling an upgraded version of your product or service to your existing customers, or "cross-selling" to other business units.

>> **Advocate:** "Always on" marketing to turn your customers into advocates.

Adopting your technology

Your customers learned a lot about your company during the buyer's journey. Their purchase was the beginning of a deeper understanding of you and your product or service. Now that they bought from your company, you must set them up for success. If your users can't learn how to use your product or service, they will churn very quickly.

Account-based marketing strategies focus on the customers' positive experiences by keeping them engaged. Directly after purchase is the time for you to keep in contact with customers by offering them support and training, helping them to optimize their use of your product or service.

A successful adoption process for new customers includes

>> **Collaboration:** Working with your professional services, solutions, and product teams on the requirements for implementing your new customer.

>> **Project management:** Ensuring that delivery of the product, platform, or service to your customer is on time and in-scope.

When your customer receives access, you must train your customers on how to use your product or service. Depending on your company and the size of your customer accounts, this training includes

>> **Champion training:** Hosting your new customers for intense training, creating "champion" or "power" users. This training typically lasts for several days or a full business week, and is hosted at your own office or a neutral location.

The benefit of champion training is to create one or two "champions" who can help instruct other users at their company.

>> **On-site training:** Having a member from your support, product, or professional services team go to your client's office. The cost for this training should include an hourly rate, plus travel, hotel, and other logistical expenses.

TIP

A powerful benefit of on-site and champion training is that it's easier to build stronger personal relationships with your customers in person, and you can connect with them during social time outside of the scheduled training sessions.

>> **Virtual training:** Presenting training sessions on webinar platforms, such as GoToWebinar, WebEx, or Join.me. With software-as-a-service (SaaS) purchases, the cost for this training typically is included in the agreement as part of the on-boarding process.

The benefit is that these sessions can be recorded and replayed at your customer's convenience.

Marketing and sales should provide support while your new customers are going through training. Here are the types of activities to execute during the adoption phase of the account's journey:

>> **Follow up:** The sales account executive who closed the deal should stay in communication with the primary contacts in the new customer account. Sales representatives should send emails or make phone calls to check in during this on-boarding process. This helps establish your brand's reputation as a trusted partner.

>> **Provide content:** Tutorial content should be hosted in a virtual knowledge center or resource library. This type of content includes

- Checklists in bulleted steps and numbered lists for what to do beginning, during, and after implementation.

- "How To" guides with steps walking through different actions.

- Videos recordings showing different functionality.

- Ongoing training webinars on various topics. These webinars should happen in a recurring and regular cadence, at least monthly (possibly weekly, depending on the size of your organization).

TIP

The more content you can provide your customers during training, the less hand-holding you will need to give after your customer is ready to "go live."

Engaging end-users

Your customer at this point is becoming a user. After the initial on-boarding and implementation, the account will be handed off to a customer success manager (CSM). The goals of your customer success team are client satisfaction and retention. Every company has its own approach to this ongoing relationship with customers that goes beyond the purchase decision. You must continue to engage your customers after he initial implementation of your product or service.

TIP

In the same way you created a marketing plan for targeting all the contacts in the account, your customer success team should have a list of all the users in the account, their roles, and their responsibilities.

The knowledge of all the users in the account will help supply content. Staying in touch with relevant marketing messages will keep your customer engaged, and may increase their usage of your product and service as you continually elaborate on it as a solution to their problems. Here are ways to engage your end-users:

>> Regular communication from your customer success manager (even just a weekly email to check in or a monthly status call).

>> Send a monthly customer newsletter sharing new content, product developments, upcoming events, or a customer "spotlight" column.

>> Host customer-only events, such as an annual user conference.

>> Have your CEO host a regular town hall webinar every year or every quarter to talk about company news.

>> Review issues or tickets that have been submitted, then personally follow up with an email to the client.

The success metrics you'll see from increasing engagement with your customers include

>> **Increase in usage:** Enabling them to successfully use your product

>> **Increase in retention:** Renewing their contracts or annual agreements

>> **Decrease in churn:** Reducing the number of users who cancel or don't renew

Continuing education

There are a wide variety of methods to stay in touch with your customer as they continue to use your product. With all the stages of account-based marketing, it's extremely valuable to know the channels through which your customers most frequently interact with your company. By knowing these channels, you can deliver the right content to educate and empower your customers to be successful. Examples of content for continuing education include

>> Hosting in-person training events

>> A regular webinar series with new one-hour digital events each month

>> Implementation guides and "how-to" content for your platform

>> Checklists with step-by-step instructions for different activities

>> Creating new videos with product overviews or deep-dive instructions

TIP

To encourage continuing education, look for ways to offer credit for participating in training. Many professional associations and trade organizations require a number of training hours to earn and maintain certifications. Depending on your industry, find out whether there is an association you can join to offer continuing education credits to your accounts.

Selling to Existing Customers

Remember the mantra that 80 percent of your revenue will come from 20 percent of your customers? Account-based marketing is built on relationships with your high-value customers. When your sales teams know the needs of their accounts, marketing can be actively targeting those clients with relevant upsells and cross-sells to solve new problems and continue to satisfy the customer's needs and pain points.

With account-based marketing, you are continuously looking for additional revenue opportunities within your customer accounts at their initial time of purchase, and after. Offering your accounts an upgraded product or service, additional features, or other products that complement their initial purchase can increase their engagement with your company.

For existing customers, marketing should consider which channels to use, focusing on where an account typically connects with your company, whether it's email, social, or mobile. It's essential to have a detailed account plan of how you will continuously market to existing customers with relevant and beneficial features and upgrades.

WARNING

If the sales team hasn't followed up regularly with the accounts they closed, selling inside your customer accounts will be incredibly difficult.

The relationship your sales team has established becomes essential during this stage of the account's journey. During your efforts to initially close the deal with a client, your marketing and sales teams should have discovered the needs that the customer had within their company. Understanding the needs across a company can help your marketing and sales team to begin selling your product or service to other departments that could benefit from your product.

Landing and expanding accounts

The landing and expanding stage of the customer journey refers to identifying and reaching out to new contacts within an existing account. Your sales team has *landed* the account as a new customer. There can be an opportunity to *expand*, or develop additional business within the account.

With ABM, you continue to develop your business by winning more revenue from your existing customer base. Dealing with your customers as "accounts," rather than just companies, helps to consistently increase revenue from any single account by expanding within a company's contacts, departments, and other business units.

Furthermore, familiarity with a company's practices, procedures, and personality can give you insight about how you can continue to partner with them outside your current contacts. You may only be working with a single office of a company, while they have a large network of satellite groups throughout the country. The opportunity to grow within that company is only dependent on your ability to get in contact with other offices and demonstrate how you already have a successful relationship with their company.

Here are some of the marketing activities needed for landing and expanding within an existing account:

>> **Gather case studies and customer testimonials**: Collect data to support this value. When you are planning to expand within a company, it is important that your new contacts can see how you have added value for both their colleagues and their industry.

>> **Create detailed use cases based on the industry:** Discuss how different departments within the company or organization use your product.

>> **Demonstrate your value proposition in every interaction:** When your existing customers are familiar with your value proposition, they can be advocates within their own company to reinforce your messages.

TIP

Look at your scores of these contacts in your marketing automation system. The score tracks the engagement of contacts with your marketing activities. An uptick in the customer's score shows an increase in engagement.

The primary success metric you'll see from increasing engagement with your customers is an increase in current customer revenue.

Cross-selling in the account

A cross-sell can have different meanings. It depends on your organization. One example of a cross-sell is when your sales team offers more than one product or an additional service that could be beneficial to your customer. This product or service provides something new that the customer didn't have before. To do this, a salesperson must identify a need, then demonstrate how your product or service can meet the need.

Cross-selling is a common practice for B2B marketing and sales teams who are targeting large enterprise accounts. For example, you may have initially been working with an executive team, but your sales and marketing teams recognize the relevance of your product or service for the company's accounting or HR department. Every satisfied customer is an opportunity to expand and grow within an existing account.

TIP

This is why you need to have an account plan with organizational hierarchy for the business units in the account who can use your product or service.

Your key success metric is revenue from new business within an existing account; an increase from the original deal size you sold.

Upselling new or upgraded products

An upsell is when you sell your customer an upgraded version of the same product. For example, this could be a top-tier product that gives them unlimited access. An upsell gives your customer information tailored to their specific account, with an additional benefit (or benefits) of the same product or service that they already use.

To successfully upsell, sales must show added value in a product or service. The type of content needed to support an upsell includes

>> **Announcement:** Blog post or press release announcing a product upgrade

>> **Webinar:** Virtual demonstration of your latest upgrades, demonstrating the ROI and the value of purchasing an upgrade

Your success metrics in this step are increased revenue from existing accounts, and increased deal sizes with your accounts.

Chapter 16

Valuing Customer Advocacy

C ustomer advocacy is the most authentic type of marketing. According to a Nielsen survey spanning more than 100 countries, 92 percent of people surveyed said they would choose the recommendation of a family member or friend over any other marketing channel. This statistic demonstrates how there is no longer an effective form of mass media. Marketing must be highly personalized and based on trust.

As the proliferation of social media continues to make our world hyper-connected, you must deliver organic messaging that builds trust. Establishing relationships makes it easier for sales to close more business, faster, by using customers to help sing your company's praises. The recommendations from your customers will be exponentially more impactful than any piece of marketing content you can create. You can use your own customers' voices to tell a story about how your company helped them in an unbiased way.

In this chapter, I tell you how to leverage your customers to make them champions of your brand. I discuss why making your customers your marketers will be a much better ROI and even spark innovations for your company's product or service offering.

The Rising Influence of the Customer Voice

Your customers have more power than ever before, and they'll keep getting more influence. It is important to note that the customer voice is one of many voices shouting into the endless abyss of the internet. Other influences are coming from such sources as consultants, industry analysts, thought leaders, media, and bloggers. These voices may be louder and have a broader reach, but they aren't nearly as authentic, nor organic, as the voices of your own customers.

Authenticity is the most important quality of your customers' voices. When your prospects or opportunities read a customer case study or watch a customer video testimonial, they hear from your own customers about the success they've had with your product or service. The *most* authentic form of marketing is unsolicited and offered by the customer on their own channel, whether it's talking to a peer, writing on their own blog, or posting on social media. This is why you must provide value at every interaction to give your customers a better overall experience.

Providing customer joy

Customer joy is defined by delighting your clients. At every point where they interact with your company, your customers should have a positive experience. These points of interaction include

» **Content:** Every communication, such as a blog post, case study, newsletter, webinar or customer-centric content created by marketing, should leave a positive impression.

» **People:** Each time one of the employees at your company talks to a customer, these interactions should be positive. This includes

- The first time you made contact at the beginning of the buyer's journey as a prospect

- Working with your salespeople throughout the purchase decision as an opportunity

- During implementation for going live with your product or service

- On-boarding and training with your product

- Collaborating with your customer success team

» **Product:** If your product offering isn't stable, you're fighting a losing battle. An unstable product filled with bugs will wreck your customer's experience.

» **Support:** A system like Zendesk (www.zendesk.com) is used for submitting tickets if/when your clients need help with your product. This offers you the capability to look for ways to improve your clients' experiences.

WARNING

When your customers aren't happy, you'll hear about it, one way or another, especially in the age of social media. When customers aren't happy, they will leave. It is much less expensive to retain an existing client. The cost to acquire new customer accounts through marketing is expensive.

Surprising your clients

Your customers need to continue finding value in your business. B2B companies have a dedicated customer success team in order to provide ongoing service and support to your clients. The idea of "surprise and delight" is a big part of customer success. Your customers need to be elevated from the mundane tasks of their everyday jobs. Here are ways that your company can surprise your clients:

>> **Go beyond your value proposition:** The solution you presented to your accounts in the buyer's journey is why they chose to purchase from your company. Your clients expect you to honor what was promised in the terms of the purchase agreement. Attempt to deliver services beyond whatever your customer was expecting, to help them realize your value immediately. One way to do this is to meet deadlines earlier than expected, or overachieve on goals you set together.

>> **Provide added-value:** Providing additional value to your clients is becoming an expectation, not an add-on. Look for ways to meet and exceed their expectations, such as offering additional products or upgrades at a lower cost.

>> **Host events:** Whether it's your annual user conference or taking them to dinner, an invitation to an event is a great way to surprise your clients and engage them.

>> **Engage them on social media:** Posting Tweets, retweeting posts from their company accounts, or commenting on LinkedIn posts will be a pleasant surprise.

>> **Send them mail:** The same way you sent direct mail to your sales prospects and opportunities, you should continue sending fun packages to your clients. Examples of items to mail include:

  • Sweets (cookies, candy, or brownies) or healthy fruit baskets

  • Hand-written thank you notes from you and/or your company's CEO and executive leadership thanking them for their business

  • Branded items, or "swag", from your company, such as t-shirts, water bottles, notebooks, coffee mugs, or other fun giveaways

TIP

Send your clients a "welcome kit" after the purchase decision and the contract has been signed. This welcome kit should contain swag from your company's logo to start engendering brand value as soon as on-boarding starts.

Establishing relationships

Account-based marketing is a continuous cycle. Marketing and sales have worked to gain new customers. Your entire organization is responsible for keeping your customers happy to prevent them from leaving. The term for losing a customer in business is *churn*. One way to prevent churn is by having strong relationships with your customers. These relationships are based on trust and providing good service.

Your account's journey is a symbiotic relationship. Contacts in the account interact with all facets of your organization during their experience as your customers. Here are the ways your clients have relationships with various departments in your organization:

>> **Marketing:** The first touch point your customers had was with marketing. Each customer clicked on an ad, came to your website, met at an event, or downloaded a piece of content.

ABM marketers continue to build a relationship by supplying content (such as training webinars, checklists, and how-to guides) and meeting your customers at events such as your annual user conference.

>> **Sales development:** The call with your business or sales development representative (BDR/SDR) to schedule that first discovery call or demo.

After the customer comes on board, the BDR/SDR should send an email thanking the customer for their business and offer to help in any way.

>> **Sales:** Throughout the account's journey, the account executive who signed the customer should continue to reach out. ABM goes beyond the buyer's journey, and sales should, too. Checking in periodically (at least once a quarter) to see how the customer is progressing with your product or service is a great way for sales reps to stay engaged.

>> **Support:** The dedicated team of support staff who answer your customers' service tickets and provide training.

A support team should actively monitor each customer account to escalate issues quickly and follow-up after resolution of these issues. Providing technical support and the ability to resolve issues can make or break a relationship with your customers.

>> **Product:** Your clients spend tons of time interacting with your brand and using your product or service. Your company's offering will ultimately have a

strong impact on the customer's experience. After all, it's what they're paying your company for.

WARNING

The key here is providing a good product. When the product isn't stable, or is filled with bugs, then you'll be continuously fighting a losing battle to keep your customers happy.

>> **Customer success:** The forces on the front line servicing your accounts are the customer success or client relations team. The customer success manager (CSM) is the main point of contact who owns the relationship with their assigned accounts. A good CSM knows the ins and outs of the account, including vital information:

- *Primary users:* Who from the account is most active with your product or services?

- *Organizational hierarchy:* Who are the stakeholders, champions, decision-makers, and executive leaders?

- *Usage:* How is the account using your product or service, what is the functionality, and how often are the account's users active?

- *Contract terms:* What level of product or service is the account using, and when is the agreement is up for renegotiation?

REMEMBER

This is important. Sales usually must get involved with any contract renewals or upgrades. The primary task of customer success is to service the account.

>> **Executive team:** Getting your C-level executive leadership involved in the account takes the relationship to a higher level. A great way to surprise and delight your contacts is personal communication from the CEO. Having a senior executive send an email (even just a few sentences to check the status and see how things are going) will leave a great, lasting impression with your customers.

WARNING

Before having your executive leadership communicate with the account, be sure you're fully aware of the account's status. Check your CRM and support platform to see whether there are any issues or recently submitted tickets that impact the current status of the account.

There are many different ways to build a relationship with a customer account. Like the initial buyer's journey, working with the account during their experience as a customer is about engaging them on their terms. Here are ways you can create a solid foundation of your relationship with the account during their initial on-boarding:

>> **Have a communication plan:** The CSM should set the expectation for contact frequency, whether it's a weekly email status update or phone call to

check in during the ramp up period, or monthly for on-going communication after the account is live and using your platform.

>> **Know your champion:** The primary user in the account will be your VIP in the account. This contact is the person you want to develop into your customer advocate.

Making Your Customers Your Marketers

According to research from Texas Tech University, 83 percent of satisfied customers are willing to refer a product or service, but only 29 percent actually do. This problem stems from the fact that traditionally B2B marketing teams didn't have a customer marketing program. B2B marketers were focused on lead generation. There wasn't much budget dedicated to customer marketing, if any.

All throughout the industry, the idea of rallying around your customers and the importance of customer success continues to gain traction. There are horror stories from companies that had an amazing product, but suffered from not being focused on customer success. Marketers are starting to understand that the next customer will come from your current customers. Letting your customers tell the story about the success they've had with your company is the most authentic type of marketing.

Word-of-mouth has always been the most important marketing channel. It's marketing that's based on a foundation of trust. Hearing a story from someone you know instead of an unknown sales rep is much more impactful. Even with colleagues, peers, or friends of friends, you trust these people more and are much more likely to listen to their experience than a vendor. This is why it's important to get your customers talking about your company within their own personal networks.

Getting your customers talking

A huge payoff from a satisfied customer is when they tell their friends and colleagues about your product or service. Happy customers are a great way to attract new customers. Your happy customers may become brand advocates for your product or service. Such brand advocates move beyond spreading the word to friends and colleagues, and can influence any number of prospects in the general public. These practices help to get your customers talking about your business:

>> **Do a good job.** Provide a product that works effectively without bugs or issues, and support your customers with any questions they have in a timely, courteous manner.

>> **Measure to know you're doing the right things.** Ask your customers for feedback by email, send out quarterly or annual surveys, and look at support tickets to identify areas for improvement.

>> **Segment your customers into people who had a good experience.** You do this by reviewing the feedback from surveys, examining the notes in your CRM or support systems, and talking to your customer success managers. These information sources can quickly name your happy customers.

>> **Give them tools to talk their experience.** Your customers need a neutral place to come and share their stories. A few places online to do this include

- *G2Crowd (www.G2crowd.com):* A business software review platform, leveraging more than 50,000 user reviews read by nearly 400,000 software buyers each month to help them make better purchasing decisions. G2Crowd users get unfiltered reviews from peers who use similar solutions. This is the first review site to recognize an account-based marketing product category.

- *LinkedIn Groups (www.linkedin.com):* The Groups feature on LinkedIn provides a place for professionals in the same industry, or with similar interests, to share content, find answers, post and view jobs, make business contacts, and establish themselves as industry experts. You can create your own group for your customers to share their experiences.

- *Net Promoter (www.netpromoter.com):* This review site asks a simple question: "Using a 0-10 scale: How likely is it that you would recommend [brand] to a friend or colleague?" Your customers then rank your business on a scale of 1 to 10; 10 is the highest Net Promoter Score® (NPS®). Respondents who gave your company a score of 9-10 are the ones you should target to develop into customer advocates.

FRED REICHHELD, THE LOYALTY GURU

The Net Promoter Score® is the brainchild of Fred Reichheld (@FredReichheld). A Bain Fellow and founder of Bain & Company's Loyalty Practice, he introduced NPS to the world in a 2004 Harvard Business Review article. Since then, NPS has become the go-to source for customers to leave their candid feedback about products and software they use. In Fred's latest book, *The Ultimate Question 2.0: How Net Promoter Companies Thrive in a Customer Driven World*, he explains how NPS can be used by businesses for customer advocacy to help turn your clients into your marketers. His additional titles include *The Loyalty Effect: The Hidden Force Behind Growth, Profits, and Lasting Value*; *Loyalty Rules! How Today's Leaders Build Lasting Relationships*, and *The Ultimate Question: Driving Good Profits and True Growth*.

A rising category of marketing technology (MarTech) software solutions are focused primarily on customer advocacy. By providing a platform just for your customers, you're giving them a safe, dedicated space to voice their opinions. Using technology platforms built for your customers helps to get them talking. Here are a few software solutions to consider:

>> **Trustfuel (`www.trustfuel.com`):** Trustfuel is a B2B word-of-mouth platform that turns your happiest customers into brand ambassadors to drive new business. The platform helps to discover potential candidates via industry standard techniques such as Net Promoter Score®. Then, Trustfuel intelligently recruits these unique customers to refer their friends, provide testimonials, amplify your messaging on social media, write online reviews, and act as references for sales.

>> **Ambassador (`www.getamabassador.com`):** Ambassador empowers marketing teams to increase revenue by leveraging the power of recommendations. Their flexible referral marketing platform automates enrolling, tracking, rewarding and managing loyal customers, affiliates, partners and fans. This allows B2B companies, consumer brands, and agencies to scale, and optimize referral marketing programs. Ambassador's open API also seamlessly integrates with existing technologies, enabling companies to create a custom experience that aligns with their brand.

>> **ChurnZero (`http://churnzero.net`):** ChurnZero powers subscription businesses to engage customers, generate more revenue, and prevent churn. You can see real-time insights into customer activity to get alerts on contacts in accounts, such as when there is a lack of engagement. You can also communicate to your customers while they're using your application or platform to serve up content, like an ad promoting your next users meetup.

>> **Gainsight (`www.gainsight.com`):** Gainsight allows companies to monitor and engage with a variety of customers — without compromising scalability. You can structure, streamline, and optimize your team's workflow around the customer lifecycle, knowing that you're sending the right message to the right customer contacts at the right time. This helps to deliver a personalized, unified experience to your customers.

>> **Influitive (`www.influitive.com`):** B2B buyers are tuning out marketing and sales messages, but prospects are more interested in listening to the advice, recommendations and reviews of knowledgeable peers when making purchase decisions. Influitive helps B2B marketers tap into this trend by capturing the enthusiasm of their advocates, then turning that into measurable improvement in marketing and sales effectiveness. With AdvocateHub, marketers build powerful advocate communities where members systematically increase their status, access and network as they participate in activities like referral programs, reference calls, product reviews, and focus groups.

- » **RO Innovation (www.roinnovation.com):** RO Innovation activates and amplifies the "Voice of the Customer" to accelerate revenue in the B2B sales process. RO's software serves as the critical link between happy customers, sales activity and closing new prospects. RO ties together the critical marriage of customer reference management and sales enablement.

- » **Boulder Logic (www.boulderlogic.com):** Acquired by RO Innovation in 2015, BoulderLogic's easy to use customer reference software helps to increase revenue by closing deals faster. The powerful, intelligent matching algorithm identifies and delivers the most effective reference at exactly the right time. Achieve more with fewer program resources by saving time searching for references, maintaining a continuous pipeline of new testimonials and increasing adoption through integrations with other software including Salesforce and Influitive.

- » **Smync (www.smync.com):** For building customer advocacy, Smync searches social networks and integrates with your CRM to create an SRM (Social Relationship Manager), identifying your most engaged customers across all social networks. The Smync platform provides the toolkit to activate social relationships with the customers wanting to share their experience with your brand on a one-to-one and one-to-many basis.

  Smync provides several utilities, such as

  - • Share, which generates shareable branded landing pages for offers or email sign-ups

  - • Shout, which aggregates social posting rights from customers to create buzz around bigger events or launches

  - • Community, which builds branded advocate communities that generate trusted reach, user generated content and customer insights

Interviewing your customers

To really understand your customers' sentiments, the marketing team needs to have conversations with them. Developing a relationship between your clients and marketing is essential for creating customer advocates. One of the first ways to start building this relationship is through an interview. When marketing interviews customers, the content from this interview can be repurposed for such collateral as a case study, a quote for your website, or a blog post.

REMEMBER

Always ask for your customers to approve their statements before publication. Send an email with the quote you want to feature, or the draft of the content, for your customer to review and edit. This will increase trust as you continue to collaborate for creating content.

Marketing team members typically don't have a close relationship with customers. When marketing wants to reach out to a customer for an interview, the initial communication should come from the person who owns the relationship. The people to ask are your team members who have directly helped the customer. These primary team members will most likely be either

>> **Customer success manager:** The main point of contact on your client services team who is responsible for supporting the account.

>> **Sales account executive:** The salesperson who closed the deal.

The person who owns the relationship should send an email to the client, connecting them with your marketing team member who will produce the content. In the email, they should introduce the marketing contact, explain the marketing contact's role, clarify why marketing wants to interview the client, and ask whether the client will agree to spend time with marketing.

REMEMBER

Whoever manages the relationship with the account will be the person from your team whom *all* communication should flow through. Even after the interview has been conducted, marketing should send drafts of communication to the primary account manager before reaching out directly to the customer.

WARNING

When the client says now isn't a good time, there may be an underlying issue that should be investigated by customer success and support.

When the client agrees to an interview, the marketing team member interviewing the customer at the account should treat this interview as a reporter or journalist. The interview questions should be based on the 5W's and an H:

>> **Who?** Ask your customers details about themselves. Where are they from originally? How long have they been in the industry? How long have they been with the company?

These questions will help you get to know your customers better before you dive into specifics about how they interact with your company.

TIP

>> **What?** What are their responsibilities in the company? Have they had various roles or titles in the organization? What's the typical day like?

>> **When?** When did they make the decision to purchase from your company? Was there a catalyst for making a purchase decision?

>> **Where?** Where does your solution fit in with their organization's business objectives? Is your product/service being used at just one of their office locations, or only within one business unit?

>> **Why?** In their own words, why did they decide to purchase from your company? Why do they continue to do business? What need is being fulfilled? What do other people in the organization like about your company's offering?

>> **How?** How often are they using your product or service? How can your offering be improved? Are there opportunities to use your company's offering in a different way?

TIP

Before the interview, meet with both the account executive who closed the deal and the customer success manager to get as much information as possible about your customer, such as why they chose to purchase from your company, and how they use your product/service. This will help give you an understanding of the relationship before your interview.

There are several formats in which this interview could be conducted. The goal is to record as much information as possible during your time with your customers. Here are ways to capture the conversation:

>> **Use call-recording software:** Applications, such as GoToMeeting, WebEx and Google Hangout, allow you to interact digitally then record the entire conversation.

>> **Send them the questions via email:** Asking your clients questions over email allows them to edit their answers. This can add an additional level of comfort, because they can review their responses before sending the email back.

>> **Include them as a panelist on a webinar:** Inviting your clients to be a speaker on a webinar, which you'll record, lets you capture their quotes in real time. This adds an authentic element to your webinar content, because your customers are sharing their own stories.

TIP

Consider using a transcription service, such as Rev.com. It charges you $1 per minute to transcribe your audio recordings and videos. This saves you time and gives you a document of your customers' quotes to repurpose for content.

Driving referrals and references

According to Edelman Trust Barometer, 84 percent of B2B businesses start the buying process with a referral. When your customers have a good experience with your company, they will talk about it with their colleagues and peers. This type of authentic word-of-mouth marketing influences perceptions more powerfully than any other type of marketing activity.

There is a difference between a customer referral and a reference:

>> **Reference:** You ask your customers to be a reference for you. When a customer agrees to be a reference, you can use them on a sales call to help close a new account. You can also interview them for a testimonial video, create a case study, or use a quote for your website.

>> **Referral:** Your customer sends you new business. Your customer contacts in an account connect you with a new contact or prospect in their network who might become an opportunity.

WARNING

You must understand your customer well enough to ask them to be a reference or give you referral business. Don't treat all of your customers alike. You can't just send an email from your marketing automation system to all of your customers asking for them to give you a Net Promoter Score®. You may reach a few happy people, but you will also reach unhappy customers. Asking your unhappy customers for a referral is like rubbing salt in a wound.

When it comes to getting customer referrals and using customers for references, it's truly a partnership. Many customers are nervous about agreeing to be references, because they're worried about getting asked to be on sales calls all the time. The process for asking your customers to be references should include

>> **The initial conversation:** Ask whether they would be willing to serve as this person, and how often an account executive will reach out to them (once a week, month or quarter) and how you'll police it.

>> **Follow up on the conversation:** Explain how you'll collaborate with them in the future. Start with a small task, such as requesting a quote from them to put on your website.

>> **Make them thought leaders:** If they've agreed to be your reference, promote them to your customers as thought leaders. You want to demonstrate how they're smart and innovative, and why your product is great to check out. Feature your customers in such content as

- Case studies

- Blog posts

- Video testimonials

- Social media posts

THE VALUE OF REFERRALS

Research from Influitive and Heinz Marketing shows how customer referral programs are essential for closing more new business faster, and at a lower cost to marketing. "The responsibility for generating referrals can't rest solely on the shoulders of front-line sales reps," says Jim Williams, Vice President of Marketing at Influitive. "Simply asking individual prospects and clients for one-off referrals won't get you to your revenue goals."

Their research shows that only 30 percent of B2B companies have a formalized referral program. Companies who participated in the survey who have a more formal referral program experienced faster revenue growth, and were much more likely to achieve their revenue goals than organizations lacking a referral program.

Reaching new contacts

As mentioned in SiriusDecision's 2015 Study on Customer Advocacy and Engagement, 83 percent of B2B companies say references are "critical" or "valuable" to the sales cycle. Your customers have networks. The networks of peers, colleagues, family, and friends can present new revenue opportunities. The idea of human-to-human (H2H) marketing really comes into play here, as the customer advocates who you've tapped to be references can provide introductions to their networks. You need to enable them to speak highly about your business.

TIP

Send an email to your customer advocates with this question: "How likely are you to recommend (NAME) to someone you know?" This is an opportunity for your customer to think about how their overall experience. Also ask, "Is there someone you know who would benefit from our product or solution?"

WARNING

Don't offer ridiculous cash bonuses for referrals. Your customers won't have a great impression of your company.

Event marketing with your clients

A great way to get your customer advocates talking about you is to bring them to your events. Because your marketing team is investing its time and money to attend events, bringing your customers along for the ride will make your company's presence at the event more impactful.

TIP

Before hitting the road, send an email to your customer base to see whether they're attending the same event. "See you at (event)?"

When you know your clients will be at the same conference, whether you're exhibiting or not, meet up with them to walk the conference floor together. Offer them an opportunity to come to your booth, to give them "swag" or whatever your show giveaway may be, or buy them a meal. It's about taking the time to have these one-on-one connections to further establish your relationship.

Here are ways to include your clients in marketing events:

>> **Bringing clients to your booth at a tradeshow.** When show attendees walk up, you can introduce them to your customers who can talk about their experience.

>> **Inviting them to attend a dinner with your clients.** This is a great opportunity for them to make new connections in their industry, and sit down with your company's team members.

>> **Host an event in their hometown.** Pull your list of client companies in your database to see whether there are clusters in certain cities, such as San Francisco, New York, and Boston, then plan a meetup event, such as a breakfast, happy hour, or one-day training session.

Building buzz

Getting good buzz can be a daunting task. As a marketer, when I see a company who has a lot of buzz, I often wonder how they got people talking about their brand. For generating buzz or word-of-mouth marketing, it's about promoting your business in an unbiased and positive way. It's authentic, and not just another spin that marketing is putting on content.

Such brand advocates move beyond spreading the word to friends and colleagues. They can influence any number of prospects in the general public. Here are ways to get your customers' help in building buzz:

>> **Thought leadership:** Feature your clients in blog posts and "customer of the month" spotlights on your website, then ask them to share the links on social media.

>> **Press release:** When you're announcing company news or debuting a new product, include a quote from one of your customer advocates discussing why they're excited about this new development.

>> **Connect them with influencers:** Your company should be collaborating with industry influencers, such as reporters and speakers. Also, you can engage them by introducing them to your customers.

>> **Webinar:** Consider putting one of your customers and an industry influencer on a webinar together, with one of your company's executives serving as a moderator. The combination of these voices will create a powerful buzz.

TIP

Host a "CEO Town Hall" webinar at the beginning of the year. This is an opportunity for your company's leadership to communicate with your clients. In this webinar, discuss achievements from the past year, opportunities for improvement, and what's to come for the year in product development. Transparency is essential with this type of communication and helps to build buzz for the year to come.

Engineering Product Development

Companies that don't innovate die. Your marketing and sales team won't be successful if they must keep coming up with new ways to sell the same thing. Your customers also want innovation. When you look at your product roadmap for new features, get your customers involved in the process. They will be the ones who will actually use it.

Reviewing your existing product

Feedback is a powerful tool. Asking your customers what they think about your product is a great way to get feedback. There are several ways to engage your customers for reviews about your product. Here are a few solutions:

>> **Send in an email:** This is an opportunity for the customer to step back from the product and holistically respond to the question: "How likely are you to recommend us to someone you know?"

>> **Create a survey:** Tools like Survey Monkey (www.surveymonkey.com) have an easy-to-use function for capturing your customers' anonymous feedback. When you need to know who your customers are, be sure to include a "Name" field in the survey. For anonymous customer satisfaction feedback, Suggestion Ox (www.suggestionox.com) is a free platform for 100-percent anonymous feedback.

>> **Prompt your customers:** Include a survey or form inside the application, asking for feedback. There's a higher chance of getting responses, because you're catching them in context of using your product or platform. Your customers can then respond to this survey after doing something with your product. Tools such as Trustfuel aid this action.

WARNING

Your customers can be frustrated. Putting a survey in your application may not be the right time to ask. This is why it's important to look at data in your CRM or support ticket system to get these insights about what your customers currently are experiencing.

Asking for input on your product roadmap

Depending on how closely your marketing and sales teams know the people in a certain account, the information from a survey could help guide the content and support that are offered during a customer's first experiences with the product or service. As your marketing team strives to build a relationship with your customer advocates, your product and engineering team needs to have a select group of customers to reach out to for input on development of future product features and enhancements.

TIP

Create a group of your VIP customers who can be a sounding board for product developments.

Commonly called a customer advisory board (CAB), there are several benefits for forming a core group of customers to provide feedback on product developments. This should be a small, limited group only available to an exclusive selection of customers. A product/customer advisory board is a great way to empower your customers. If they'll be your advocates, they must believe in the product and be invested in your mutual success.

REMEMBER

Be very selective in this process. These customers should be doing something novel with your product, such as pushing and testing the product's limitations if you're a software company.

It's also good to make sure the customers are aligned with your ideal customer profile (ICP). Consider including one or two outliers or innovators who may not fit perfectly with your ICP as they offer a unique perspective.

WARNING

Don't put a customer on there just because they're a strategic account you want to upsell or cross-sell.

In the long run, it's about appointing customers who will be partners. If you get the wrong people on your CAB, it can create a precarious situation. One of your customers may want an update that applies only to their industry vertical, or specific use case, and is not prudent for all your customers using your product.

It's also important to keep in mind how sales can sell any new product developments. When your CAB is comprised mostly of customers who fit in your ICP, any feedback they give about product development should align with how your set of target accounts can also benefit from these new enhancements. Consider how any new feature sets would be viewed from your target accounts in a certain vertical.

Factoring in feedback

In the process of gathering feedback, input, and reviews from your customers, you'll hear many differing opinions. It's up to your executive team to take this feedback and determine what should be considered for future product developments or improvements in your offering. What's important is being able to rank and prioritize feedback with what's in line or already on the list for your product roadmap.

WARNING

Asking for feedback can be a double-edged sword. When you ask clients for feedback, they'll expect you to take the feedback and do something with it.

TIP

Document all of your customers' sentiments and feedback. This way, you can list why you didn't take their suggestions if your customers prompt you for an explanation later on.

Chapter 17

Aligning Marketing, Sales, and Customer Success

For too long, marketing, sales, and customer success departments had different success metrics. Marketing was concerned about generating new leads for sales. The sales team's mission was to take those leads and entice them to become opportunities, then win the deal, creating customers. Customer success was tasked with ensuring clients successfully adopted the product and service, preventing customers from leaving ("churning") and keeping them happy. This is how it's always worked in the B2B world.

Account-based marketing (ABM) flips this model upside down with marketing, sales, and customer success aligned with one mission: Get and keep revenue. The previous standard for B2B marketing teams was looking at a customer marketing program as a luxury. But, as you grow your business, you must ensure your customers are growing with you. ABM makes customer marketing a must-have initiative. It is through communication, education, and events that you turn your customers into advocates. This helps with both retaining your current customers and growing new business.

In this chapter, I show how to put together marketing programs for your customers by collaborating across multiple departments in your organization. I discuss how viewing your customers as prospects who represent potential revenue shifts the focus toward creating content and activities specifically tailored for your revenue-generating clients.

Nurturing Never Stops

Nurturing never stops with ABM. To keep and retain your customer accounts, your company must continue demonstrating value. Marketing should continue to nurture customers the same way it nurtures prospects who are making a purchase decision. Your customers need to be nurtured with content and activities that are designed specifically with their wants, needs, and pain points in mind. Nurturing is an ongoing process of continuing to supply your customers with messaging, training, and collateral. This process of nurturing clients strengthens your relationships and reduces customer churn.

Advertising to your customers

With ABM, you're using advertising to target prospects and opportunities, based on who they are, and where they are in the buyer's journey. The account's journey is a lifecycle that starts as a prospect, and continues when the account becomes a customer. Therefore, the same techniques you used to engage your prospects should be used to connect with your customers.

TIP

Advertising with specific messages targeted at your customer accounts helps to keep your brand top of mind. Your company's logo and message appear in advertising as your customers surf the web and engage on social media.

REMEMBER

The final stage of the flipped funnel for account-based marketing is to create customer advocates. Promoting your brand through advertising will help the advocacy process.

Here are the types of advertising you can do with your customer accounts.

>> Promoting a case study driving to a non-gated landing page. If you just wrote a case study, start an advertising campaign to promote it to your customer base to learn something from their peers.

>> Registering for your events, such as webinars, user conference, or roadshow. Invite customers to join the same content you're promoting to prospects, such as webinars.

>> Sponsoring social media posts on Twitter and LinkedIn.

Figure 17-1 is an example of an ad that was designed for your customers and uploaded into your ABM platform, along with the list of the customer accounts you want to target.

FIGURE 17-1:
Example of advertisement targeted to your customers.

REMEMBER

The same way you targeted prospects, segmenting by industry and role profile, you need to target your customers. A marketing manager should be targeted with a different advertisement than the one you created for a C-level executive client.

Advocating for your users

In the same way you need to turn your customers into advocates, you should be an advocate for them. Your customers don't have a voice in the daily happenings within your own office. The voice of your customers is in their communications, most often with customer success. As customers continue to get more active on social media, posting Tweets to your company's Twitter handle when there are issues, internal resources should be dedicated to responding to customer sentiments.

As part of aligning "smarketing" with customer success, there are several ways marketing can hear what customers are saying about their experience with your company. Here's how marketing can gauge what customers are thinking and feeling:

>> **Read product reviews.** Find out what they're experiencing by reading review sites, such as G2Crowd and Net Promoter®. Customers also are leaving reviews on Google Plus, Facebook, and Yelp (depending on your industry and offering).

>> **Connect with your customers.** Follow them on Twitter, invite them to connect on LinkedIn, or send them an email (copying the CSM on the correspondence). Ask for their time to chat about how things are going, for input on your next piece of content, or help plan an upcoming customer-centric event.

>> **Read support tickets.** This is the best source for what customers are experiencing with your company's product or service. Support tickets are submitted when your customers have issues and need resolution. Reading these issue tickets can help show whether there is an actual problem, or if there might be a lack of training.

WARNING

Customers who constantly submit tickets or leave negative reviews may need more training, or they can be detractors who will never be satisfied no matter what. Use discretion, and ask the CSM for input, before reaching out to customers with negative experiences.

When you understand your customers' joys, pains, frustrations, and opportunities for improvement, marketing can be the internal advocate for improving these areas.

Promoting customer content

The same way marketing created content for a Resources section on your company's website for prospects to download content, a customer-centered library of content, or "Knowledge Center," should be established to provide your customers with resources. A big way "smarketing" can serve as a user advocate is to design training programs to empower customers to use your product or service. Publishing training content to the customer Knowledge Center helps, as it is easy for customers to go online and download the resources they need. Here is the type of customer content that should be included in the Knowledge Center:

>> **Checklists:** A checklist with Before, During, and After steps helps customers with preparing, executing, and measuring their activities.

For example, one checklist could be how to execute an account-based marketing campaign with creating a list of prospects, designing your ads, launching your campaigns, and measuring the results.

>> **How-to guides:** How to use a different features of your product or service. These guides can include the checklists as well as going into more detail about running programs at scale. Similar to the *For Dummies* book you're reading, the how-to guide should give your customers a blueprint for using your product or service.

>> **Training videos:** Have a member of your product, engineering, or customer success team record a step-by-step process of how to use the features in your product or service. These instructional videos can be replayed at your customer's convenience while he or she works with your offering.

>> **Case studies:** While case studies are typically provided to prospects and opportunities during the purchase decision, they can also be added to your Knowledge Center. Your customers can read from their peers about how they have found success.

>> **Webinars:** Schedule a regular webinar training series for your customers. The same how-to content you created with the checklists, guides, and tutorial videos can be used in a live, on-air demonstration. The format should be at least 30 minutes, preferably 60 minutes, giving your customers time for a Q and A session with the webinar moderator.

WARNING

Your company team member moderating the webinar should be trained to use the product to the best of his or her availability to ensure competency in answering your customer's questions. The last thing you should say live on air is "I don't know."

TIP

However, even the best webinar moderators get stumped sometimes. If a tricky question is asked during the Q and A, he or she should respond with something along the lines of "Great question! I'm not 100-percent sure, and I'm eager to find out. I'll confirm with my team and email you today to let you know what I learned." Tell the customer you'll follow up with them with an answer via email, and (ideally) get back to them within 24 hours of the webinar's broadcast.

TIP

Recordings of customers' webinars should be posted into the Knowledge Center, the same way prospect webinar recordings are shared in the Resources section on your website.

REMEMBER

Customer content doesn't need to be gated. This content should be uploaded as files into your marketing automation system, then placed on landing pages. The landing page is the website your customers will click on to download content. Because it is stored in marketing automation, you can track what your customers download and how often to see what content is the most effective. Another place to host your Knowledge Center is in Zendesk (www.zendesk.com), the same system used for submitting support tickets.

Every quarter, your "smarketing" team should get together to determine the types of content that marketing needs to produce for sales enablement. Marketing should do the same thing with customer success. Syncing with customer success on the topics and the key takeaways for each piece of collateral will help create a comprehensive Knowledge Center of content solely for your customers.

TIP

Every time a new piece of content is added to the Knowledge Center, send an email to your customers alerting them. Your marketing automation system can send emails just to your customers. You can create a list with only your customer accounts, then send emails with links to the new content.

Collaborating with Customer Success

Traditionally, customer success and marketing departments in B2B organizations had very little interaction. It was the responsibility of marketing to help sales "sell the dream," then customer success had to "service the nightmare." The results of this isolation include higher customer churn, and communication silos between departments. With account-based marketing, it's important that your sales and marketing team are aligned as one "smarketing" unit to target and close your ideal customer accounts. Think of aligning "smarketing" and customer success as "smarketing success" to take those accounts and turn them into your customer advocates. Customer success will be the team you work closest with to turn your champion customers into your marketers, and this requires "smarketing success" to be a tightly knit team. Marketing can work cross-functionally across departments to create a comprehensive customer experience. This collaboration will help ensure customers have a successful adoption of your product or service, preventing churn, and retaining revenue.

Thinking of customers as prospects

Your customers represent monthly and annual recurring revenue (MRR/ARR). It's your customers paying their bills that keeps the lights on in your office. Your clients are prospects in this regard, as you must keep your customers happy so they will continue to do business with your company. Depending on your business model, your customers will either be on automatic renewal or have a contract with your company. When a contract is in place, then you will need to designate a team member who is responsible for managing this agreement. Most often, this responsibility falls on customer success.

To successfully manage a relationship with your clients, you need a few key pieces of information on your customers. This information will help empower you to keep and retain clients, including

>> **Contract terms:** The length of the agreement, renewal date, and what is included with your company's offering.

A calendar reminder should be set at least 90 days before your clients must renew their agreement to continue doing business.

>> **Account score:** Like you manage your prospects' activities in marketing automation, use a scoring system done for your customers. Keeping track of your customers' scores shows you which content they have found most useful.

TIP

Scoring your customer accounts shows you whether there's potential to upsell an upgrade of the product, or additional services. For example, when a client constantly replays the same training video, customer success can offer a one-hour training program or consulting services to ensure your account can properly use your solution.

One of my favorite things to do with my customer success managers is to meet with them one-on-one to examine their entire list of accounts. Each CSM is designated with a list of customers which he/she is responsible for servicing. By thinking of your customer accounts as prospects, you'll keep them top of mind. This also gives you insight into the status of each account.

REMEMBER

It's important for "smarketing" to do an account review with customer success on a recurring basis.

During this account review, the CSM should have a spreadsheet of all their accounts and the primary contact. Marketing should make notes, such as "Mary has agreed to be a case study," or "John went dark and, hasn't been responding to emails from his CSM." This will aid marketing's efforts to create and empower customer advocates. Table 17-1 is an example of a CSM's account list, with notes.

TABLE 17-1   **Example of Customer Account List**

Customer Account	Notes	Action
Company A	Happy. Good check in call last week.	Reach out to for video testimonial
Company B	Customer advocate	Ask about webinar panel
Company C	Went dark. No contact in 30 days	CSM needs to re-engage
Company D	Customer advocate	Invite to CMO dinner in NYC
Company E	Okay. Not very active	Send new checklist on "how to"
Company F	Churning	Not a right fit, not successful
Company G	Good. Customer is content	Marketing call to discuss options
Company H	Customer advocate	Participating in case study
Company I	New - going through on-boarding	Send implementation guide

REMEMBER

Meetings like this are important when you're planning a user conference. As marketing is preparing a "VIP" list of customer advocates to attend and speak at the event, customer success will provide insight about those customer advocates are.

Customer success should also tell marketing which clients aren't in a good place. The last thing you want at your user conference are "naysayers" or "detractors" who only gripe about the issues they have with your company's product or service.

TIP

"Smarketing success" can successfully collaborate together by meeting at least once a month, ideally bi-weekly. In this meeting, marketing can share what they're working on for content, and customer success can provide feedback in the creative process to ensure the content will provide answers and training the customers are looking for.

Producing effective customer case studies

The purpose of customer case studies is to demonstrate how clients have been successful with your product or service. A solid case study addresses the problem or pain the customer was experiencing and how your business provided a solution. Effective customer case studies demonstrate:

>> **The Customer:** A customer case study should focus on your champion contact in the account, as this brings a human element to telling a business use case.

>> **The Problem:** How the customer and his or her team was struggling in a certain area, the business need, and the pain points associated.

>> **The Solution:** What the customer realized needed to be put into place for resolving the area of need or pain. Demonstrate proof points and metrics from using the solution.

Framing a customer case study in this context allows the reader to connect with a story, instead of starting with "Here is why our customer thinks we're great." It introduces a narrative, then lets the customer tell the story of how your business helped with resolution. There are many ways to publish a customer case study, including

>> **Multiple-page .pdf:** Customer case studies are most commonly produced as a document in .pdf form that can be shared digitally or printed to distribute. Digital customer case studies should be loaded into your marketing automation system then added to a landing page to download. Printed customer case studies can be handed out at user conference, tradeshows, or (if you're prospecting to an account) given out during meetings with new sales opportunities.

>> **Customer spotlight:** A shorter version of a case study. Commonly done in a blog post, these spotlights can be featured in your company's monthly newsletter or linked in social media posts.

>> **Video testimonials:** Interview your customers on camera and ask them to share a story of how your business helped them solve a problem. Seeing and hearing from your own customers about their success is a powerful way to do a customer case study.

TIP

After conducting the interview with your customer to get the content for a case study, you can repurpose this into multiple forms.

A longer case study in a .pdf can be abbreviated into a blog post, with a link to a landing page to download the full case study. Figure 17-2 shows an example of a customer case study.

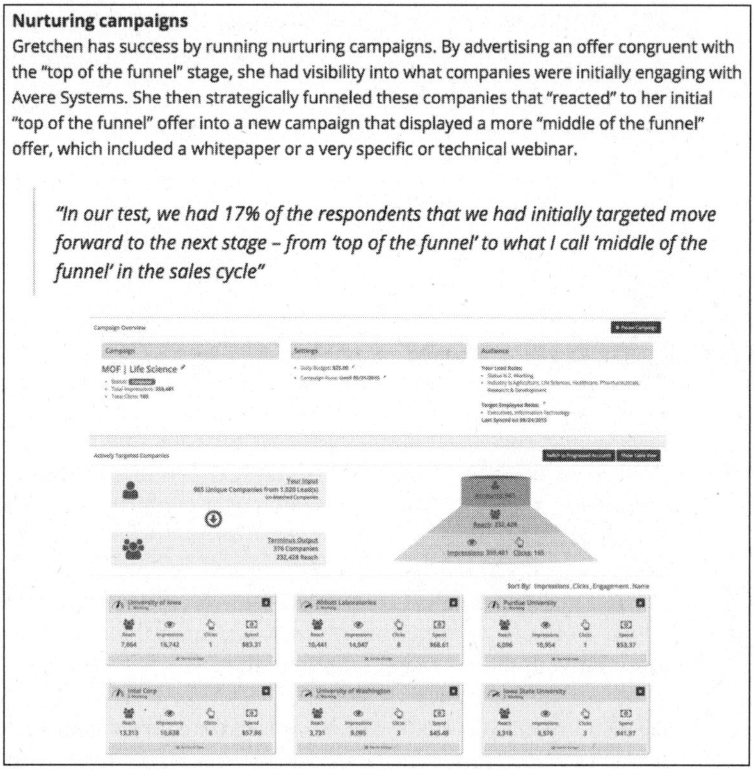

Nurturing campaigns

Gretchen has success by running nurturing campaigns. By advertising an offer congruent with the "top of the funnel" stage, she had visibility into what companies were initially engaging with Avere Systems. She then strategically funneled these companies that "reacted" to her initial "top of the funnel" offer into a new campaign that displayed a more "middle of the funnel" offer, which included a whitepaper or a very specific or technical webinar.

"In our test, we had 17% of the respondents that we had initially targeted move forward to the next stage – from 'top of the funnel' to what I call 'middle of the funnel' in the sales cycle"

FIGURE 17-2:
Example of customer case study.

REMEMBER

Testimonials, customer spotlights, blog posts interviewing your customers, and longer case studies can be used in place of customer references for sales. The sales account executive can provide these upfront and early in the purchase decision (when they get past the initial demo or discovery call), and leverage this content to help close business, instead of continuously bugging your customers for their time to get on referral calls.

Sharing best practices

One of the goals of these customer-centric content initiatives is to share best practices. Sharing best practices demonstrates thought leadership on the subject matter, and shows why your company is a leader in your industry. There are many ways to share best practices, using

>> **Content:** Checklists, blog posts, and case studies sharing tips.

>> **Advertising:** Targeted messaging to your customers linking to the landing pages where the content on best practices is hosted.

>> **Webinars:** Putting your customer advocate on a training webinar, so your other customers can hear best practices from a peer.

>> **Events:** Host training breakfasts in cities where your customers' offices are headquartered, a meetup, or user conference.

Planning Your User Conference

A user conference is an annual meeting for your customers. These events can be one day, or held over two or three days, depending on the type of content and activities at the event. The purpose of a user conference is to bring together your customers and staff.

REMEMBER

Whether you're a small startup or a large enterprise organization, it's important to host an event, or multiple events, throughout the year that provide an opportunity for your clients to gather together.

The primary reasons customers want to attend a user conference include

>> **Content:** Thought leadership and presentations on subject matter they're interested in discussing best practices.

>> **Training:** The opportunity to learn something new that can help improve their day-to-day jobs.

>> **Networking:** Connect with their peers and meet new people, especially your team members (such as your CSM and account executive).

TIP

Invite late-stage opportunities to attend your user conference. New accounts that are close to becoming customers can learn a lot at your annual customer event, and this will help to seal the deal.

Picking the right venue

Location, location, location! Choosing the right hotel or conference center for your user conference is a critical element to a successful event. It's the one time a year where your customers are all coming together with your team, and the place for this user conference needs to be special. When selecting the location, consider the following elements:

>> **Convenience:** Hotels with conference centers or on-site meeting rooms that can accommodate your guests, so they don't have to travel between their rooms and your central meeting location.

>> **Logistics:** Because your customers are geographically dispersed, you need to select a venue that is easily accessible from a major airport.

>> **"Wow" factor:** The goal of a user conference is to treat your customers like VIPs. The venue you select should be modern, well-appointed, and representative of your brand. Amenities should include free Wi-Fi, a workout facility, pool or relaxation area, and the necessities to make your customers feel at home.

WARNING

A five-star hotel at $300+ per night is luxurious, yet may be out of range for your customers. Consider a three- or four-star hotel with room rates in the $129 to $199 range (keeping it under $200 per night before tax).

TIP

Tour the property with a member of your "smarketing success" team, so you can decide together whether this is the best place for your event. On your tour, look at the guest rooms and meeting rooms where your event will be hosted. When you're planning a cocktail reception or dinner, look at this space, and consider asking to sample the menu for food selections.

Treating your clients like VIPs

Your user conference should be a balance of work and fun. From 8 a.m. to 5 p.m., your customers are in meetings, presentations, and training sessions, breaking for lunch and snacks. Throughout the day, there are ways to treat your clients like VIPs.

A few things that have worked well for me these events:

- >> **Keep 'em fed:** You know how sometimes you go to an event and you're wondering whether they'll ever serve food? You must feed your brain when learning tons of new material. Give your attendees welcome bags with snacks, such as granola bars and bottled water, to keep them full and focused throughout the day.

- >> **Get up and move:** To keep your audience pumped up throughout the day, a few of our team members lead the audience in Zumba or stretching exercises after lunch. Additionally, our attendees played around with some beach volleyballs bouncing throughout the conference room (but beware of hot coffee to avoid a spill).

- >> **Engage them:** One thing I hate about attending conferences is when I just sit in the audience listening to a speaker. During the presentations, you should find ways to engage your clients, like these:

  - Inviting them to present on a panel with fellow customers.

  - Have presenters ask questions, and include time for a Q and A in each session.

  - Set up a camera booth to give video testimonials at the event.

After 5 p.m., it's time to party. I joke that my name Sangram sounds a lot like the ginger ale brand Seagram's. Happy hours and dinners are one of my favorite parts about attending a user conference. When planning your cocktail reception or dinner party, consider the following:

- >> **Food:** Get creative with your menu selections beyond the typical cheese board. Consider having a theme based on your location, such as Southern food like fried chicken if your event is in Atlanta.

- >> **Drinks:** Premium open bar can get expensive. Check pricing to for a drink package, instead of paying for drinks based on consumption. Think about a specialty themed cocktail or ordering cocktail napkins and koozies with your logo. It's your event. Brand it!

- >> **Location:** Go offsite if you've been at the same hotel or conference center all day. While taking your clients to a nice restaurant for dinner, consider such alternatives as

  - Club-level seats in a stadium for a sports event

  - Touring a local brewery or winery

  - Calling in a few food trucks

TIP

Hire a certified meeting planner (CMP) or additional events coordinator. This person should be a professional host, not an intern or marketing team member, who can help host your event. After all, you spent all this time planning an excellent customer event. You should enjoy it!

Programming the best content

The sessions at your user conference should be short, sweet, and engage the audience. Your content should keep the customer top of mind, not be a product push. The sessions should be a mix of customer-centric content, including

>> **Keynote:** To welcome attendees in the morning and a closing keynote session in the afternoon

>> **Panel presentations:** Putting three, four, or five people on a panel; find a balance between customers and thought leaders

>> **Breakout sessions:** Focused on specific "tracks" tailored to role profiles, such as marketing, technology, and leadership

WARNING

Beware the hidden cost of audio and visual (A/V). Most hotels and conference centers don't include A/V in the standard meeting package. The costs for A/V, such as projectors, screens, and microphones for each session, can add up. Be sure to get an estimate to budget accordingly.

The presentations should be a mix of thought leadership and educational content. Because your customers have already purchased from your company, the content of each session should focus on a key message or takeaway. Table 17-2 shows a sample user conference agenda for one day of meetings, breakout sessions, and presentations, with meals and break times scheduled throughout the day.

TIP

Offer additional training sessions the day before or after for an additional charge. There will be customers who want to take advantage of these extra training opportunities.

Partnering with sponsors

You can invite your partners to attend the conference as sponsors. Your partners include any other business or organization that serves your same client base, industry, or vertical. These partners are referred to as "channel partners," for example, if you're a email marketing software provider hosting a user conference for digital marketing managers, you can invite such channel partners as a CRM

TABLE 17-2

Example of a User Conference Agenda

Time	Session	Room
7:30 - 8:30 a.m.	Registration, Networking & Breakfast	Lounge
8:45 - 9:15 a.m.	Welcome	Conference Room 1
9:15 - 10 a.m.	Morning Keynote	Conference Room 1
10 - 10:15 a.m.	Break/Attendee Meet & Greet	
10:15 - 11 a.m.	Breakout Sessions 1	Conference Rooms A, B, C
11 - 11:45 a.m.	Breakout Sessions 2	Conference Rooms A, B, C
12 - 1 p.m.	Lunch & Sponsor Expo	AREA
1: 15 - 2 p.m.	Panel Presentation	Conference Room 1
2 - 2:15 p.m.	Break	
2:15 - 3 p.m.	Breakout Sessions 3	Conference Rooms A, B, C
3 - 3:45 p.m.	Breakout Sessions 4	Conference Rooms A, B, C
3:45 - 4:30 p.m.	Customer Panel Presentation	Conference Room 1
4:30 - 5 p.m.	Closing Thoughts	Conference Room 1
5 - 6:30 p.m.	Cocktail Reception	Lounge
7 - 10 p.m.	Dinner	Off-site

software provider or website hosting service provider. The benefit of having channel partners sponsor your event includes

>> **Revenue:** User conferences are expensive, costing upwards of $20,000, depending on the size and scope of your event. By structuring sponsorship packages at $1,000, $2,500, $5,000, $10,000, or more, you can offset the costs of your event.

>> **Thought leadership:** Combining forces with industry leaders and channel partners reinforces your company's position as an industry thought leader.

>> **Value:** when you plan to continue hosting a user conference each year, your company will need to establish this event as a must-attend for your channel partners.

The sponsors at your event should be vendors who target a similar ideal customer profile (ICP) for their products or services. This way, your sponsors know that there will be a good return on their investment (ROI) for participating in your user conference. Here are ways you can integrate partners and sponsors into your event:

>> **Invite them to present:** Panel presentations or short solo addresses that are thirty minutes or less. These are sometimes called "flash presentations" to highlight their product or service.

>> **Give them a booth:** Designate an exhibitors area or "vendor village" where your channel partners can set up a display or table.

>> **Inclusion in your goodie bag:** Add a small item or tchotchke, such as a key chain, pen, notebook, or other "swag" giveaway branded with their company's logo.

>> **Host part of the event:** Breakfast, lunch, snack, cocktail reception or dinner can be sponsored by one of your partners. Include their logo on signage at this part of the event.

TIP

Before your user conference, you need to prepare a "run of show" walking through each element of the show. The "run of show" helps your team to finalize all the details. It also helps for sticking to the schedule as there are many moving pieces. The items you need to prepare for the show include

>> **Final agenda:** Your schedule for the event. Verify that the room numbers where all the meetings and sessions take place are accurate. If you must switch rooms or draw partitions down a conference room, confirm with your venue on the logistics.

>> **Presentations:** All the slide decks and PowerPoint presentations from your speakers. When materials need to be printed out for breakout sessions or training, print those in advance so you're not scrambling.

>> **Confirm with sponsors:** Make sure you know which items they'll put in the goodie bags, whether they need power for their booth, or any other house-keeping items. Your sponsors and channel partners are paying to be there, so you need to make sure it's all set.

>> **Finalize attendee list:** Check the list of registrants to confirm everyone has a nametag or badge printed.

TIP

For late or walk-up registrants, have a printer on-demand or blank name tags to fill in their names.

There are two technology platforms I've found to be particularly helpful with planning our events:

>> **Attend (www.attend.com):** Integrated with Salesforce, Attend makes it easy to customize and collect important data about who came to your event. Everyone in your "smarketing success" team can access real-time registration data anywhere with the Attend app. If you have VIP customers arriving at the registration desk, you can get an alert when they arrive.

>> **Cvent (www.cvent.com):** Cvent provides online software for event management, web surveys, and email marketing, as well as a global event venue directory for more than 150,000 venues. The platform also has a robust communication tool to send targeted email invitations, and advanced social media integration to connect with your VIPs. There are also more than 100 built-in reports to provide insights on attendance, ROI, and more.

Announcing new product developments

Your user conference is a great opportunity to unveil your product roadmap for the coming year. This is when you can discuss updates or new versions of your product, or enhancements to your service offering. A demo should be prepared to showcase these new features, so your attendees can get a glimpse at the latest innovations at your company.

REMEMBER

If you have a customer advisory board (CAB), do a practice run or preview of this presentation to get their input before showing it to all of your customers and partners at the conference.

TIP

Survey guests at the conference for feedback. This announcement should be fresh in their minds, and you need their candid thoughts on these product developments.

6

Putting It All Together

IN THIS PART . . .

Managing account-based marketing campaigns and all the moving pieces

Seeing your success and progression at the account level

Modifying campaigns by adjusting budgets and testing your creative content and copy

Demonstrating the effectiveness of your ABM programs

Chapter 18

Measuring the Success of Campaigns

B efore account-based marketing, the success of marketing campaigns was measured by the number of leads generated. Marketing didn't worry how many of those leads turned into revenue-generating customers.

Sales and marketing work for the same company and therefore need to have the same goal: generating revenue. Generating more revenue begins with creating more engagement within your target accounts. Moving to a new approach with account-based marketing is about the quality of engagement. Your marketing team is focused on driving awareness, influence, and engagement from within your target accounts. This engagement is driven through strategic marketing campaigns and activities at individual contacts in those accounts. To create this engagement, you must know what's working. Are you seeing a progression from accounts to the next stage in the buyer's journey? Is your marketing creating velocity and putting new opportunities in pipeline?

Measuring the success of your account-based marketing campaigns is just like measuring any other marketing campaign, except you're restricting your measurements to key accounts. Your metrics depend on your business goals and the type of campaign you're running.

In this chapter, I tell you which metrics to measure for your ABM campaigns. I discuss how to test your message, graphics, and creative content to help drive more engagement within your target list of accounts. I also explain how to review your metrics to know you're efficiently using every dollar dedicated to your campaigns.

Setting Key Performance Indicators

With ABM, the main goal is revenue. You've aligned your sales and marketing ("smarketing") tetvam to focus on one goal: growing more revenue for your company. With the main goal being revenue, it's important to have key performance indicators (KPIs). The KPIs let you know whether you're on track to meet your revenue goals.

The most important KPI is progression of your target accounts. This is measured by using data in your CRM. Your CRM stores all the data on accounts. An account progression is when your account moves from one stage to the next in the account's journey. From your list of best-fit accounts, do you see them advancing from one stage to the next?

Your "smarketing" team needs to define what the next meaningful stage or status that these accounts go to, with the ultimate goal of making these accounts your customers. Here is an example of stage progression for your accounts and the associated KPIs.

>> **New/Prospect:** The number of accounts that were qualified as a best-fit with your ICP and persona criteria.

>> **Qualified:** The number of accounts generated by marketing that went through a discovery call or demo to become a revenue opportunity.

>> **Opportunity:** The number of accounts that became revenue-generating customers.

   The number of opportunities added to pipeline through marketing activities is called *marketing-sourced pipeline*.

>> **Customer Upsell/Cross-sell:** Customer accounts that will purchase more from your company, or purchase a better/upgraded version of your offering.

>> **Customer Advocate:** The number of customers who serve as advocates for your brand, refer new business, or collaborate for marketing.

Attributing metrics at the account level

Account-level attribution means you can see the activity at each of the accounts you're targeting. You must know which content and marketing activities are creating velocity and advancing accounts to the next stage of the buyer's journey.

REMEMBER

Because there will be different activities at each stage of the account's journey, you need to examine all of the touch points that influence account. You can't say "This account closed because they came to this event," but it's a combination of all the activities that lead to revenue.

Before account-based marketing, it was nearly impossible to report on account-level metrics. B2B marketers were used to lead-based metrics. This caused a lot of friction with the sales department. Sales didn't report on what happened with the leads they got from marketing. The sales team reported on accounts that became customers.

If marketing tried to report which leads turned into customers, there were many missing pieces. That's because marketing was focused on an individual lead or contact, not on all of the contacts in the account. With lead-based marketing, it was a hope that one of the leads that came in became a customer. But leads don't pay your company money. Your accounts that became customers are what keeps the lights on at your office. This is why, as a marketer, you need to look at the activities that helped generate new customer accounts.

Lead-based attribution reporting doesn't give marketers enough credit for all their activities. If a lead came through from downloading an ebook two years ago, but the lead's company just became a customer, how do you know which touch point to credit with a deal? You wouldn't. The initial lead may have downloaded an ebook, but you wouldn't know that one ebook download started the account's journey to becoming a customer.

What marketing wants to know from account-level attribution is how the contact's action impacted this deal being closed? Account-level attribution is about getting more insight into all of the account's activities. Part of this influence is getting your message in front of the right contacts in the account. One of the C-level executives you're targeting is much less likely to click an ad to download an ebook or fill out a form.

This is why account-level attribution is so important. You need to examine the activities of all the contacts in the account to find what's driving them to progress to the next stage and purchase from your company. Account-level attribution should recognize any and all of your "smarketing" efforts. Your efforts include the activities and content that are used to create velocity and accelerate an account through the buyer's journey to generate new revenue.

REMEMBER

When starting with your first ABM campaigns, revenue won't come immediately. It takes time to grow your business by developing opportunities in your best-fit accounts.

Account-based "smarketing" is about identifying the path your best-fit customers take, and replicating it again and again. There's good news: there are other KPIs to determine whether you're on track to meet or exceed your revenue goal. Using metrics and KPIs, you can track the success of all your activities and campaigns. These metrics show you what's working to generate velocity in accounts. KPIs also help demonstrate where campaigns can be refined for success in the future. Here are the smaller KPIs to check

>> **Timeline of stage-progression:** From the first touch as a prospect, the amount of time for the account to become an opportunity

>> **Engagement in accounts:** Showing an uptick in the account's score in your marketing automation system

>> **Expanded engagement in accounts:** More contacts from a targeted account coming to our site and engaging with our content

REMEMBER

It's important to watch the progression of accounts. This information can be found using reporting in your CRM.

However your CRM is organized, you need to set progression rules. Progression rules are a specific type of feature in the CRM. Your sales database administrator or marketing operations manager would someone need to set up a workflow rule or automation rule. These progression rules will let you know whether accounts are moving from one stage to the next. When you're running a targeted advertising campaign at qualified accounts who have completed the first discovery call or demo, then your KPI will be how many of those accounts turned into opportunities.

REMEMBER

The results of your marketing activities and campaigns will be different for every B2B organization. There's no right or wrong answer. The question to ask is how do you measure *influence?* What are we doing to drive awareness and engagement in accounts?

Whatever phase or stage you're looking at, the KPI you need to monitor is the time it typically takes to move to the next stage. This is part of the calculation of sales velocity.

REMEMBER

The formula for sales velocity = `distance/time`

The sales velocity is what marketing wants to create in order to progress the account to a revenue-generating customer. All of marketing's daily activities should increase the number of appointments or demos sales can set. Your marketing is running an advertising campaign in conjunction with sales activities such as calls and emails. The efforts from marketing include monitoring web engagement with your advertisements and contacts downloading content. The "smarketing" efforts all come together to impact the movement of that account from one stage to the next of the buyer's journey to becoming a customer.

TIP

Run weekly reports in your CRM to show how marketing is working to progress your target accounts to the next stages.

In your CRM, you can run reports to see how many accounts are in which stage. Because your sales team should be updating the CRM every time an account moves to the next stage in the purchase decision, you can run a report on this progression. Every week, the reports my "smarketing" team runs include

>> Content downloads

>> Demo request forms completed

>> Inbound demos scheduled

>> Inbound demos completed

>> Inbound opportunities created

>> Inbound Closed/Won opportunities

The goal is to monitor and report on the progression of accounts, and illustrate how marketing activities are contributing to this progression. You can consolidate these metrics into a single Excel spreadsheet to show your "smarketing" team. Table 18-1 is an example of the weekly "smarketing" metrics report for the number of accounts and their stage-based progression.

TABLE 18-1 **Example Report of Inbound Marketing Activity for Account Progression**

Week Ending In	Week 1	Week 2	Week 3	Week 4	Week 5
Content Downloads	19	22	10	9	30
Demo Request Form Completions	8	4	7	5	5
Inbound Demos Scheduled	8	5	2	6	14
Inbound Demos Completed	5	7	7	2	0
Inbound Opportunities Created	3	2	6	1	0
Inbound Closed/Won Opportunities	5	3	1	1	1

All of your account-based marketing campaigns should be focused on progression from one stage to another. The goals for your campaigns include

» Generating demand within your target prospect accounts

» Increasing number of accounts moving into qualification, such as marketing qualified accounts (MQA) or sales qualified accounts (SQA)

» Increasing the number of opportunities in your qualified accounts

» Increasing Closed/Won deal size

» Increasing revenue or increasing contract length

» Decreasing in time from initial contact to Closed/Won, resulting in a shorter sales cycle

» Decreasing churn (the number of customers who came on board, then didn't renew or continue doing business with your company)

» Increasing the number of customers who successfully adopt and implement your solution

» Creating new customer advocates

Attributing metrics at the campaign level

Each campaign will have metrics you need to monitor. When you're running an advertising campaign targeted at your accounts, there are two main metrics you'll look at:

» **Impressions:** The number of times your ad appeared to a contact in your target account. Every time your message appears, it is counted towards the impressions.

» **Clicks:** The number of times contacts you're targeting clicked on the CTA (call to action) in your ad. It's all about getting your message in front of the right people.

The success of your advertising campaigns should be measured by impressions, not clicks. What you need to show is how a targeted advertising campaign provided an uptick in engagement. It's this engagement that will help progress the account further in the purchase decision. You're running targeted advertising campaigns, according to the stage in the account's journey. By showing how many impressions you had for a certain campaign, you can correlate this to a progression of the account.

Here is an example: You're running an advertising campaign that targets accounts in the opportunity stage. These are high-priority opportunities targeted to close within the next 30 days. Because these accounts are associated with a revenue opportunity in your CRM, you can pull this account list and run an advertising campaign to accelerate these accounts. This is called an *opportunity accelerator campaign.*

The campaign runs for a full month. You set the campaign to run for one month because these are accounts you want to close in 30 days. At the beginning of the campaign, you check how many accounts are in the opportunity stage. At the end of the campaign, you check how many of those accounts turned into Closed/Won customers. This will help show whether the advertising campaign worked to create velocity and progress the opportunity to closed/won.

REMEMBER

Because you're running this campaign from an account-based marketing platform, when the deal comes in and becomes a Closed/Won customer. The contacts in that account will need to be removed from the campaign.

Your ABM campaign is synced with your CRM. Because the stage of the account has been updated in your CRM, and your ABM campaign is running based on the stage, the account will be removed from an opportunity accelerator campaign. However your data is organized in your CRM, set this as a progression rule. You can target these companies with advertising for a certain amount of time (such as 30 days for accounts that a high priority to close). In 30 days, you want to progress those high-priority accounts from the SQA or opportunity stage to becoming a customers. At the end of 30 days, examine how many of these accounts have moved to a progressed stage.

Comparing cost per click

Every marketing team has a budget. The budget is set by the Chief Financial Officer (CFO) of your company. The CFO wants to see an ROI from the amount of money the company has invested in marketing initiatives. One of the big questions B2B marketers always get is "How many leads did you generate this quarter?" But that's a vanity metric, because the number of leads generated doesn't correlate to the amount of new revenue the company brought in.

Your CFO should be delighted that you're going to cut costs by taking an account-based approach. An ABM approach to your digital campaigns means rethinking your metrics. If you've run search engine marketing (SEM) or other digital advertising campaigns before, you know the two big metrics are

>> **Cost-per-click (CPC):** How much you spent to get a person to click on the advertisement.

>> **Cost-per-thousand impressions (CPM):** How much you spent to get your advertisement to appear 1,000 times.

These metrics worked for a lead-based approach, but they weren't targeted. If you were running an SEM campaign, there were many wasted marketing dollars. Marketing must bid on each click and impression, and you can't get account-level attribution with most SEM campaigns. This is because the campaigns are run through search engines. It doesn't make sense to continue investing marketing budget in clicks and impressions, especially when marketing can't tie that investment back to an account they're trying to nurture for sales.

What makes more sense is to run a targeted advertising campaign through your account-based marketing platform. Because the ABM platform is synced with your CRM, you know exactly who you want to target. You can get in front of the decision maker with an impression, even when he doesn't click on your ad. Marketers, especially those familiar with SEM, know this isn't typically what they're used to doing with advertising and retargeting.

The account is more important than getting a lower CPC or CPM. Because you aren't running advertisements to anyone who searches your keywords, the overall cost will be much lower. In 2014, the average click-through rate for standard image ads in the software industry was 0.08 percent, according to Google Rich Media Gallery data. This means that 99 percent of advertisements never got clicked on. Talk about a waste of money when you look at how much you spent on CPC for leads that ultimately would never turn into customers.

Showing impressions

Dynamic CPM is another option that is far less expensive for targeting at the account level. The dynamic CPM is based on the value of each impression. Using your account-based marketing platform, you can bid for a flat CPM at the beginning of a campaign. This dynamic CPM is based on impressions (not clicks) for the individual contacts you want to target in the account. You're running targeted advertising campaigns according to your account's industry, the job roles of contacts in the account, and the stage of the buyer's journey. The key metric here is the number of impressions within your target accounts: How many times your message appeared throughout your account-based advertising campaign. The reporting you'll need to show includes:

» Number of accounts you actively targeted

» Number of contacts reached

» Total number of impressions from your campaign

This reporting will show how your campaign surrounded your account with your message to achieve a halo effect and keep your company top of mind throughout the purchase decision. Figure 18-1 is an example of a campaign report showing the number of targeted accounts, contacts reached, and impressions achieved.

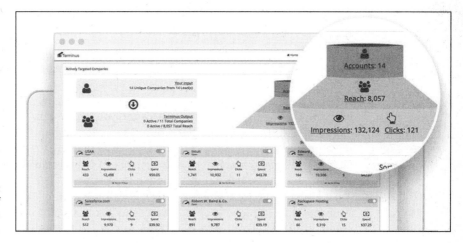

FIGURE 18-1:
Report of
impressions from
a campaign.

REMEMBER

Traditional lead-based success metrics were such numbers as clicks, click-through rates, and form completions. These generated more leads. But it's truly about what's business-centric: increasing revenue by bringing on the right accounts. These are accounts that fit your ICP and are the best fit for your business.

Expanding your audience

With account-based marketing, you don't go after just one contact in the account. You must get in front of as many stakeholders as possible. You can expand your audience by using an account-based marketing platform that pulls in data on your ICP accounts and personas.

TECHNICAL
STUFF

The power of an ABM platform for advertising is the ability to sync with your CRM. You plug in the company names you want to target. This is accomplished by syncing the contact information in your database with cookie- or IP-based targeting of all of the devices that meet the criteria and expand on what you have in your CRM. This will give you the capability to show account-level attribution across digital channels because your ABM platform is integrated with your CRM.

REMEMBER

If you only have one contact for the account in your CRM, you need to reach more than person at the contact's company to move the purchase decision forward. You may be reaching the right person, but you need to expand your audience to connect with all the decision-makers involved. It's about reaching all the contacts in the account on their own terms.

Engaging accounts

You only have a few seconds to engage a contact and keep their attention, so more than one activity is needed to grab their attention for the entire account's journey.

TECHNICAL STUFF

For a full view of engagement in an account, you must marry the data in your CRM and ABM platform with your marketing automation system. That system is tracking all the activities for the contacts in your accounts. The data from your ABM platform and marketing automation system can also be transferred into your CRM to see an account score.

Your reporting needs to show whether there was a specific activity or interaction that triggered a stage progression of the account. At the account level, you need to see whether marketing created the halo effect to influence individuals.

Everything is truly focused on progression of accounts. The faster you can progress your accounts, the quicker you can accelerate your accounts through the sales pipeline to generate more revenue.

MEASURING ENGAGEMENT IN MINUTES

Founded by Marketo co-founder Jon Miller, Engagio is an account-based outbound marketing platform for B2B companies with complex, enterprise sales. Engagio's ABM platform complements marketing automation platforms, (such as Marketo) with account-centric capabilities. It helps companies to engage target accounts, expand customer relationships, and deepen sales and marketing alignment.

The company's first solution integrates with marketing automation and Salesforce to streamline account-based reporting and analytics. By matching leads to accounts, the solution helps companies know which marketing investments work best to reach target accounts and accelerate deals, understand which accounts have the best engagement and opportunity for growth, and measure the impact and ROI of your ABM programs — all without spending tons of time in Excel.

Engaging accounts continues after you have landed accounts as your new customers. Marketing must continue to nurture them and develop them into customer advocates. Advocate marketing helps you to retain your existing customers. By developing your customers into advocates, they become "champion" users of your business. Customer advocates also help you create awareness in more new accounts through word-of-mouth referrals.

To know whether you're effectively engaging your customer accounts, you need to see an increase in moving your customers through the account's journey. It's all about the increase in revenue within an account, or creating a new sales opportunity in your customer account. These types of customer engagement metrics can include

» New sales opportunity, such as an upsell for a new product

» Cross-selling the same product to a different business unit in the account

Testing Your Campaigns

Marketing is a science. Before starting a marketing campaign, you have a hypothesis about it you think will work. There's a goal you want to achieve. You'll test it the marketing message and creative, like a scientist would test a hypothesis, then modify them as needed.

When you plan your account-based marketing campaign, you likely already know which group of companies you want to target, and the roles within those companies. The next step is to develop a persona with the needs, wants, and desires of the target roles.

A/B creative testing

Many traditional marketing strategies don't allow you to optimize until after a campaign has run its course. But advertising at the account level lets you optimize your campaigns on the fly through A/B testing. You can see which advertising creative and marketing messages are falling flat with your target audience as the campaign runs, then replace copy or ads that aren't having much success. The success is measured by the number of clicks on your advertisement that take the contact to your landing page.

A/B testing is a common capability in marketing automation platforms. It allows you to test two versions of an email or landing page to see which one delivers better engagement. You can do A/B testing with your account-based marketing campaigns to see how your advertisements are performing.

TIP

To make sure switches are seamless, have alternate messaging and creative ready to go for your advertisements. In your account-based advertising platform, you can load two variations of the same advertisement. These variations include simple changes, such as

>> Slight revisions in the copy, or the message on your content

>> Graphics, such as design, images, color, and font

>> CTA (the call to action, such as "Read More" and "Learn More")

Figure 18-2 shows A/B testing of an advertisement in an ABM platform.

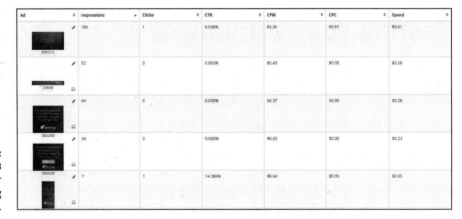

FIGURE 18-2:
Example of A/B
testing your
advertising
creatives.

Trying new content

Content marketing is a much softer way of selling. With content that educates your prospects and contacts about your thought leadership position, your brand stays top-of-mind when it's time for a purchase decision. In a non-pushy way, this content helps educate your contacts about your business.

The marketing campaigns you're running should be linked to a piece of content. You can replace the content in the campaign by changing the link. When you're running an advertising campaign, the CTA will be linked to a piece of content. When you're running a drip email nurturing campaign, a CTA to download content will be included, too.

After you've performed A/B testing to find which graphics, message, and creative content works best for your targeted audience, you can test which content resonates the most. When you're running an advertising campaign designed to progress qualified accounts into opportunities, you can test different pieces of content; for example, comparing a .pdf customer case study to a customer video testimonial.

From your test group, which subset of accounts saw more progression to the opportunity stage? Did the accounts who received the CTA to watch the video testimonial progress to opportunities faster than the accounts who downloaded the case study? Testing different pieces of content in the same campaign can provide you with these types of insights.

Combining your offers

A comprehensive account-based marketing strategy means you're offering up lots of different content and activities to the contacts in the account. When you need to build awareness in a new account, you have an SDR sending emails, marketing running advertising campaigns, and the account may be on a nurturing drip, too. You're driving your message and your name brand in multiple places. How do you know what's working in this combination of activities?

It comes back to the time required for the account to move to the next stage of the buyer's journey. Because you're running campaigns and emailing content, and sales reps are calling and emailing accounts, you know that one activity doesn't necessarily mean that's what triggered the account to progress to the next stage. Account-based marketing has many activities and efforts that make up a comprehensive strategy.

Knowing You Aren't Wasting Money

There's a famous quote from advertising legend John Wanamaker: "Half the money I spend on advertising is wasted. The trouble is, I don't know which half." The allocation and attribution of advertising spend are hot topics for marketers. We all strive to wrap our heads around how much we should spend, and whether the amount we're spending can be attributed to success. The incredible part of account-based marketing is that you can be laser-focused on where your advertising dollars are going, and directly connect this amount with engagement metrics for each account.

You need to show a return on investment (ROI) to prove to your executive and leadership and finance team why ABM works to drive business, not leads. Lead generation was an easy sell, because it gave marketers the ability to demonstrate tangible, quick results. "Look, we generated 1,000 new leads this quarter." But, according to Forrester Research, less than 1 percent of leads actually close. That's a lot of wasted money. Marketing to only the right accounts will have a much more significant impact on revenue. You won't be wasting 99 percent of your money.

At the same time, you are likely facing greater pressure to show return on investment from your ad spend. Simply put, your ad campaign success is important. Here's how to look like a hero.

Budgeting the right amounts

Account-based targeting doesn't require nearly as much of an investment as other types of digital advertising, such as SEM. You're focusing only on the contacts in accounts you want to get your message in front of, so you can be more conservative with your advertising spend. When you're preparing a budget for how much you want to invest in your account-based advertising campaigns, consider the following factors:

>> The number of accounts you're targeting.

>> The stage of the accounts you're targeting (MQA, SQA, opportunity, or customer).

>> The industry (or number of industries, if you're targeting one type of job role, such as a CMO).

>> The number of job roles, if you're targeting one type of industry. For example, if you're targeting marketing managers, directors, and CMOs of marketing technology companies.

From here, you will set a daily budget for your advertising campaigns. The daily budget is the maximum amount you want to spend to get your advertisement to appear to those contacts in your target accounts.

TIP

Test a smaller group to determine how much budget was needed, then scale from there.

Attributing advertising spend to revenue

With your targeted advertising campaigns, you can show a direct correlation to how much you spent at the account level and whether the account became a customer.

This is a significant proof point for account-based marketing. If your company is currently making any type of SEM or CPC investment, you know you can't attribute how much you spent on digital advertising to grow revenue. You don't have enough visibility into targeting accounts. Using an account-based marketing platform for targeted advertising, your can run reports to see the performance of your campaigns. These reports will show you the following metrics:

>> How much you invested (dollars spent)

>> The number of impressions (how many times your advertisement reached one of your targeted contacts)

>> The number of clicks (how many times a contact clicked on your advertisement to go to a landing page)

Using your CRM platform, you can see how many accounts in these campaigns progressed to becoming your customers, ultimately tying back your advertising dollars to new revenue generated.

Showing engagement in the buyer journey

Gathering feedback from your sales team is an important part of the optimization process. It which should happen continuously as you run your ABM campaigns. The goal of your ABM campaigns is to move accounts faster through the buyer's journey. To know just how fast accounts are moving through your pipeline, you can use reports in your CRM to see the number of days an account moved to the next stage.

At the account level, you want to demonstrate how your advertising campaigns created a halo effect. A halo effect describes how a contact in an account is surrounded by your message. This increased messaging helps to keep your brand top-of-mind and progress the account through the various stages of the buyer's journey to close a deal.

Chapter 19

Tracking Metrics for Every Account

You've got a lot going on at work. Everyone is busy. The to-do list is endless. Someone always needs something else. And now you must get everyone on board with this idea of account-based marketing, which will revolutionize the way your sales and marketing ("smarketing") team works together to grow new revenue for your business. It's going to be worth it.

When your team fully commits to doing account-based marketing, you can watch the progression of an account across all stages of the account's journey from prospect, to qualification, then opportunity accounts, as well as your customer accounts. Your "smarketing" team can monitor how every account is contributing to the growth of your company. For new accounts, it's powerful proof that marketing is working when you can see engagement building within an account by connecting with more contacts in who see the value in working with your company and become revenue opportunities.

Potential revenue exists in all stages of the account's journey. You want to look at accounts currently generating revenue, as well as the accounts who represent opportunities. Metrics matter for every account. They're different depending on the stage, and the activities required. So how can you be sure, with everything going on in your office, that your "smarketing" team doesn't let anything fall through the cracks?

In this chapter, I discuss how to track metrics for every account depending on their stage in the account's journey. I outline the process your "smarketing" team should take for an ongoing review of your target accounts, and how marketing can work with customer success on monitoring engagement within customer accounts to look for potential revenue opportunities. I also discuss how marketing can continue to provide added value to accounts by sticking to the core of your company's value proposition.

Ongoing Account Maintenance

The account's journey is a comprehensive lifecycle, starting from the time they first connected with your company. Depending on where the account is on this journey, different people in your company will need to support the account in a variety of ways. Marketing will provide continuous support for sales as they target new accounts by serving up content, planning activities, and executing campaigns together. After accounts come on board, marketing must work with customer success on maintaining relationships with customers and developing accounts into advocates. In account-based marketing, the marketing team will always play an integral part in landing new accounts and retaining them as customers.

Delivering reports and results

Because you're using marketing technology (MarTech) for account-based marketing, you have the ability to produce reports to gain visibility on your activities and campaigns. Depending on the stage of the accounts, you'll want to report on different metrics. Customer success doesn't really care how many accounts progressed from prospect to qualification, because these are potential opportunities that aren't yet customers. On the flipside, sales account executives *should* care about the status of accounts they worked so hard to bring on, as they're the ones who invested time in building those initial relationships with accounts.

Your marketing team can serve as the connector for bringing all this information together. From your MarTech stack, you can pull different reports to show vital information to sales, customer success, and your executive stakeholders. These reports will provide insights into the health of your business and make everyone aware of potential issues. Here are the types of reports marketing will want to produce and the sources.

>> **CRM:** Stage progression for accounts. The reporting can be done by setting a filter or running a query in your CRM to product a list of accounts in each stage. This is vital for sales and your executive team to look at the health of

your sales pipeline and accurately forecast revenue. Marketing will want to pull reports on stage progression including:

- New accounts which came in that week from inbound
- Demos were scheduled by SDRs
- Demos completed by sales
- New opportunities created
- Deals Closed/Won or Closed/Lost

» **Marketing automation:** This reporting shows your sales team what's working to move the needle on engagement. Reports can be produced for both accounts in the buyer's journey and the sales journey. Here's the type of engagement reporting you'll want to see, based on the types of activities and campaigns:

- Demo request forms completed by qualified accounts
- Form completions to download content, such as ebooks, case studies, whitepapers, and infographics
- Webinar registrants and attendees
- Event registrations for in-person events

REMEMBER

Filter the results suppression list. Filters can be set in your CRM to show the results of activities for just your target account list.

TIP

The same way you run these reports to see which content is resonating with accounts in the buyer's journey, you can pull reports for your customers.

It's important to show customer success and your executive stakeholders what activities and content are helping develop your clients into advocates. This type of reporting will also come from your marketing automation system, including registrants for training webinars, on-site workshops, your user conference, and content downloads from your Resource Library or Knowledge Center:

» **ABM platform:** Show the results of advertising campaigns launched using your ABM platform. What's really cool is to how it's far less expensive and more precise for targeting at the account-level. Account by account, see the cost to reach these decision-makers at the account is far lower compared to the CPC of other campaigns.

REMEMBER

You aren't looking at reports for a CPC or average CPM. You'll be reporting on the number of impressions for your target accounts, and the actions which were taken on that ad.

>> **Support ticket system:** Marketing will need to work with customer success and your support team, as marketing typically doesn't have access to this system. Although the B2B industry is starting to see some new support service providers operate with database-based pricing models instead of seat-based pricing models. This gives marketing access to support channels. It's important for marketing to see the types of tickets your customers submit. This allows you to report:

- When several clients say they can't get a certain feature to work.

  This could be either a product issue or a lack of training contributing to this pain.
- Response time of support.

  If the support team is lacking in the turnaround time to get resolution for tickets, marketing needs know it. This harms the development of advocates, and will lead to negative customer sentiments (possibly bad reviews posted about your company online).

People inherently are impatient. Replying quickly, and frequently, to your customers support tickets helps to set the right expectations about resolution time. Ongoing and consistent communication helps customers, even if the issue takes several weeks to fully resolve, because at least you set that expectation in your response to the customer's support ticket.

Creating a review process

Not all accounts are created equal. In order for your "smarketing" team to be at its most productive level, all of your sales and marketing team members must focus on one goal: closing revenue. Marketing needs to own an account review meeting, holding sales accountable for coming to the meeting with a list of accounts that marketing can help close. This review process should include

>> Target account list for each SDR and sales account executive

>> Editorial calendar from marketing with upcoming content and activities

>> Engagement report from marketing automation on active contacts in targeted accounts

>> Pipeline report with opportunity accounts

This review process will help ensure your "smarketing" team members are aligned on what's happening within each account, and help develop a plan for generating even more velocity within those accounts. In the same way marketing will work with sales on these target accounts, marketing needs to regularly meet with customer success managers for status updates on your key customer accounts. The type of reporting marketing needs to prepare for customer success should include

>> Engagement with contacts in customer accounts (from your marketing automation system, filtered using a customer list)

>> Tickets from support signaling potential issues

>> Any recent reviews or feedback posted on the internet

Marketing needs to meet with all the customer success managers to review their list of accounts they own. From this list, marketing can get insight into who your "VIP" customers are. These VIPs are the power users who are happy with your product or service and can be leveraged for case studies or video testimonials.

REMEMBER

The importance of marketing and customer success working on these reports is to help develop customer advocates for word-of-mouth marketing. These customer advocates will help promote your business in an authentic, organic way and drive new revenue for your company.

Executing on tasks

The importance of project management can't be overstated. Good project managers know how critical it is to document every task, assign an owner, and a due date. Your "smarketing" team needs to develop a list of tasks for each person and how they will work together. This helps ensure your team is tracking the status and deliverables for every account and nothing is falling through the cracks.

TIP

Set tasks in your CRM for each account. There should always be a next step with an account based on the stage.

Here are examples of tasks which your "smarketing" team will need to execute based on the stage of the account:

>> **SDR:** New inbound form completions need to be sent an email and call as soon as possible. If the account doesn't respond within 24 hours, set a reminder task to follow up the next day.

>> **Account executive:** When a qualified account has been handed off from an SDR and the demo has been scheduled, make a note in your CRM on the next steps to follow up.

- » **Marketing:** After your weekly "smarketing" meeting, document what content sales has requested. Assign a due date for delivering this content and next steps.

- » **Customer success:** Follow up on tickets and issues need to be remedied. Your clients can't wait forever to get resolution. If you can't get clients resolution, then they'll perceive your company negatively.

TIP

Customer success managers need to send an email to check in at least once a week with users in the account. It helps develop a relationship with assists in customer retention. After each check in, the CSM needs to email the account with next steps, follow up, and deliver on those action items.

Gauging Potential Opportunities

The steps you're taking internally with your "smarketing" and customer success team will help make all the stakeholders aware of the status of each of your target accounts. For sales, this means seeing how accounts are advancing to the next stage of the buyer's journey and what else can be done to move the account forward. For customer success, this means having inherent knowledge of how the account is doing with your company to look for opportunities to upsell your product or service.

Limiting the margin for error

Tracking success metrics for every account means you're reducing the room for error. The primary error that occurs in account-based marketing include is the lack of follow-up. Lack of follow-up includes

- » When a qualified account downloads content and an SDR doesn't send an email to send an email or calls the contact

- » Sales account executives who hold a demo, then don't send a follow-up email, or when an opportunity sends an email that goes unnoticed because of a stacked inbox

TIP

You can sync your CRM system with your email to monitor all of these email activities and ensure your salespeople are following up accordingly.

REMEMBER

This is why it's important to do a weekly review of your target account list. It provides transparency for what every "smarketing" team member should be doing to grow revenue.

For customer success, limiting the margin of error means ensuring you're aware of the terms of service and what sales promised your company would do for the account after they became a customer. One of the biggest ways B2B companies fail is when sales promises certain things that don't come to fruition. During the sales process, marketing and customer success need to be involved in looking at late-stage opportunities.

Providing a statement of work (SOW) helps limit the margin for error. An SOW will spell out exactly what your company will provide for the account after they become a customer. SOWs should be shared internally with the account's future customer success manager so they understand expectations.

When you have a contract in place for your accounts, customer success managers need to set a reminder for several months before this contract expires.

Your sales team worked hard to bring on best-fit accounts. When there's a contract or service agreement with an expiration date, the customer success manager *must* be aware of that date. Most times, an account must give notice that they will no longer do business with your company. The CSM must be aware of when that deadline is, keeping it top of mind, so he or she can ensure your team is doing everything in your power to make sure the account is happy and will renew their contract.

Anticipating future needs

The needs of your account will constantly change. Every contact in your accounts is different. You can't please everyone, no matter how hard you try. What you can do from a service perspective is mutually agree on what your contacts in your account need now. These types of needs are stage based.

Having designed personas for use cases will help you understand the needs of your contacts in your accounts based on their stage in the buyer's journey.

Having an SOW for each account helps customer success managers to anticipate future needs of accounts after they come on board as clients.

Building an engagement report

Your marketing automation system will provide you with the data needed to build an engagement report. In order to build an engagement report, you need have a scoring system in place with your marketing automation system. Points are assigned for each marketing activity. As a contact engages in different marketing activities, such as downloading content or attending a webinar, points are added to the contacts score. You can then run a report to show all the contacts in the account to see all of their scores.

The value here is looking within your target accounts to see engagement across all the accounts who can influence the purchase decision. When there are upticks in activity, you can see this through the account's score. Because your marketing automation system is synced with your CRM, you can run engagement reports for accounts based on stage in the accounts journey. The types of engagement reports you should run include

>> Prospects

>> Qualified accounts

>> Opportunities

>> Customers

>> Engagement with contacts in those accounts

TIP

Look at churned customers who are no longer doing business with your company, as well as Closed/Lost customers to see whether there's any sign of engagement. If they're still downloading content even though they told your company "No," this may be a sign it's time to reengage or warm up the account to get them back on board.

Providing Value Add

With account-based marketing, you're establishing a relationship throughout the account's journey. As you started building a relationship, you asked the key decision-makers in the account about the problems they were trying to solve. You wanted to understand their pain points so your company could provide a solution. The sales team told the account about your company's value proposition in their calls, emails, and product demos, then marketing provided content to support these go-to-market claims.

Living up to expectations

If you were successful, the account came on board as a customer believing, in good faith, that your company could deliver on what was promised: to alleviate whatever pain the account was experiencing through your company's solution. Customer success managers must ensure your company delivers. As a team, your company must work together making sure your clients always receive what they were promised.

REMEMBER

Always go above and beyond to provide added value to your customers. At each stage in the account's journey, meet or exceed what you told the contacts in the account you would do. Meeting expectations is essential. This helps to build trust and keeps the relationship going strong so your accounts continue to do business with your company.

Continuing to improve

There's always room for improvement. If your team members don't think about new ways to grow, then they don't develop professionally. As a team, you should push each other to think about ways to improve. Account-based marketing helps you think about improvement strategically because you're considering what also will be best for your best-fit accounts.

Here is how each team member can look to improve:

>> **Marketing:** What type of content can you produce that will increase engagement? Do you see your contacts in target accounts engaging with one type of content more than another? Does sales have questions or objections from prospects which you can answer with content?

Thinking through these questions will accelerate the brainstorming process for new content and activities, continuously improving your content marketing efforts and increasing engagement.

>> **Sales:** Are there places where you can generate more velocity in the sales process? Do you see there's more time wasted from converting qualified accounts to opportunities?

Think about what can be done to expedite the process of progressing account's to the next stage. Get marketing involved to help. Supplying more content, inviting a qualified account to an account, or sending direct mail can all help generate velocity and improve the time it takes to win new business.

>> **Customer success:** For CSMs, looking to improve means finding new ways to surprise and delight the accounts you're responsible for.

Getting your customers involved in planning your marketing activities is a great opportunity for improvement. Ask your customers:

- What type of content do you want to read?

- What topics would be helpful for a training webinar?

- Would you like to contribute to planning our user conference?

- Do you want to attend this event with us?

» **Product**: Ask both prospect accounts and customers for feedback on your product. Where is there room for improvement? What features are lacking?

When you're planning on introducing a new product, or an upgraded version of your product to the market, then create a plan for introducing it to your existing customer accounts (or late-stage opportunities) for their input. After all, you're in business to serve these accounts with products and solutions they'll want, need, and use.

7

The Part of Tens

Chapter 20

Ten Reasons B2B Companies Need Account-Based Marketing

When account-based marketing succeeds, it pays off with increased revenue for your organization. Becoming laser-focused on your targeted accounts helps your whole company see the biggest potential growth. With ABM, you're either focusing on current customers you want to turn into advocates (the best-fit customers who have proven success with your product or service) or hyper-targeting the companies that meet the best-fit criteria.

At the FlipMyFunnel event that my company, Terminus, hosted in August 2015, Megan Heuer of SiriusDecisions presented an amazing business case for why companies need account-based marketing. If you don't know about SiriusDecisions, get online now (www.siriusdecisions.com). They're one of the top research analyst firms for the intersection of B2B marketing, sales, and technology. At SiriusDecisions, Megan leads the organization's account-based marketing and marketing operations services. Her goal is to help her clients build a bridge between best-practice theory and real-world requirements. In her FlipMyFunnel session, she discussed why account-based marketing makes sense to start implementing at your company now. She has given us permission to use her content for this book.

In this chapter, I expand on her initial findings about where companies are on the ABM journey. I show why marketers need to think about marketing to accounts throughout the entire customer experience (the lifecycle of the account). If you have a list of companies that your salespeople care about closing, and a list of customers that your company cares about keeping, then you need account-based marketing.

Doing the Math

It's essential to map your marketing budget against potential revenue opportunities. Before you start account-based marketing, look at the data in your CRM for recently Closed/Won accounts. Which activities did contacts in those accounts engage in during the buyer's journey? Review how much your marketing team invested in those activities to determine whether the expense was worthwhile. For example, if you spent money hosting webinars, how many Closed/Won deals attended them?

Marketing must align its efforts to the accounts, sellers, and actions most likely to deliver growth. Then, marketing must execute in a way that respects and engages individual accounts according to their needs, preferences and timing. "Here is what we spent last year on these things and here's how much we're going to add," Megan said. "Start with the math. Where will growth come from? When you know that, you are on the road to doing ABM."

Needing a Strategy

A football team doesn't take the field without a plan to score a goal. Why would a marketing team do any activity that doesn't help sales bring in revenue? If you've "done the math" to identify which activities helped close business from your existing customer base, then you know where your growth potential exists. You know the marketing activities and tactics that help to close business. If you can develop and organize those tactics into a strategy, then you're on the road to targeting and engaging accounts to bring in more revenue for your company.

Focusing on Sales Productivity

In order for your sales team to be most productive, your salespeople should be focused on one goal: closing deals for revenue. Marketing needs to provide support for sales enablement. "What we need to do is help our sellers spend most of their time working with them on things that matter, in front of customers, helping to close business, helping to develop relationships," Megan said.

Utilizing Your Technology Stack

When you decide which tools you need for the buying cycle, the modern B2B marketer should also consider tools you need for the customer lifecycle. CRM stands for *customer relationship management* for this reason. It contains information about your prospects and (more importantly) the customers who are currently paying your company revenue.

One of most important stages of the account-based marketing funnel is creating customer advocates. To create customer advocates, you must never stop nurturing your existing customers in the same way that you actively nurture your prospects. You can even use your marketing automation system to send nurture emails and drip campaigns to your prospects. For example, if you're promoting a recent case study and you emailed this to your prospects, consider sending it to your customers, too.

If you're using display advertising technology to surround your best-fit prospects with your message about why they should buy your product or service, then you should also create display advertising targeted at your customers. Think about MarTech tools that you're using to engage your prospects, and identify how you can further engage your customers, too.

Prioritizing Tech Investments

According to a recent SiriusDecisions survey, 61 percent of B2B companies said that they're planning to invest in technology to help with account-based marketing this year. MarTech is a critical resource for executing digital marketing campaigns, but you must define the metrics for measuring the success of those activities.

"I have companies come to me very often and say, 'Hey! I put this great technology in it. I was really excited about it, but I'm just not seeing the results.'" Megan explained. "I ask, 'What was your goal? What were you hoping to get from it? What kinds of things did you think would work?' If there's a pause after I ask that question, I know what the problem is. Know why you're acquiring a technology, and make sure that your marketers can use it."

If your company makes an investment in new marketing technology, such as an account-based marketing platform that lets you target your accounts with display advertising, then it's essential to train your team on how to successfully use your technology. Many B2B marketing teams have a designated in-house "marketing technologist" who is tasked with managing these tools. If you don't have a MarTech person, then it's an opportunity for you and/or another team member to develop a new skill.

Building New Skills

About 47 percent of companies doing account-based marketing said their marketers don't have skills they need to be successful, according to SiriusDecisions. "This was a finding that made me sad," Megan said. "About half of companies who are doing ABM told us they didn't think their marketers had the skills they need to be successful. That isn't okay. Make sure your marketers are learning what's different."

You need two plans to help develop these new skills:

>> A communication plan for communicating your ABM strategy to upper management

>> A training plan for educating yourself or your team members

Account-based marketing isn't hard to execute if you have the skills to

>> Identify leads in your CRM who are the best fit for your business.

>> Build a contact profile for those best-fit leads, then turn those contacts into accounts.

>> Engage them through content marketing, social media events, direct mail, and advertising.

>> Measure the success of those activities.

Leveraging Customer Experience

"Customer experience trumps everything in B2B buying decisions," Megan stated. "We need to prioritize our marketing efforts accordingly." The SiriusDecisions survey asked, "What was the most significant driver of decision to select vendor of choice?" Here are just a few statistics from SiriusDecisions:

>> Customer experience generally is 71 percent of the reason buyers said they purchase from a company. "If we forget that, we fail," Megan said.

>> Just 18 percent of survey respondents said their buying decision was based on the promise of the product to meet their needs.

>> Only 9 percent of survey answers said that their purchase decision was based on price.

Treating Clients Differently

Your customers are your best marketers. If they like working with your company, then they'll be willing to sing your praises through word-of-mouth marketing. You should plan customer marketing efforts the same way you plan how you'll market to your prospects and opportunities. The content must be different, so your customers continue to find value by working with your company. "Buyers are trying to buy something. They want to make a purchase," Megan said. "Your customers have already done that. They want to get value."

Megan went on to say the buyer's journey and the customer lifecycle are two different things. "Think of the buyer's journey as an episode, it's *Law & Order*. It all gets wrapped up in a nice bow," she said. "The customer life cycle is a soap opera — it never ends." Helping B2B buyers make a decision is different than helping customers get value. This is why account-based marketing is needed because the marketing efforts are continuously going for both your buyers and customer accounts.

Developing ABM Relationships

With account-based marketing, you have a buying cycle and a customer lifecycle happening at the same time with different people at different places, Megan explained, and as such, there are two different sets of goals.

>> **Opportunity goals:** What else am I going to sell?

>> **Relationship goals:** How do I make sure this company wants to stay my customer?

"If your account-based marketing only focuses on opportunity, and God forbid, top of the funnel opportunity, you're missing the boat," Megan stated. "This is a holistic view of your customers and your prospects and what they need from you whether they're buying or whether they're customers."

Measuring More Than Leads

You can't do account-based marketing if all you're measuring in marketing is leads. "It doesn't mean you can't bring value, it just means the value you bring must be measured differently," Megan said. "If marketing is going to be engaged to focus on customers after they buy and not just to sell them more, you're not generating leads." It's all about measuring the progression of the accounts you're targeting.

Chapter 21

Ten Obstacles Facing Account-Based Marketing

D espite all the industry buzz about account-based marketing, you'll most likely face roadblocks for implementing ABM strategies and goals. Change is hard, even when it means doing what's best to drive new revenue and find new ways to surprise and delight your internal and external customers.

The success stories of ABM are slowly starting to arise, but the case studies are few and far between. It's a relatively new practice of aligning marketing, sales, and customer success with the same metrics. For so long, these teams had different goals. Marketing focused on generating leads, sales focused on growing revenue from new business, and customer success focused on keeping clients happy. With ABM, all three teams are focused on the same metric: revenue. This shouldn't be a hard sell to your executive team, but it can be a surprisingly daunting task.

In this chapter, I cover the ten biggest hurdles for your team running as fast as it can with account-based marketing.

Measuring Leads as Success

The status quo success metric in the B2B marketing industry has been leads. Success was defined by the number of leads generated, then the percentage of those marketing qualified leads (MQL) handed over to sales. These sales accepted leads (SAL) then were qualified through various activities, such as discovery calls and product demos, to become sales qualified leads (SQL). These turned into revenue opportunities. Along the way, leads fell out of the pipeline as they failed to move onto the next stage of qualification. The buyer's journey could be a painful one for the sales team as they waited for leads to become opportunities, but marketing continued to count leads as its key success metric.

Trying to change the status quo is never an easy process. To tell a marketing team that they need to focus on revenue, not leads, takes time. Your marketing team has the tools it needs to start: a CRM full of contacts and a marketing automation tool to track the engagement and activities of those contacts. Now, it's a matter of identifying those best-fit contacts who could turn into potential revenue.

Blasting Emails Too Quickly

Marketing automation platforms have made it easy to send thousands of emails in a few seconds. Marketers use open rates and click thru rates to gauge the success of those emails. If 1 percent of 10,000 people open, that's 100 people who are potential leads, right? *Wrong!* Those 100 people could be customers, people who already told your sales rep that they weren't interested, and the message in your email isn't personalized at all. Email marketing needs to be a well-planned activity.

Email blasts are a powerful asset of a marketing automation platform. Having the ability to email thousands of people at once is pretty cool. But you can't personalize content for each individual person. Yes, you can code in the person's name, title, and the company they work for, but so can everyone else. Your email must be a love letter to the prospect so they want to see where this relationship might go with your company.

Expecting to Engage Every Time

Wayne Gretzky famously said "You miss 100 percent of the shots you don't take." True as this is, marketers can't expect to make 100 percent of their shots. Different marketing tactics will have varying rates of success. The success metric of your individual campaigns will have different outcomes, depending on your content, message, and the targeted audience. Using display advertising, for example, the number of impressions and click-through rates to landing pages will be different for each campaign. This is why it's called providing *always-on* air cover.

You can't engage every contact at every account every time you reach out. What's important with account-based marketing is *impressions*. Even if the contact you're targeting doesn't click on your ad, they're still seeing your ad. This counts as an impression. You want to measure the number of impressions you get, as this helps for branding and keeping your company top of mind.

Relying on Marketing to Do It All

It's called account-based marketing, but a true ABM program includes both *account-based selling* (ABS) and *account-based sales development* (ABSD). The ultimate goal of these new B2B marketing and sales tactics is to identify your best-fit companies (accounts) at the start of your marketing initiatives. To identify these companies, you must agree on the ideal customer profile (ICP), which takes input from customer success to tell you which accounts have been the hardest to service. These criteria include such measurements as company size, industry, and job titles of your end users. This information is in your CRM, but you need customer success to validate your assumptions about which companies are in your ICP.

From there, marketing can design campaigns with specific activities aimed at engaging potential new customers. The process must planned to provide a comprehensive customer experience throughout the entire lifecycle of the account.

Sending All Leads to Sales

Leads come in all shapes, sizes, and forms. The trick is to identify the right kind of leads. That isn't an easy task. The faster you figure out which leads are important, the better for the sales team. If your salespeople aren't happy with the leads you give them, then you're doing it wrong. The leads that marketers get can be divided into three categories:

» **Hot Leads:** Prospects who are ready to buy.

» **Warm Leads:** Prospects who are qualified, but aren't ready to buy.

» **Cold Leads:** Prospects who love your content (they download from your website and always register for your webinars) but will never buy from you.

If your sales team starts calling every lead, they won't be very productive, because they aren't focusing on the right kind of leads. The result is misalignment of sales and marketing, leading to lower pipeline and revenue numbers. Here's how to start categorizing your hot, warm, and cold leads:

>> **Hot Leads:** These leads are the hand-raisers. These leads request demos, watch recorded demos and product videos, and attend in-person events that you host. They show interest, intent, and need. These are the activities that sales reps need to take the conversation forward.

>> **Warm Leads:** These are leads that do the right activities showing interest, but not necessarily intent to buy. For example, they attend webinars, download content, read blogs, and engage with you on social media. Using scoring criteria in your marketing automation system can help you rank and prioritize these warm leads for sales.

>> **Cold Leads:** These leads bloat the top of the traditional funnel. The people looking at your content include researchers, analysts, consultants, interns, employees, competitors, and agencies. None of these folks will ever buy your product. Don't hand these leads directly to sales without qualifying them as potential customers.

Asking for More Leads

More leads seldom is the answer to the chronic problem of not enough qualified leads. If you already have 10,000 leads in your CRM and marketing automation system, how much value will more records add? It will make your contact database larger, but are these the *right* contacts?

For example, if you get 1,000 new leads in your CRM and marketing automation platform every month, and about 100 of these leads meet your qualification criteria, this is a good number, as you need to close about 10 deals a month to meet your revenue goals. That means a 10 percent win rate.

If the new revenue numbers need to grow to 20 deals a month, then there are two ways to do it: increase the win rate, or add more leads.

But more leads may not mean qualified leads that are ready to close. It's better to study existing qualified leads, then figure out how to drive more of the same type of leads and behaviors to create velocity for potential sales.

Not Paying Attention to Customer Retention

There's an adage that *80 percent of your revenue comes from 20 percent of your customers.* I've seen this as true, especially for enterprise companies that sell large deals and have complex sales cycles. In these deals, it costs a lot of time, money, and resources to acquire new business. After you've landed these customers, you have to keep them happy.

Customer loyalty is a big deal, not only because the cost of customer acquisition is very high, but also because your customers can serve as your marketers. The voice of the customer is one of the most authentic and organic types of marketing. Companies should turn head over heels to keep these customers happy. For marketing to pivot and pay attention to customer success requires a shift in focus and a change in metrics.

Forgetting About Your Customer Advocates

Renowned author Seth Godin proposed flipping the traditional B2B marketing and sales funnel so it becomes a megaphone giving your customers a voice. The best companies focus on turning customers into advocates. This is because advocates are the new customer acquisition engine.

For example, suppose that one of the top video marketing companies is your customer. You could reach out to other video marketing companies with a success story about how your company has helped a leading video marketing company to success. That's powerful marketing from one of your customer advocates. The rest of the video marketing companies will look at this see how they can achieve similar, if not greater, success. Forgetting about your customer advocates is a huge detriment to succeeding with ABM.

Selling Instead of Serving

One of my biggest pet peeves is when I get a cold call from a number I thought I recognized, and the sales rep on the other end immediately launches into a product pitch. This rep hasn't taken the time to ask me about the work I'm doing, or any potential pain points to identify my problems. He just wants to sell me his product or service. I'm not buying.

Regardless of how many technological advances there have been in the MarTech industry, human touch will be important (until one robot sells to another robot). Humans are social animals. We like compliments, smiles, a joke that breaks the ice, and small gestures that build connections. These human elements separate a to salesperson from an average one.

Your company's mission should helping solve a problem for your customers and helping them to achieve their goals. Account-based marketing is about serving up helpful content and educating your potential customers. This requires a shift in focus and a change in marketing strategies instead of just cold calling and emailing prospects.

To serve means to help solve a problem and help your customer achieve their goals. When sales processes focus on these type of goals, they can achieve greater success by selling instead of serving. This requires a shift in focus, instead of constantly calling and emailing prospects to follow up.

Changing the C-Suite's Assumptions

Your executive team expects marketing to perform certain functions. The marketing team is responsible for brand, communications, content, product promotion, and a variety of activities and efforts that are supposed to help enable sales to win more deals. Your higher-ups in the C-suite probably assume that everything is going well when the sales team hits its quota every quarter. While that may be true today, companies that don't innovate ultimately die. This is true for B2B marketing and sales teams.

If your marketing team doesn't innovate, all those leads you've been bringing in will dry up. You can only fish in the same pond so long before you've caught all the fish. The same is true for trying to bring in tons of leads. Try to explain this to your executives in the C-suite. They have to understand why it's important to implement account-based marketing before there are no more new leads to bring in.

Chapter 22

Ten Account-Based Marketing Blogs to Read

The blogosphere for account-based marketing is growing exponentially. The B2B marketing and sales blogs that have been around for years recognize the power of the keyword *account-based marketing*, and feature even more posts dedicated to the idea and best practices of ABM. These blogs typically are easy to digest and offer email subscriptions for free.

This chapter presents ten of the blogs that are the most useful for news and featured content on ABM, and how it impacts the world of B2B sales, marketing, and technology.

MarketingProfs

MarketingProfs' (www.marketingprofs.com) mission is to offer real-world education for modern marketers through training, best practices, research and other content. With more than 300,000 Twitter followers and over 111,000 Facebook followers, MarketingProfs promotes the latest news for innovative marketing professionals across multiple platforms. The Chief Content Officer at Marketing-Profs, Ann Handley (@annhandley), is a thought leader for the marketing industry. The subject matter at MarketingProfs covers the dozens of applicable topics for modern marketers. The ROI and metrics blog category can be particularly useful for your account-based marketing efforts. MarketingProfs also hosts events, both in-person around the country and online in a virtual conference series (www.marketingprofs.com/events).

Follow MarketingProfs on Twitter (@MarketingProfs).

ClickZ

ClickZ (www.clickz.com) is home to the latest and greatest in digital marketing news and analysis. The blog's expert advice includes such categories, email, analytics, media, social, stats and tools, videos, and breaking news. ClickZ provides global coverage including North America, the UK, and Asia. The account-based marketing content from Matthew Sweezey, author of *Marketing Automation For Dummies*, is particularly impactful, as well as the author's insights on the world of B2B marketing software best practices. The ClickZ Academy (www.clickzacademy.com) offers free webinars, as well as paid training and e-learning sessions.

Follow ClickZ on Twitter (@ClickZ).

Funnelholic

Funnelholic (www.funnelholic.com) is a blog by Craig Rosenberg, an innovative B2B marketing and sales leader. Craig's obsession with the funnel comes from his lifetime on the West Coast helping companies — ranging from startups to large enterprises — improve their sales and marketing strategies to drive revenue. The content that Craig posts to Funnelholic includes aligning your sales and marketing teams to exploring the technologies needed to execute account-based marketing at scale. He also provides helpful insights on account-based sales development, encouraging sales professionals to take an active role in demand generation. There's great content here on predictive analytics, prescriptive analytics, and how these tools help you obtain the data for ABM. Also, if you aren't an active blogger, his tips will help you to take your B2B blog to the next level.

Follow Funnelholic on Twitter (@funnelholic).

Business2Community

Business2Community (www.business2community.com) is more than just a blog: it's a content aggregator. The platform sources original content on account-based marketing from a variety of B2B marketing and sales companies. The community of contributing bloggers and editors covers the top trends in content marketing, digital innovations, social media, social selling, and more. You'll find tons of original content, such as predictions for the next wave of B2B digital marketing, plus trending U.S. news and global reports. It's a go-to site for everything modern B2B marketing and sales professionals need to know about the latest news and trends. Business2Community offers free webcasts and whitepapers to readers.

Follow Business2Community on Twitter (@B2Community).

CustomerThink

CustomerThink (www.customerthink.com) is focused on customer-centric business management topics. This is a must-read for account-based marketing, because putting your customer first is an essential part of the process for turning your customers into your advocates. The site's columns, articles, and interviews are contributed by writers from around the world. The Think Tank category includes posts that are handpicked by the blog's founder, Bob Thompson (@Bob_Thompson) who is the author of *Hooked on Customers: The Five Habits of Legendary Customer-Centric Companies.* On CustomerThink, the featured resources include a range of B2B customer-centric content that's readily available for download, such as Marketo's *Definitive Guide for Demand Generation* and *Definitive Guide for Social Media.*

Follow CustomerThink on Twitter (@customerthink).

MediaPost

Media Post (www.mediapost.com) is a central source for marketing and advertising professionals who need comprehensive coverage on the ever-evolving media industry. Account-based marketing topics on the MediaPost blog include best practices for using display advertising, designing creatives, targeting your ideal customers, and more. Email updates are delivered multiple times a day, depending on which categories you select when setting up your user profile on MediaPost. The Events page on MediaPost (www.mediapost.com/events) includes major shows, such as SXSW (South by Southwest) and OMMA (Online Media, Marketing and Advertising), summits, workshops, and more. If you're looking for a claim to fame, you can apply for a number of awards (`www.mediapost.com/awards`).

Follow MediaPost on Twitter (`@MediaPost`).

Heinz Marketing

Heinz Marketing (`www.heinzmarketing.com`) is a consultancy dedicated to essential programs to successfully execute account-based marketing, such as content strategy, demand generation, sales enablement, and pipeline management. The founder, Matt Heinz, regularly blogs about a variety of ABM topics including "Best Practices for Implementing a Winning Account-Based Marketing" and "Ten sales & marketing tactics that are allegedly dead." The site also has a bevy of additional resources for implementing ABM at your own company.

Follow Heinz Marketing on Twitter (`@HeinzMarketing`).

Chief MarTec

Chief MarTec (`www.chiefmartec.com`) is the B2B marketing industry's source for the news and innovations for marketing technology, commonly referred to as MarTech. As the blog's founder and editor, Scott Brinker, said, "Marketing has become a technology-powered discipline and therefore marketing organizations must infuse technical capabilities into their DNA." As account-based marketing leverages best practices for marketing and using technology to execute ABM at scale, the content posted on Chief MarTec will provide additional insights and be incredibly helpful. There are also ongoing MarTech events, including annual conferences in the United States and Europe that are vendor-agnostic. They're designed to bring together marketing and tech-savvy professionals.

Follow Chief MarTec on Twitter (`@chiefmartec`), and keep up with the latest trends in marketing technology by using `#MarTech`.

MarketingLand

MarketingLand (www.marketingland.com) is a go-to source for CMOs and marketing leaders. Blog topics include best practices and thought leadership for SEO, SEM, paid search, advertising, mobile, email marketing, MarTech, and (of course) account-based marketing. Applicable ABM topics include "Account-Based Marketing: New Buzzword Or New Reality?" and "Account-Based Marketing: Back to Basics." MarketingLand hosts tons of events, such as the annual Search Marketing Expo (SMX), smaller SMX events, and the SocialPro conference.

Follow MarketingLand on Twitter (@Marketingland).

MarTech Advisor

MarTech Advisor (www.martechadvisor.com) has more than 350,000 subscribers to its blog and newsletter. This site is unique in how it divides its main categories. The "Experiences" category focuses on content marketing topics, such as email marketing, events, webinars, social media, sales enablement, and ad tech. There are other categories, such as "Operations" for analytics, "Middleware" for customer data management platforms, and "Backbone" for the essential marketing technology platforms, including CRM, marketing automation, and website content management. MarTech Advisor's Editor-in-Chief, Ankush Gupta (@thelearnedman), runs an interview series called "MarTech Maven." It features guest authors and thought leaders from the marketing technology world.

Follow MarTech Advisor on Twitter (@MarTechAdvisor).

Chapter 23

Ten ABM Thought Leaders to Follow

Account-based marketing is the culmination of many facets of B2B marketing, sales, and technology. Across the industry, marketers and salespeople look to social media for guidance on initiating ABM and implementing it successfully at their own companies. The best and brightest B2B thought leaders are active on Twitter, LinkedIn, and their own websites. This chapter presents some of the top account-based marketing experts who can help guide you on your way to doing ABM at scale.

Jill Rowley

Jill (@jill_rowley) is more than just the queen of social selling. She's the master of the #SocialSelling universe. Jill held top positions at Salesforce, Eloqua, and Oracle before launching her own consultancy. Jill says she's a sales professional trapped in a marketer's body, and that she eats failure for breakfast so she can dine on success for dinner. *Forbes* magazine named Jill one of the "Top 30 Social Salespeople In The World," and she isn't slowing down.

Jill's definition of account-based marketing starts by engaging the right contacts on social media. According to Jill, social selling includes using social networks to research and build relationships that drive revenue. Social selling is all about "social proximity," or degrees of separation based on social networking. Her B2B marketing and sales framework includes metrics to measure the ROI of #SocialSelling. These metrics include size of network, volume of content shared, meetings booked, pipeline, and (most importantly) revenue generated. Jill said, "The modern consumer is digitally driven, socially connected and mobile empowered. Sales reps need to adapt or be replaced."

www.linkedin.com/in/jillrowley

David Raab

David (@draab) is a graduate of the Harvard Business School who has spent almost 30 years in the B2B marketing and technology industry. David views account-based marketing as the "Integration of advertising with marketing technology potentially gives salespeople another route for generating their own prospects."

David has written hundreds of articles on marketing technology for publications, including *Information Management, DM Review, DM News,* and *The Journal of Database Marketing.* He's the author of *Guide to Demand Generation Systems, Marketing Performance Measurement Toolkit, B2B Marketing Automation Vendor Selection Tool,* and *Guide to Customer Data Platforms.* His new research appears regularly on http://customerexperiencematrix.blogspot.com.

Craig Rosenberg

Craig (@funnelholic) is the brains behind the Funnelholic blog (www.funnelholic.com). Craig is the co-founder and Chief Analyst of TOPO (www.topohq.com), a research and advisory firm that studies the marketing and sales patterns of the fastest growing companies in the world and uses that data to help their customers drive more revenue. One of their chief areas of focus is account-based marketing. Craig is legendary in the B2B world for his insights on best practices for demand generation. Craig believes that sales and marketing work together in account-based marketing, to create an "always-on" series of touches and relationship-building aimed at these accounts.

According to Craig, one meeting with an account is just the beginning — not the end — of an ABM program. "ABM requires a truly coordinated effort between sales, sales development, marketing, and executive staff," Craig says. His analyst team at TOPO is spending more time than ever before answering client inquiries about ABM, and he anticipates ABM becoming a critical sales and marketing capability for B2B companies.

Jon Miller

Jon (@jonmiller) is the CEO and co-founder of Engagio, an "all-in-one" platform for account-based marketing (www.engagio.com). Previously, Jon was a co-founder at Marketo (Nasdaq:MKTO), a leader in marketing automation. He is a speaker and writer about marketing best practices, and is the author of multiple marketing books, including *Definitive Guide to Marketing Automation, Definitive Guide to Engaging Email Marketing,* and *Definitive Guide to Marketing Metrics & Analytics.* Jon has a passion for helping marketers everywhere, and is on the Board of Scripted and is an adviser to Optimizely and Newscred. In 2010, The CMO Institute named Jon a Top 10 CMO for companies under $250 million in revenue. Jon holds a bachelor's degree in physics from Harvard, and an MBA from Stanford.

Chris Engman

Chris (@chrisengman) is the CEO and founder of Vendemore (www.vendemore.com), a global account-based marketing company based in Stockholm, Sweden, and operating in regions around the world. Chris says that his company's goal is to be the SAP of the account-based marketing world, targeting Fortune 500 companies.

Vendemore has been a pioneer in account-based marketing. Seven years ago, the B2B marketing industry didn't know the term "account-based marketing." Chris and his team called it *pipeline marketing,* as it used targeted advertising to influence the sales cycle. Now, the MarTech industry recognizes the capabilities of account-based marketing to eliminate the process of collecting tons of leads, and align marketing spend with a revenue opportunity. As Chris says, account-based marketing starts with good knowledge about both your existing top accounts and your most wanted new accounts.

Ann Handley

Ann (@MarketingProfs) is the Chief Content Officer at MarketingProfs (www.marketingprofs.com). She's the author of *The Wall Street Journal's* best-seller *Everybody Writes: Your Go-To Guide for Creating Ridiculously Good Content,* and the co-author of *Content Rules: How to Create Killer Blogs, Podcasts, Videos, Ebooks, Webinars (and More) That Engage Customers and Ignite Your Business.*

www.annhandley.com

Matt Heinz

Matt (@HeinzMarketing) is an expert in B2B revenue acceleration using a combined sales and marketing strategy, demand generation, sales pipeline, and process improvement, with a keen focus on customer retention and renewals. He has more than 15 years of B2B marketing, business development, and sales experience. In 2007, he launched his firm Heinz Marketing to help his clients focus on their business goals for marketing and customer acquisition opportunities.

Matt has published several guides to best practices on such topics as marketing automation, secrets to productivity (work/life balance and success), and sales for startups.

Megan Heuer

Megan (@megheuer) is the Vice President and Group Director at SiriusDecisions, a research analyst firm dedicated to empowering sales, marketing and product leaders to make better business decisions and accelerate growth. With more than 20 years of professional experience in the world of B2B marketing, Megan has seen firsthand the shifts in technology which allow marketing and sales professionals to become laser focused on the best-fit accounts. At SiriusDecisions, she leads the organization's account-based marketing and marketing operations services.

Megan's goal is to help her clients bridge the divide between best-practice theory and real-world requirements to deliver exceptional customer experiences. According to Megan, account-based marketing represents the future of the B2B marketing industry. "We have to embrace the reality of how our buyers buy and what our customers want from us," Megan said at the #FlipMyFunnel 2015 conference. "Salespeople talk about accounts, they talk about customers. . .they don't talk about leads. Salespeople think about how they'll win accounts in the first place, then how they'll keep and grow those accounts."

Scott Brinker

Scott (@chiefmartec) is the co-founder, president, and CTO of ion interactive (www.ioninteractive.com) for content marketing and software programs. Scott's a mastermind when it comes to the intersection of marketing and technology, especially when it comes to account-based marketing. His main claim to thought leadership fame is his blog Chief Marketing Technologist (www.chiefmartec.com).

Since 2008, Scott has kept the B2B marketing and sales industry informed of the latest trends in marketing technology at Chief MarTec and helped to coin the term "marketing technologist" as an essential employee to any successful B2B marketing team. Every year, Scott produces an infographic outlining the marketing technology landscape that examines 40 different categories of software, systems, and applications. He has a B.S. in computer science from Columbia University, and M.B.A. from MIT, and a master's degree in computer science from Harvard.

Jim Williams

Jim (@jimcwilliams) is the Vice President of Marketing at Influitive , a SaaS platform that makes it easy for B2B marketers to recruit, mobilize, and recognize advocates to support marketing campaigns, refer new clients, and close deals. Over the course of seven years at Eloqua, he held a number of senior marketing positions, including Senior Director of Product Marketing, where he was responsible for product go-to-market strategy and tactics. He's the go-to-guy on how to turn your customers into advocates using account-based marketing. Customer advocacy is definitely the name of his game.

Index

A

A/B creative testing, 295–296

ABM. *See* account-based marketing; account-based marketing platform

ABS (account-based selling), 321

ABSD (account-based sales development), 108, 321, 326

account lists
  of customers, 273
  prioritizing, 218–219
  tiered, 121, 132

account managers
  football analogy, 216
  roles and goals of, 148
  "smarketing" tasks, 234

account marketing plans, 41–42

account scoring system, 273

account-based marketing (ABM)
  Advocate stage, 17, 25
  buyer's journey, 24–25
  customer's journey, 26–27
  defined, 1, 10
  driving more revenue from, 28–30
  Engage stage, 16–17, 25
  Expand stage, 16, 25
  Identify stage, 15, 25
  lead-based marketing versus, 10–13
  making case for, 20–22
  number of companies using or planning to use, 21
  obstacles facing, 319–324
  reasons for using, 313–318
  resources needed for, 23

account-based marketing (ABM) platform
  integrating other software with, 54
  marketing technologist and, 57
  overview, 51
  reports, 303
  tying back to accounts, 57

account-based sales development (ABSD), 108, 321, 326

account-based selling (ABS), 321

accounts. *See also* target accounts
  as data point in CRM, 83
  defined, 14
  Engage stage, 16–17
  Expand stage, 16
  leads versus, 22

account's journey, 106–108, 148–152, 183, 222–230, 232–233

account-specific plans
  champions, 114, 117
  decision-makers, 114
  defined, 114
  detractors, 118
  power sponsors, 114, 118
  stakeholders, 114–117

Act-On, 79

Adobe Design Suite, 61

Adoption stage of customer's journey, 26, 242–244

AdRoll, 182

advertising
  as air cover, 145
  automation, 185–186
  campaigns, 178–181, 186, 232–233
  changing message by stage, 183–185
  connecting outside of business hours, 173
  to customers, 268–269
  display ads, 53, 58, 119, 177
  mobile ads, 53, 58, 172–177, 180
  nurturing throughout buying process, 164
  outbound marketing, 129
  pipeline acceleration campaigns, 161
  purpose of, 58
  pushing the envelope, 181–183
  search ads, 53

BuiltWith, 86–87

business intelligence, 53

business software review platform, 120

Business2Community, 327

business/sales development representatives (BDRs/SDRs)

connecting through LinkedIn, 188

converting accounts to opportunities, 105

as CRM account owner, 94

defined, 39, 141

establishing relationships, 252

football analogy, 216–217

gauging interest, 100–101

generating velocity, 169–170

handling prospects, 223–224

qualifying revenue opportunities, 107–108

roles and goals of, 146–147

"smarketing" tasks, 234, 305

buyer's journey

ABM compared to, 25

Closed/Won stage, 24–25

Demand Generation stage, 23–24

Opportunity stage, 24–25

showing engagement in, 299

stages of, 218

with traditional lead-based marketing, 47

buying centers

defined, 122

identifying, 123

C

CABs (customer advisory boards), 282

calls and call centers, 53, 66

calls-to-action (CTAs), 65, 179, 184, 210, 296

Canva, 62

case studies

adding to Knowledge Center, 271

advertising to customers, 268

content for marketing activities, 62

in content library, 194–195

producing content by industry vertical, 201

producing effective, 274–276

certified meeting planners (CMPs), 279

CHAMP acronym, 102

champions

account-specific plans, 114, 117

as customer advocates, 84

defined, 114

enabling and empowering, 117

establishing relationships, 253

pipeline acceleration campaigns, 159

training, 243

channel/local marketing, 53

Chief Marketing Technologist, 335

Chief MarTec, 52, 328

churn

defined, 30, 252

preventing, 30

ChurnZero, 256

C-level executives

changing assumptions of, 324

content development based on, 204

generating velocity, 169

roles and goals of, 148

as stakeholders, 116

clicks metric, 32, 58, 235

click-through rates metric, 65

"click-to-close," 158

ClickZ, 326

closed accounts, 95

Closed/Lost stage, 150, 165–166, 219

Closed/Won stage, 24–25, 166, 235

Cloudingo, 93

CMPs (certified meeting planners), 279

CMS (content management system), 50–51

cold leads, 321–322

communities, 53

company lists

applying ideal customer profile to, 78–80

tiering targets, 77–78

company size

content development based on, 200–201

in ideal customer profile, 73

identifying stakeholders, 115–116

segmenting by, 71–72

specifying, 71

tiering targets by, 79

Consideration stage of lead-based marketing, 11

G

G2Crowd, 120, 255, 269
Gainsight, 256
gamification, 53
gating content, 127, 179, 186, 192
Ghostery, 87
Godin, Seth, 14, 323
The Golden Circle, 165
Google Alerts, 212
Google Hangout, 63, 259
Google Plus, 269
GoToMeeting/GoToWebinar, 63, 259
grading, 137–138
Grammar.ly, 62
graphics, 179, 181
Gretzky, Wayne, 320
Gupta, Ankush, 329
Guru, 62

H

halo effect, 146
Handley, Ann, 326, 333–334
Heinz, Matt, 328, 334
Heinz Marketing, 328
Heuer, Megan, 313–318, 334
historical backtesting, 89
Hooked on Customers (Thompson), 327
hot leads, 321–322
how-to guides, 270
HubSpot, 49, 79

I

ideal customer profile (ICP)
    applying to tiered company list, 78–80
    comparing customers with, 84
    creating personalized sales messages, 35
    defining personas, 74–75
    example of, 73
    general discussion, 72
    identifying best-fit contacts, 15–16
    personas' motivations, 75
Identify stage of ABM

buyer's journey compared to ABM funnel, 25
data
    creating new accounts, 91–95
    general discussion, 81–82
    managing existing, 82–84
    obtaining new, 84–90
    protecting quality of, 95–98
lessons learned from Mad Men, 184
overview, 15
qualifying target accounts
    account's journey, 106–108
    agreeing on sales-ready opportunities, 108–109
    converting to opportunities, 104–106
    finding multiple opportunities within one, 109–110
    gauging interest, 99–103
    holistic view of, 109
sustainable "smarketing" process, 151
targeting best-fit accounts
    criteria for, 70
    general discussion, 69
    ideal customer profile, 72–75
    segmenting by industry and company size, 71–72
    specifying company size, 71
    specifying industry, 70–71
    tiering targets, 77–80
    value proposition, 76–77
impressions metric, 58, 235
inbound marketing and activities, 100, 107, 126–128, 146–147, 222–223
Infer, 89–90
influence metric, 36
influencers
    connecting customer advocates with, 263
    content development based on, 203
    pipeline acceleration campaigns, 159
    webinars, 64
Influitive, 153, 176, 256, 261
infographics
    content for marketing activities, 62
    in content library, 193–194
    cross-promotion, 213
InsightSquared, 61, 200
Instagram, 190

general discussion, 51
networking through, 174
sponsoring posts, 190
tracking clicks, 196
Twitter handles
Ankush Gupta, 329
Ann Handley, 326, 333
Bob Thompson, 327
Business2Community, 327
Chief MarTec, 328
Chris Engman, 333
ClickZ, 326
Craig Rosenberg, 39, 332
CustomerThink, 327
David Raab, 332
Fred Reichheld, 255
Funnelholic, 326
Gary Vaynerchuk, 198
Heinz Marketing, 328
Jason Jue, 208
Jill Rowley, 331
Jim Williams, 335
Joe Chernov, 200
Jon Miller, 36, 333
MarketingLand, 329
MarketingProfs, 326
MarTech Advisor, 329
Matt Heinz, 334
Matthew Sweezey, 134
MediaPost, 328
Megan Heuer, 334
Sangram Vajre, 5
Scott Brinker, 52, 335

U

Uberflip, 210
The Ultimate Question (Reichheld), 255
The Ultimate Question 2.0 (Reichheld), 255
Upsell and Cross-sell stage of customer's journey, 26–27, 247–248
upselling, 26–27
urgency, detecting among accounts, 143–144

user conferences
agendas, 280
content, 279–280
defined, 276
new product development announcements, 282
sponsors, 279–282
treating clients like VIPs, 277–279
venues, 277

V

value proposition
defined, 76
differentiating value based on roles, 76
going beyond, 251
personalized messages, 76–77
preventing churn, 30
vanity metrics, 24
Vaynerchuk, Gary, 198
velocity to advance accounts
advancing opportunities to Closed/Won deals
converting opportunities, 165–166
general discussion, 163
nurturing throughout buying process, 164
selling value, not product features, 164–165
general discussion, 157
growing revenue
case study, 168–170
creating clear metrics, 167
general discussion, 166
linking strategy to revenue, 167–168
pipeline acceleration campaigns
executing with sales team, 160–161
focusing on the right deals for, 161–163
general discussion, 158
launching, 158–160
types of, 162
pipeline velocity, 225–227
progression of opportunities, 241
sales velocity, 227–230
Vendemore, 120, 333
vertical markets, 70, 200–201
vice presidents (VPs), 116–117

Notes

Notes

About the Author

Sangram Vajre is the CMO and co-founder of Terminus, an account-based marketing platform. Before launching Terminus, Sangram was Head of Marketing at Pardot, a marketing automation platform that was acquired by ExactTarget, and subsequently Salesforce in 2013. His passion for innovation drives him to constantly question the status quo of B2B marketing and sales. Sangram is a passionate marketing geek at heart and loves to solve problems, both analytically and creatively. In today's marketing world, when companies need to rapidly adapt to changing buyer-centric communication, Sangram finds comfort in all things technology to keep pace with this challenge. Originally from Nagpur, India, the first time Sangram came to America was to attend the University of Alabama, where he achieved his master's degree in information science. He lives with his wife and two kids in Atlanta.

Follow Sangram on Twitter: @sangramvajre

Dedication

This book is dedicated to my father, who passed away shortly after I began this project. He was always very proud of me, no matter what I did. I used to be a D and F student! One year, I barely passed, but he threw a party to make me feel happy. He passed away before his time, and I wanted him to have the first copy of the book. I know he is still proud of me, and I dedicate this book to him for his unconditional love and faith in me against all odds.

Author's Acknowledgments

First, I have to thank my wife, Manmeet, who has been my rock through this crazy and challenging year of growing a startup, losing my dad, and still writing a book. You, Krish, and Kiara are the best! I love you guys. I have to thank my team at Terminus. This book wouldn't have been possible without each and every one of you: Nikki Nixon, Tonni Bennett, Sydney Smith, Amanda Faillo, Karen Topham, Josh Fowler, Kipp Ramsey, Lucas Ulloque, Chris Reene, Kirby Oscar, Brad Wilkerson, Brandon Cummings, Steve Vines, Stu Maron, Zach Patterson, and my co-founders Eric Spett and Eric Vass. I want to especially give thanks to Lauren Patrick, our storyteller, who helped bring this book to life and made it much better in every aspect. The thought of writing a book is exciting, but doing it is a completely different ball game. With Lauren's amazing support, we made it happen.

To the innovative B2B marketing and sales thought leaders who agreed to interviews and read our work: Megan Heuer of SiriusDecisions, Jon Miller at Engagio, David Klanac at Trustfuel, Jim Williams at Influitive, Sean Zinsmeister of Infer, Adam New-Waterson at LeanData, Jeff Epstein at Ambassador, Jim Hopkins at Salesforce, Ted Wright of Fizz and guru on word-of-mouth marketing, Craig Rosenberg "The Funnelholic" at TOPO, Jason Jue at Triblio, Anisha Sekar at Datafox, Daniil Karp at 6sense, Matt Heinz of Heinz Marketing, and all the Funnel Flipper rockstars.

Thanks to Wiley's acquisitions editor, Amy Fandrei, for giving us a shot at changing the status quo of B2B marketing; to our project editor Pat O'Brien, for his continued patience and support; and to Melanie Crissey, our technical editor, for sticking with us. Hat tip to Seth Godin for writing the first-ever book on flipping the funnel to give your customers a megaphone, and Joseph Jaffe, my colleague and author of *Flipping the Funnel*.

Account-based marketing is going to change the B2B "smarketing" industry in so many ways, and I'm blessed and thankful to be part of the conversation. I have tried to acknowledge everyone who helped with this project. Here's a big thank you to everyone who provided support, guidance, and help along the way. Now it's time to go flip more funnels.

#FlipMyFunnel

Publisher's Acknowledgments

Project Manager: Pat O'Brien
Technical Editor: Melanie Crissey
Special Help: Lauren Patrick
Sr. Editorial Assistant: Cherie Case

Production Editor: Selvakumaran Rajendiran

Apple & Mac

iPad For Dummies,
6th Edition
978-1-118-72306-7

iPhone For Dummies,
7th Edition
978-1-118-69083-3

Macs All-in-One
For Dummies, 4th Edition
978-1-118-82210-4

OS X Mavericks
For Dummies
978-1-118-69188-5

Blogging & Social Media

Facebook For Dummies,
5th Edition
978-1-118-63312-0

Social Media Engagement
For Dummies
978-1-118-53019-1

WordPress For Dummies,
6th Edition
978-1-118-79161-5

Business

Stock Investing
For Dummies, 4th Edition
978-1-118-37678-2

Investing For Dummies,
6th Edition
978-0-470-90545-6

Personal Finance
For Dummies, 7th Edition
978-1-118-11785-9

QuickBooks 2014
For Dummies
978-1-118-72005-9

Small Business Marketing
Kit For Dummies,
3rd Edition
978-1-118-31183-7

Careers

Job Interviews
For Dummies, 4th Edition
978-1-118-11290-8

Job Searching with Social
Media For Dummies,
2nd Edition
978-1-118-67856-5

Personal Branding
For Dummies
978-1-118-11792-7

Resumes For Dummies,
6th Edition
978-0-470-87361-8

Starting an Etsy Business
For Dummies, 2nd Edition
978-1-118-59024-9

Diet & Nutrition

Belly Fat Diet For Dummies
978-1-118-34585-6

Mediterranean Diet
For Dummies
978-1-118-71525-3

Nutrition For Dummies,
5th Edition
978-0-470-93231-5

Digital Photography

Digital SLR Photography
All-in-One For Dummies,
2nd Edition
978-1-118-59082-9

Digital SLR Video &
Filmmaking For Dummies
978-1-118-36598-4

Photoshop Elements 12
For Dummies
978-1-118-72714-0

Gardening

Herb Gardening
For Dummies, 2nd Edition
978-0-470-61778-6

Gardening with Free-Range
Chickens For Dummies
978-1-118-54754-0

Health

Boosting Your Immunity
For Dummies
978-1-118-40200-9

Diabetes For Dummies,
4th Edition
978-1-118-29447-5

Living Paleo For Dummies
978-1-118-29405-5

Big Data

Big Data For Dummies
978-1-118-50422-2

Data Visualization
For Dummies
978-1-118-50289-1

Hadoop For Dummies
978-1-118-60755-8

Language & Foreign Language

500 Spanish Verbs
For Dummies
978-1-118-02382-2

English Grammar
For Dummies, 2nd Edition
978-0-470-54664-2

French All-in-One
For Dummies
978-1-118-22815-9

German Essentials
For Dummies
978-1-118-18422-6

Italian For Dummies,
2nd Edition
978-1-118-00465-4

e **Available in print and e-book formats.**

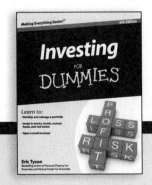
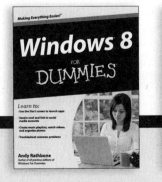

Available wherever books are sold. **For more information or to order direct visit www.dummies.com**

Math & Science

Algebra I For Dummies,
2nd Edition
978-0-470-55964-2

Anatomy and Physiology
For Dummies, 2nd Edition
978-0-470-92326-9

Astronomy For Dummies,
3rd Edition
978-1-118-37697-3

Biology For Dummies,
2nd Edition
978-0-470-59875-7

Chemistry For Dummies,
2nd Edition
978-1-118-00730-3

1001 Algebra II Practice
Problems For Dummies
978-1-118-44662-1

Microsoft Office

Excel 2013 For Dummies
978-1-118-51012-4

Office 2013 All-in-One
For Dummies
978-1-118-51636-2

PowerPoint 2013
For Dummies
978-1-118-50253-2

Word 2013 For Dummies
978-1-118-49123-2

Music

Blues Harmonica
For Dummies
978-1-118-25269-7

Guitar For Dummies,
3rd Edition
978-1-118-11554-1

iPod & iTunes
For Dummies, 10th Edition
978-1-118-50864-0

Programming

Beginning Programming
with C For Dummies
978-1-118-73763-7

Excel VBA Programming
For Dummies, 3rd Edition
978-1-118-49037-2

Java For Dummies,
6th Edition
978-1-118-40780-6

Religion & Inspiration

The Bible For Dummies
978-0-7645-5296-0

Buddhism For Dummies,
2nd Edition
978-1-118-02379-2

Catholicism For Dummies,
2nd Edition
978-1-118-07778-8

Self-Help & Relationships

Beating Sugar Addiction
For Dummies
978-1-118-54645-1

Meditation For Dummies,
3rd Edition
978-1-118-29144-3

Seniors

Laptops For Seniors
For Dummies, 3rd Edition
978-1-118-71105-7

Computers For Seniors
For Dummies, 3rd Edition
978-1-118-11553-4

iPad For Seniors
For Dummies, 6th Edition
978-1-118-72826-0

Social Security
For Dummies
978-1-118-20573-0

Smartphones & Tablets

Android Phones
For Dummies, 2nd Edition
978-1-118-72030-1

Nexus Tablets
For Dummies
978-1-118-77243-0

Samsung Galaxy S 4
For Dummies
978-1-118-64222-1

Samsung Galaxy Tabs
For Dummies
978-1-118-77294-2

Test Prep

ACT For Dummies,
5th Edition
978-1-118-01259-8

ASVAB For Dummies,
3rd Edition
978-0-470-63760-9

GRE For Dummies,
7th Edition
978-0-470-88921-3

Officer Candidate Tests
For Dummies
978-0-470-59876-4

Physician's Assistant Exam
For Dummies
978-1-118-11556-5

Series 7 Exam For Dummies
978-0-470-09932-2

Windows 8

Windows 8.1 All-in-One
For Dummies
978-1-118-82087-2

Windows 8.1 For Dummies
978-1-118-82121-3

Windows 8.1 For Dummies,
Book + DVD Bundle
978-1-118-82107-7

e Available in print and e-book formats.

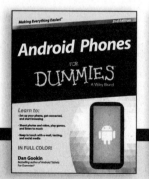

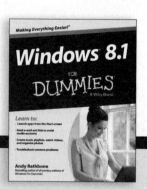

Available wherever books are sold. **For more information or to order direct visit www.dummies.com**

Take Dummies with you everywhere you go!

Whether you are excited about e-books, want more from the web, must have your mobile apps, or are swept up in social media, Dummies makes everything easier.

Visit Us

bit.ly/JE0O

Like Us

on.fb.me/1f1ThNu

Follow Us

bit.ly/ZDytkR

Watch Us

bit.ly/gbOQHn

Join Us

linkd.in/1gurkMm

Pin Us

bit.ly/16caOLd

Circle Us

bit.ly/1aQTuDQ

Shop Us

bit.ly/4dEp9

Leverage the Power

For Dummies is the global leader in the reference category and one of the most trusted and highly regarded brands in the world. No longer just focused on books, customers now have access to the For Dummies content they need in the format they want. Let us help you develop a solution that will fit your brand and help you connect with your customers.

Advertising & Sponsorships

Connect with an engaged audience on a powerful multimedia site, and position your message alongside expert how-to content.

Targeted ads • Video • Email marketing • Microsites • Sweepstakes sponsorship

21 Million Monthly Page Views & 13 Million Unique Visitors

For Dummies is a registered trademark of John Wiley & Sons, Inc.

# of For Dummies

Custom Publishing

Reach a global audience in any language by creating a solution that will differentiate you from competitors, amplify your message, and encourage customers to make a buying decision.

Apps • Books • eBooks • Video • Audio • Webinars

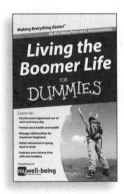   

Brand Licensing & Content

Leverage the strength of the world's most popular reference brand to reach new audiences and channels of distribution.

For more information, visit www.Dummies.com/biz

FOR
DUMMIES
A Wiley Brand

Dummies products make life easier!

- DIY
- Consumer Electronics
- Crafts
- Software
- Cookware
- Hobbies
- Videos
- Music
- Games
- and More!

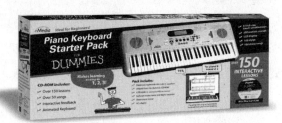

For more information, go to **Dummies.com** and search the store by category.

For Dummies is a registered trademark of John Wiley & Sons, Inc.

FOR
DUMMIES
A Wiley Brand